D0621056

THE BROADVIEW BOOK OF

DIPLOMATIC ANECDOTES

THE BROADVIEW BOOK OF

DIPLOMATIC
ANECDOTES

edited by
Gordon Martel

broadview press

Cataloguing in Publication Data

Main entry under title:

The Broadview book of diplomatic anecdotes

Includes index
ISBN   0-921149-85-9

1. Diplomacy — Anecdotes. 2. Diplomats — Anecdotes. I. Martel, Gordon,
1946–   . II. Title: Diplomatic anecdotes.

JX1662.B76   1991   327.2   C91-094892-5

broadview press   OR   broadview press
P.O. Box 1243   269 Portage Rd.
Peterborough, Ontario   Lewiston, NY
K9J 7H5   Canada   14092   USA

printed in Canada

Table of Contents

For Nancy and Freddy,
—who tried to smooth some of the rough edges

> "History will be kind to me, for I intend to write it."
>
> *Winston Churchill*

*　　　　*　　　　*

Diplomatists, especially those who have entered into the higher levels of the craft, are sensitive to the question of how they will be regarded "by history". And, recognizing that history does not make itself, but is made partly by those who leave a record of it, they are usually determined to leave their own account of their career and, if possible, to influence the accounts of others. The stories that follow are those that have been told by the diplomats themselves; they should not be confused with history.

Cautionary Tale

In London in 1942 the Foreign Ministers of the United States, Britain, Germany and France were meeting to discuss a number of delicate, and potentially volatile issues involving NATO and the European Defense Community. The British Foreign Secretary, Anthony Eden, hosted a dinner one evening at his residence at Carlton Gardens. Dean Acheson, the American Secretary of State, found himself between Robert Schuman, the French Minister for Foreign Affairs, and André François-Poncet, the French High Commissioner; across the table was Konrad Adenauer, the Chancellor of West Germany (and his own foreign minister), who was seated next to Eden. During the evening, the discussion turned to the writing of memoirs.

"I will be kind to you in my memoirs," Adenauer told François-Poncet, "if you will be kind to me in yours."

François-Poncet agreed to the bargain.

Schuman turned to Acheson and whispered: "Adenauer will lose; he will die first."

*

Adenauer, who was ten years older than François-Poncet, outlived him by four years.

Preface

My main objective in producing this book has been to entertain. I have tried to restrain the professional historian's impulse to indulge in pedantry and pedagogy, although I am sure that some readers will find that these continue to break through the surface occasionally. Like the best jokes, however, I hope that these stories do tell some truths about diplomacy as a craft and about diplomats as people.

I have tried to select stories that would illustrate the multi-faceted nature of diplomatic life in the twentieth century, but I decided early on that I would rely on the diplomats themselves (broadly defined to include consular officials, service attachés and translators) for the stories. Since I first began to study international history in the mid-1960s, I have found the lives of diplomats peculiarly fascinating—not a taste that is widely shared—and perhaps for this reason I have concentrated more on the people involved in this process than on the monumental diplomatic events of the century. I have made no attempt to corroborate, cross-reference, or check out their historical veracity in any way.

As I went about reading autobiographies, memoirs and diaries, it did occur to me, however, that it would be interesting to use the anecdotes in a more sustained way to look more closely at one historical event in a way that would show how varied the perspectives and the sources might be, that there are many stories to be told about the same event. This led to the "experiment in anecdote" contained in the chapter on the Munich Crisis. If there is a single diplomatic event in the twentieth century that has worked itself into the collective consciousness of literate citizens in the western world, it is almost certainly the crisis of September 1938. Thus, although the July Crisis of 1914 and the meetings at Yalta also offered attractive possibilities,

I decided that Munich would be the most interesting example, possibly because of the recurring references that were made to it in the days leading up to the Gulf War.

*   *   *

This book begins with a chapter on diplomats entering the profession, which seems a logical place to start; the only preliminary to this would be to look at the stories of those who sought to join, but failed to do so. Finding no such stories, I offer mine in place of them.

How Historians Almost Become Diplomats
— or —
How Would-be Diplomats Become Historians

In the autumn of 1975 I was a PhD student struggling to finish a thesis and desperately in search of gainful employment. Valerie, my wife, had given birth to our first child the previous January. Although we had been married for seven years by this time, we suddenly managed to break all known records for the speed of conception: a second child was due to be born before the first celebrated a birthday.

Two children were going to make things difficult: we lived in a one-bedroom apartment, and could ill afford anything larger. I was already using a small laundry room, complete with diaper pail and kitty litter, in which to write my dissertation. Valerie had wanted children for a long time, and wished to stay at home to raise them. Clearly, I had to find a job.

But there were no jobs. Or at least there were very few jobs for historians; in fact, at that time, there was not a single university position available in Canada for an historian of modern Europe. On the other hand, there was the possibility of employment in the public service. In 1969, when I received my Master's degree, the Canadian Department of External Affairs was so keen on finding good candidates that they had actually written to me to ask if I would like to take the annual examination. Although I decided to go on to study for the doctorate, I always had it at the back of my mind that, if a career as an academic historian did not work out, a diplomatic career would be my second choice.

But this world too had changed since 1969; where dozens of people were being hired annually in the 1960s, only a tiny handful were being selected by the mid-1970s. Nevertheless, I gave it a try and prepared for the written examination. I was told that it was not possible to prepare for such an examination, which consisted of general knowledge, an I.Q. test, and an essay, but this didn't fool me. After ten years as a student, I was confident that no test could be designed that couldn't be crammed for. I got a textbook of Canadian history and memorized all the major, most of the minor, and many of the trivial names, dates and events. I got a guide to Canadian literary criticism and culture and familiarized myself with much unknown terrain. I got a handbook of international organizations and memorized the functions, abbreviations and locations of every relevant institution. I got a book entitled *Know Your Own I.Q.* and set about practising the tests.

I was right. I fooled them all. Not long afterwards I was delighted to receive word that I was high enough up on the list to be given an interview. Valerie and I were thrilled; at the youthful age of thirty, I might at last enter gainful employment, and in a profession that I was certain I would find fascinating.

The grilling that I received from the three career diplomats in a Vancouver hotel room was daunting indeed. Unlike poor Norval Richardson (see Chapter One), they didn't actually confront me with names or places that were totally unfamiliar to me. We had quite a pleasant, if straightforward half-hour together. I didn't realize that this was only Round One. As I was leaving the room, I was told that after all the candidates had been interviewed, some would be called back for a second, more searching inquisition. And, to be called back meant that the experts deemed the candidate suitable for employment by the Department; but the ranking of the suitable candidates would be determined largely by performance on the second interview.

I didn't know whether to be overjoyed or throw myself off the Lion's Gate Bridge. The arrival of the second baby was, by this time, a little more than a month away; Valerie's maternity leave would carry her through until the following spring. If I didn't rank highly enough on the second interview, things were going to look pretty bleak: there was still no academic job going in Canada for which I could even apply. To get this close to a career as a diplomat and then to fall short would be a crushing blow.

The second interview was a real challenge. The interviewers were no longer looking for simple factual knowledge and speaking ability: now they wanted to see fast thinking when confronted with challenging problems. Would I sell a nuclear reactor to Argentina? What three changes in Canadian immigration policy would I suggest, and what would be the foreign and the domestic ramifications of each of these? If I were attending a diplomatic ball, and the wife of a foreign ambassador let it be known that she wished to dance with me—and it was an exotic dance with which I was unfamiliar—what would I do to extricate myself? And if I knew that she was a little tipsy and was known to have a violent temper, what then?

Our enjoyable little chat lasted over an hour. I was exhausted; the inquisitors, who seemed to have enjoyed themselves, appeared to be pleased and satisfied. I went away hopeful but uncertain.

I heard nothing for a month. Then one morning shortly before Christmas, and long before dawn, the telephone rang in the living room. I stumbled out of bed, trying to answer it before the baby woke up. It was Ottawa calling. The Department of External Affairs wished to let me know, "informally", that they would be offering me a position. They had discovered in previous years that some of their best candidates would be lost to them because of the time-consuming procedures that were involved in getting the offers out. Candidates who did not hear from them became become understandably anxious and accepted other offers, so they now called people directly to reassure them and encourage them to wait for the formal offer.

I went back to bed and told Valerie the good news. It was 6:10 a.m. This was my first opportunity to learn that easterners believe the entire continent works on the same schedule that they do. Dawn was still a long way off. The entire episode had taken no more than five minutes.

It didn't take long before everyone was told of our plans. Two weeks later Mireille was born, joining Lisette and the cat in our one-bedroom, ground-level quadruplex apartment. Two cribs were set up in what had been an eating area next to the kitchen; the living room was divided in two, one half of which now became a "dining room". But these cramped conditions and the difficulties of our financial situation suddenly seemed much less oppressive, as we began to envision a bright future. I worked even harder at the thesis, determined to finish it before we moved to Ottawa.

The weeks passed by, the pages piled up, and the diaper pail was always full. Although no word came from Ottawa, I relied on the Department's assurance that it would be some time before I received any formal notification. January passed. Then February. We were starting to wonder what was going on, when another form of reassurance arrived, although it was somewhat disguised.

Just before dinner time one day, as I was having a quiet drink in the bathtub, there was a knock at the front door. Valerie went to answer it; I could hear snatches of conversation, as one of the many odd features of our apartment was that the bathroom happened to be situated right next to the front door. A few minutes later I heard the door close, and Valerie came into the bathroom, laughing and shaking her head.

Could I guess who that had been? No, I couldn't.

"The R.C.M.P."

What on earth did they want?

"Was I familiar with an individual by the name of Gordon Martel, and if so, could I vouch for his character? Did I know anything about the company he kept, his drinking habits, that sort of thing."

"What did you tell them?"

"That as I'd given birth to two of his babies I felt pretty certain that I knew where he stood in the matter of sexual preferences; as for drinking, he seemed to have this under reasonable control, although this might be due more to financial hardship than strength of character."

"What did he say to this."

"Nothing."

"Nothing?"

"Absolutely nothing. He simply fidgeted a bit with the collar of his trench coat, nodded, and walked away."

As silly as all this seemed, it at least reassured us that something was happening with the appointment, and that the wheels of the bureaucracy were slowly moving. March passed by, and there was still no word. April came and went. Now we were really getting worried. What would we do if something went wrong? Had the call from Ottawa only been a dream?

I contacted the Public Service Commission office in Vancouver, to ask them if they could check into the situation. They promised that they would. A week later they called back to say that no such telephone calls were made by the Department of External Affairs, that no "early offers" were ever made.

Now we really worried. Desperately, I began checking *University Affairs* once again to see if there were any positions advertised. There was one job going, a one-year sabbatical replacement at Royal Roads Military College in Victoria, British Columbia. I decided to apply, just in case.

One day late in May the telephone rang: it was Dr. Eric Graham, the Principal of Royal Roads, inviting me to come over to the college for an interview. I agreed to go, and two days later I spent a pleasant day meeting the staff, wandering the lovely grounds, and looking through Hatley Castle. A beautiful place, I thought, but the prospects didn't look good for the long term: Jim Boutilier, the man I would be replacing for the year, took me home to dinner and to meet Bryony— but he made it clear that there were no permanent appointments to be made in History, although there was a good chance that I could stay a second year, if I were offered the job.

The next day, Eric Graham rang up to offer me the job. I told him that I'd need a day to consider it.

Now we were really stuck. Did I take a certain one-year job, or turn it down in the hope that External Affairs would actually come through? I went to the library, got an Ottawa telephone directory, and looked up the numbers of some of the offices at External. I was lucky with my very first call: the secretary who answered reassured me that I had the right office. Her boss was away for the rest of the day, but perhaps she could help? I explained the situation to her, trying not to sound absolutely desperate as I did so.

"Just a minute," she said. "I've got all the files right here in the cabinet."

I could actually hear her open the drawer and pull the file.

"Let's see...Martel, André Gordon...oh, yes, your name is close to the top of the list. We will certainly be offering you an appointment."

But if this was the case, what was taking so long? The competition had finished in November; over six months had passed. Why?

"Oh, it's all because of the Olympic Games in Montreal."

"What?" How could my future be tied up with something as remote as this?

"Well, you see, where we normally have fifty or sixty RCMP officers working on the security clearances of the qualified candidates, this year we only have five or six, because most of them have been assigned to cover the Olympics. So they are taking much longer than usual. And no offers can go out until all the investigations are completed."

*

Had it not been for the Olympic Games in Montreal that summer of 1976, I would now be working as a Canadian diplomat instead of writing diplomatic history and collecting stories about the craft.

After I spoke to the helpful secretary that day, Valerie and I spent a sleepless night trying to decide what to do. In the end, we agreed that, as a diplomatic career had always been a second choice to a scholarly one, we would run the risk that "something would turn up" after the year at Royal Roads was over. It did, and everything turned out for the best. But had it not been for the Olympics, I would never have bothered to apply for a temporary academic job, our lives would have been very different, and this book would never have been produced—or at least, not by me. Whether this is a good thing or a bad thing I leave to the reader to decide.

Gordon Martel,
Victoria, British Columbia,
On a rainy St. Swithun's Day, 1991

Enter the Diplomats: Permission to Play

There are two key features to be found in the career of every professional diplomat: a motive for entering the service and a demonstration of ability sufficient to permit entry into it. Although many diplomats maintain a judicious silence on the subject of what drew them to their vocation, it is reasonable to assume that a variety of personal, patriotic and ideological motives may be discovered to lay behind such decisions. Perhaps this silence is so often maintained because old men, reflecting on their careers when their service is finished, hesitate to admit the sometimes whimsical—even farcical—motives that led them to the craft in the first place. Fortunately some, as we shall see, are more forthright. Many are less reluctant to describe the difficulties they experienced in gaining admission; in the twentieth century, the examination and interviewing process through which most would-be diplomats must pass can be both daunting and amusing.

An American Tale

When Norval Richardson was asked the question, "Why don't you go in for the diplomatic service?" one day before the First World War, he received it with the feeling that such a career might be the most picturesque one imaginable. To an American especially, it conjured up visions of kings and queens, decorated and decorative ambassadors, "and a horde of fascinating ladies who flitted in and out of the picture, coloring it with their beauty, their wonderful jewels, their intriguing perfumes and their possibilities for finding out international secrets which, without their aid, would remain forever unknown."

1

After these picturesque visions had vanished from his mind, however, he began to concentrate on the practical problems involved, were he to pursue a career in this service. To begin with, he knew absolutely nothing about diplomacy; unlike many of those who entered the service, he had no uncles or cousins or friends to open doors for him; although he had been to Europe twice, he had never set foot inside an embassy. He decided to do some research, making use of the limited resources available in his small town in Mississippi. He found, in the "World Almanac" an entry on the "Diplomatic and Consular Service," which listed the names of ambassadors and ministers and secretaries, their posts and salaries—but it was silent on the subject of how one set about becoming a diplomat.

As he was unable to pick up any useful information in print, he asked friends if they had any idea of how he might pursue his quest. One of them suggested that getting in was entirely a matter of having the support of his state's senator—that diplomatic jobs were mere political favours. This brought him to the conclusion that the most feasible thing for him to do was to go to Washington to consult the senator from his state; and thus, only one day after the question, "Why don't you go in for the diplomatic service," had been asked of him, he found himself leaving Mississippi on a train bound for Washington.

When Richardson arrived in the capital, his senator, John Sharp Williams, received him with proper Southern cordiality, asked him to sit down while he unlocked a drawer of his desk, took out a bottle of very fine old bourbon, mixed each of them a toddy, then sat back and asked the young man to describe his plans. Senator Williams admitted that he didn't actually know what the system was for entering the service, although he understood that the former Secretary of State, Elihu Root, had prepared some sort of scheme for improving the quality of the people admitted to a career in diplomacy. But he promised to take Richardson to see Secretary of State Philander C. Knox, where they would find out everything they needed to know.

"Before he had finished speaking he picked up the telephone and ran from his words to me into a demand...to be put in communication with the State Department. I was rather surprised to find that it took only a few moments for the Senator to be talking personally with the

Secretary of State himself." It was arranged that he would meet with Secretary Knox himself at half past ten the next morning.

Richardson felt that he had made a tremendous step forward in accomplishing his goal: "That I was actually going to meet the Secretary of State appeared to me then as having torn away all barriers. I already felt a full-fledged diplomat—somewhat disturbed, however, with the realization that I was going to have my first encounter with a member of a cabinet." Knox's reputation was that of a friendly, approachable person, but Richardson took no chances; just in case he had the opportunity to express his great admiration for what Knox had done for the nation, he spent the night reading everything he could find on him.

The next morning the young man and his senator set off to the imposing and forbidding old State, War and Navy building. A tremendous feeling of stage fright overcame Richardson when a private secretary asked them to come into the Secretary's room; but the feeling began to disappear when he entered and saw a little man sitting in a chair, which was tilted back, with his feet on the desk before him. This informal position, accompanied by a hearty, "Hello, Williams; come in," was in itself a blow that almost robbed Richardson of all his romantic notions of the craft of diplomacy. While the two wily and worldly older men amused themselves by chatting about political questions of the moment, young Richardson sat off to one side, ignored.

Finally, just as he was beginning to think that his existence had been entirely forgotten, the Senator announced: "This young man wants to go into the diplomatic service. I brought him along to find out what he had to do to get into it. Is my recommendation sufficient?"

Secretary Knox smiled sagely. "Of course that's the best recommendation he could possibly have," he deftly assured the Senator, "but we've got some special regulations just now—examinations, things like that—but I'm sure your friend can pass them all right."

Richardson could feel his heart sinking. A chill ran through him as he considered what he might be examined for. He nervously put the question to the Secretary, who genially replied, "I can't tell you exactly. I haven't time to go into it myself. The Assistant-Secretary will tell you all that. He has charge of the personnel of the service."

An expressionless, formal and grave Assistant-Secretary explained that all applicants for the diplomatic service were expected to pass an examination in international law, diplomatic usages and one modern language. He gave Richardson a pamphlet outlining the requirements and sent him off to see the Chief of the Diplomatic Bureau. At this next stop, he was informed that an examination would be held in two months' time, was advised that he should engage a teacher of international law to coach him and that he would do well to take on a French instructor as well. Eventually, Richardson departed from the building, loaded down with pamphlets, the titles of books and the names of teachers. He was not feeling optimistic. "The idea of passing an examination hung over me with depressing dread. I knew nothing of the subjects that had been mentioned. International law was as totally strange as diplomatic usages." The only ray of light that he could see was his tourist's knowledge of French; at least that was not an entirely closed book to him—perhaps he did enjoy at least some slight advantage.

Still, this small ray of hope was not enough to lift the would-be diplomat out of his mood of despair; he was ready to get back on the next train for Mississippi and look for another career when the Senator reassured him that it could not be as bad as it sounded; after all, "international law was such a vague thing that no one really knew anything about it; and so far as diplomatic usages went, he supposed that was merely a matter of knowing how to say good morning in French and to eat with the right knife and fork." Young Richardson sensed that Senator Williams and Secretary Knox obviously took the whole thing pretty lightly; but he could also see that those who were actually responsible, the Assistant-Secretary and the Chief of the Diplomatic Bureau, regarded the examination very seriously indeed. Nevertheless, having come this far, he decided that he could at least take a look at the sample examination when he got back to his hotel; maybe it wouldn't be as bad as it sounded.

When he began looking through the questions, however, he began to sink into despair once more. How, for instance was he to respond to something like this: *"During a recent revolution in Constantinople one X, a member of the late Turkish cabinet, applied to the American embassy for admission and was admitted. One Y, a member of the recent government, indicted for the misappropriation of funds, secretly entered the American embassy. Z, an opponent of the revolution, pursued by a mob, seeks refuge in the American embassy. What should be the action of the American embassy in each of these cases?"* The young Mississippian was once again tempted to take the next train out, but after spending a sleepless night decided that he had little to lose in devoting a couple of months to preparation for the examination. In spite of all the odds against him, he would give it a try.

He found a teacher of international law who thought that he might possibly learn enough in two months to get through the examination—if he devoted all of his waking hours to the subject. The only respite from the law was to be a daily hour of French. It was arranged that he would receive his tuition each morning before breakfast, from 6 a.m to 8 a.m., as the tutor was already responsible for eight other students working towards the examination.

Richardson's French teacher turned out to be an eminently practical man: there were ten questions that students were usually asked in the oral examination; he advised the young man to prepare answers to them, learn these by heart, and be ready to recite them when the crucial moment came. He gave him an example: the first question to be asked might well be, *"Where have you learned French?"* Richardson was to compose a reply, which the teacher would then convert into colloquial French for him to memorize. Years later, he could still recall: *"J'ai appris le français dans mon enfance parce que ma ville natale était près de la Nouvelle-Orléans, où l'on parle français plus que dans n'importe quelle autre ville des Etats-Unis d'Amérique."* By the time the examination arrived he could let the whole sentence slip out with all the aplomb of a spirited linguist.

Richardson was becoming committed to the project and feeling somewhat more optimistic when he received a letter from a friend who insisted that he had gone off his head to attempt to enter the diplomatic service. It took years of preparation to get in, his friend assured him; in fact, he knew of no one who would even attempt the examination without having first spent two years at the *Ecole Libre des Sciences Politiques* in Paris. This depressing information only hardened Richardson's resolve: he began working by six each morning, and continued well into the night, keeping up this pace for two months. He had never worked harder, nor would he ever work as hard again. If he did reward himself with a respite from his studies by going out to something like a dinner party, he would find himself staring at the centrepiece, imagining it to be a fishing boat caught within the three-mile limit. He slept, ate and breathed international law and diplomatic usage, taking time out only to memorize French phrases.

When the fateful morning of the examination finally arrived, he found himself with twenty-five other men in a corner room in the State Department—a room that Richardson found to be filled with an oppressive atmosphere of unremitting gloom. As the passing minutes turned into an hour while they waited to begin, the scene became almost funereal: "the solemn faces, the stiff positions, the careful dressing, the silence, the awful waiting—all of it was exactly like those moments when one waits in a darkened parlour for the corpse to be brought in." At last, a young man came into the room—to announce that the examination would be delayed twenty-four hours! The despair of the candidates was aggravated as they crept away from the building and back to their rooms.

When the agonizing wait finally ended, the applicants were assembled in an examination room, where they spent the next four hours composing answers to thirty-six problems of international law. Richardson looked over the questions, instantly concluded that he was not really familiar with any of them, but began writing anyway and, before he knew it, the four hours had passed. The candidates were then sent away to come back on the following day for the language examination.

When they arrived the next morning, they were given official notes in French to translate into English. That wasn't too bad, but then Richardson turned to find that they had also been given a treaty in English to put into French. "Put a treaty into French! Ye Gods—that was beyond any one's power—even a Frenchman's! Who under the sun could be expected to know technical phrases in French? The man sitting next to me gasped....I heard him groan and curse and complain in gasping breath." When the examination invigilator left the room, Richardson's tormented neighbour turned to him desperately and whispered, "How do you write August in French?" Richardson clearly knew a little more French than at least one of the other candidates.

Afterwards, the examinees gathered for a small celebration in the grill of the Shoreham Hotel, where a spirit of friendship—probably based on mutual suffering—began to grow up amongst them. They began to cheer up as they sat around drinking beer and complaining of the delays and unfairness of the system in general, when suddenly one of their colleagues burst into the room and stood gazing at the rest of them with fixed and bulging eyes. He wanted to know how many subjects the others had been told would constitute the subjects of the examination; they all answered the same way: "international law, diplomatic usage and a modern language." He had been told the same thing—but just now had heard from a friend of his in the Department that it had been decided to examine them on world politics as well. "It's to be to-morrow morning—oral—we're to sit before six judges and stand the grilling—it's to come just after oral French. World politics! What does it include? Everything under the sun!"

The rest of the room was stunned into silence. But their informant had already conceived of a plan: he had heard of someone—"some sort of a professor of history"—who was willing to give them a lecture that very night: "just a skeleton of everything that's happened since the world began. I've talked to him over the telephone and engaged him for the evening. Any of you want to go in on this?" The roomful of desperate, would-be diplomats instantly agreed that this was the only sensible thing they could do.

So later that night they gathered for a three-hour lecture from "a shrunken old fellow" who talked to them on everything that had happened since the beginning of time. Richardson recalled that it was impossible to keep up with him: "He changed the subject as fast and as frequently as the dictionary. Before I had finished making a note on the Young Turk Party he was in the midst of the Treaty of Vienna." The whole exercise proved worthless. It succeeded only in adding to their confusion.

The next morning proved to be the very worst part of the entire experience. They were taken into a room, six at a time, and placed in chairs facing six judges. The light streamed in from windows behind the judges, making their faces somewhat indistinct, yet nevertheless formidable. The first examinee in Richardson's group, an experienced and cosmopolitan type, got through the French brilliantly, was satisfactory in international law, and provided a convincing summary of the Hay-Pauncefote Treaty. The next young man, who had earlier explained that he had intended to go in for the Consular Service, and had somehow wound up applying for the Diplomatic by mistake, failed miserably. The third, the candidate who had not known the French for "August," got nowhere with the language section.

Finally, the inquisitors came to Richardson. As if in a dream, the French examiner turned to him and asked: *"Monsieur, où avez-vous le français?"* It was almost too good to be true. Richardson rolled out his memorized reply with a convincing flourish—and said a silent prayer in honour of his French tutor.

A question on citizenship was the next hurdle: *"If an Austrian woman married an Italian, came to America, where the husband became a naturalized American, divorced him, married a German, went mad and was deserted by the second husband and left entirely destitute—what country should take care of her?"* But the gods were once again on Richardson's side; his international law tutor had grounded him in this particular case. He got through it with flying colours.

But then they wanted to know what he knew about the Barbary States. Desperately sending out thoughts in every direction, he realized that he didn't know anything at all about them. Just as he was on the verge of confessing total ignorance however, a faint recollection stirred within, and although it seemed absurd, he replied that, "all I seem to remember about the Barbary States is that when our warships used to go there and insisted upon being received with salutes, a barrel of gunpowder was demanded for each salute fired." Although one of the judges actually broke the ice by smiling at this attempt at an answer, the questions began to get worse and worse, ending with Richardson's confession of absolute ignorance concerning Secretary Root's efforts to establish a Pan-American Union in Central America.

The agony eventually came to an end however, and that afternoon the examinees submitted themselves to a physical examination. Richardson's eyes, heart, kidneys, lungs, etc. proved that they were in good working order; so he received the discouraging news that he could be sent without danger to any part of the world. "It is all very well to know that you are perfectly fit; but when this fitness subjects you to being sent to many places that you have no great desire to see, it becomes a little less exhilarating."

When all was done, Richardson and his fellow-sufferers were advised to remain in Washington for a fortnight until the results of the examination were known. The two weeks slowly dragged by, but no word came. Gradually becoming ever more desperate to know his fate, Richardson returned to his helpful friend, the Senator, telling him that the uncertainty of not knowing the result was just about killing him. The Senator promised to go to the State Department the very next day and ask a discreet question or two.

The Senator, as good as his word, called later the next day to let Richardson know that he had passed the examination—although he was amused to pass on the comment that the examiners had found his fellow Mississippian "a provincial type". Richardson didn't care. He had passed. He went to bed and slept for two days and two nights.

Several weeks later a strange-looking tubular package arrived at Richardson's door, bearing the seal of the United States, and with "Department of State" written on it. Tearing it open, he drew out a large square of parchment, which read:

WILLIAM HOWARD TAFT
PRESIDENT OF THE UNITED STATES OF AMERICA

To Norval Richardson, of Mississippi: Greetings. Reposing special trust and confidence in your Integrity, Prudence and Ability, I have nominated and, by and with the advice and consent of the Senate, do appoint you Second Secretary of the Legation of the United States of America at Havana, Cuba, authorizing you hereby to go and perform all such matters and things as to the said place or office do appertain, or as may be duly given you in charge hereafter, and the said office to hold and exercise during the pleasure of the President of the United States.

Source: Norval Richardson, *My Diplomatic Education*, pp. 1-29.

*   *   *

On occasion, however, it has been surprisingly easy to gain entrance into the diplomatic world, even when one has one's heart set on other things.

The Exchange Rate on Swiss Francs

Canadian Louis Rasminsky, in contrast, had remarkably little difficulty in winning a post on the League of Nations staff in 1930, when Rasminsky was only 22. He later attributed this early success to his "sheer effrontery" in applying. His mind, however, was not entirely on the new job. As Rasminsky tells it, he immediately sent a telegram to Lyla Rotenberg in Toronto: "Have accepted job League of Nations at 13,700 Swiss francs. Will you marry me?" The reply was swift: "What is exchange rate on Swiss francs?"

According to all reports the marriage was long, happy, and filled with a sense of humour. In later years the Rasminskys became distinguished among civil servant families for tooting about drab Ottawa in a red convertible—but by that time Rasminsky was Deputy Governor of the Bank of Canada.

Sources: J.L. Granatstein. *The Ottawa Men: The Civil Service Mandarins, 1935-57*, p. 136.

*   *   *

In the twentieth century both a written and an oral examination have become essential components of the appointment process almost everywhere, but there are some profound differences apparent between nations in the way they choose to go about this. Different states have placed different obstacles in the path of would-be diplomats at different times. At various times those entering the service have had to prove the quality of their blood line, their knowledge of ancient languages, their ideological purity, or the extent of their private income. One wonders exactly what it was that the examiners were looking for in Britain when they grilled the young Piers Dixon.

Some Idiotic Questions

Looking back on his entry into the diplomatic service, Piers Dixon regarded his interview as a silly farce. The eminent scholar, Professor Ernest Barker (whose books and theories Dixon, fresh out of Cambridge, despised) and the woman who sat on the board did most of the questioning. They asked the candidate questions along the lines of: *"Who was the French poet who never wrote anything of note after the age of 17?"* and, *"Is there any resemblance in the mentalities of the ancient Greeks and modern Athenians?"* Probably the best one was, *"Would you prefer to live in the East or the West?"* Dixon placed second in the examinations and was admitted to the Foreign Office. He felt that he was let off lightly, but "longed to have all those Examiners in a *tête-à-tête* and to tell them their questions were idiotic."

Source: Pierson John Dixon, *Double Diploma*, p. 19.

*   *   *

A young Russian diplomat discovered that who you are—or appear to be—is sometimes as important as what you know.

Who You Know

Around the turn of the century, Dimitrii Abrikossow was a promising student with a burning desire to enter the diplomatic service and to see the world. The thought of the examination that awaited him was not especially frightening: he had taken hundreds of examinations without becoming nervous. As the day of the diplomatic approached, however, he found himself becoming afraid, as he thought about the possibility of the collapse of all his carefully-laid plans for the future, as well as the dreadful blow to his dignity that failure would entail.

He did not find a warm reception when he appeared at the Foreign Office in St Petersburg. As he made his way around the Office, in order to be presented to the high bureaucrats who worked there, he found that they never seemed to have the time to receive him, and he ended up spending hours waiting in empty corridors. He began to be oppressed by the feeling that all of the people there were hostile to him, a young man who came to them from a mere merchant family.

Eventually, the day of the examination dawned. Abrikossow waited in a half-lit room until his name was called and he passed into a brilliantly-illuminated chamber, in which everything seemed to him to be gilded. He took his place at a chair in the middle of the room, alone, in front of a long table covered in green cloth, behind which sat a row of uniformed high officials who were covered in decorations. The Vice-Minister of Foreign Affairs sat in the centre of the room, staring at the humble candidate through dark glasses. And there they all sat, for some time, in absolute silence.

When the questions began, poor Abrikossow felt like a mouse being toyed with by cats. The emininent professor of international law asked him: *"Please tell me what the Red Cross is."* Abrikossow conscientiously set about reciting the history of the founding of the Red Cross, but the professor, obviously becoming annoyed, informed him that he was not interested in historical research—he simply wanted to know what the Red Cross was. Abrikossow angrily replied that it was a flag with a red cross on it. Now the professor beamed with pleasure and said that this was the answer that he had been seeking.

The other questioners repeated the tactics of the eminent professor, reducing the whole exercise, as far as Abrikossow was concerned, to a mixture of repartee and mind reading. Meanwhile, the Vice Minister continued to sit in silence, staring at the young man through his dark glasses. The comedy lasted for an hour before Abrikossow was sent back, bitter and pessimistic, into the outer room.

During the next week the young Russian became steadily more convinced that his future would not lie in the diplomatic service. When the results were finally posted however, he was pleasantly surprised to discover that, although half of those taking the examination had failed, he was one of those who had succeeded. It did not take him long before he discovered why he had been among the fortunate ones.

The Vice-Minister, when the young man was brought before him, asked if he belonged to the rich Abrikossow family. When he had been in the Crimea, the all-powerful bureaucrat explained, he had several times passed a magnificent estate belonging to a Mrs.

Abrikossow; was the young man related to her? Remembering that one of his innumerable aunts did, in fact, own an estate in the Crimea, he answered in the affirmative—even though he knew that this aunt had absolutely nothing to do with him or with his family's fortune. Nevertheless, the connection had obviously impressed the Vice-Minister, who was a rich man himself and who, Abrikossow was later to learn, adored everything that had a touch of money.

Source: Dimitrii Abrikossow, *Revelations of a Russian Diplomat*, pp. 80-81.

*   *   *

The motives that have led men, and more recently women, into diplomatic careers are as varied as the individuals who pursue them. Norval Richardson, Piers Dixon and Dimitrii Abrikossow are relatively quiet on the subject of motivation, tending to emphasize the lure of travel and romance. Other, more serious-minded diplomats, are more inclined to explain the patriotic, philosophical or professional reasons that lie behind their decision to pursue a career in diplomacy; but the motives of many others were intensely personal and sometimes unique.

The Heart of the Matter

Ideology could easily be portrayed as the dominant theme in the diplomatic initiation of Alexandre Barmine. A young Soviet officer in 1921, he found himself accompanying a recently-appointed Soviet Ambassador, Iouréniev, on a mission to Bokhara. Four years earlier a Young Bokhara party had been formed, which soon succeeded in driving the Emir out of the country and then declared its adhesion to the principles of the Russian revolution. Nevertheless, it had since remained an independent state with a government of its own, and the purpose of Iouréniev's mission was to attempt to establish a Soviet regime there.

Barmine likened the journey to Bokhara to that of a medieval exploration of an unknown kingdom: the diplomatic party filled an entire train. In addition to the diplomatic personnel, which included a cook and typists, they took a detachment of Red soldiers, a large quantity of food, medical supplies, weapons, articles for barter, and presents. As the married members of the party brought their families with them, the party numbered forty-six in all. Normally, the journey would have taken five days; it took them twenty-four. The sun beat down on them every day as they travelled through the steppes and wastelands: "Men, and sometimes women, lay half-naked on the carriage roofs enjoying the warmth. We all felt at the top of our form, conscious that we were on the way to adventure, with a great mission to accomplish, and ready meanwhile to enjoy an unexpected rest-cure."

But what had brought Barmine to join this party, which was his initiation to becoming a career diplomat: revolutionary ideology? the quest for adventure? Partly; but the primary reason was more personal: "One of my friends...had a wife—a pretty little Tartar woman..." Not long after meeting her, Barmine found himself suggesting that she should leave her husband. "I was passionately in love, and so, apparently was Khadidzé (for that was her name). Although we lived in neighbouring rooms she would write me long letters the style of which at first surprised, then enchanted, me, such magic lay in her use of words."

The husband, when he learned of the relationship, approached Barmine for an explanation. As the two men were Party members, they believed in exercising tolerance and in the application of rationality to such affairs. Barmine later recalled having the impression "that all the militants of my generation were particularly scrupulous in affairs of the heart, and careful always to respect the woman's sense of dignity. We agreed to let Khadidzé decide between us." But she did not choose him. His spirit was crushed.

What made matters worse was Barmine's discovery of, "a correspondence, quite as lyrical as ours, which she was carrying on with another officer..." He did not tell his pretty little Tartar of his discovery, but it embittered him. "Disillusioned, and quite sure that I knew all that was to be known about the perfidy of the female heart, I decided to take the first opportunity that offered of going to some distant country."

That opportunity came when Ambassador Iouréniev asked Trotsky to find him some men with a knowledge of Oriental languages to assist him in undertaking his mission to Bokhara. Barmine was taken out of military college and appointed consul.

Another career in diplomacy had begun.

Source: Alexandre Barmine, *Memoirs of a Soviet Diplomat: Twenty Years in the Service of the USSR*, pp. 120-23.

* * *

Careers, romance and the expectations of youth seem to intermingle repeatedly at the outset of entering into the diplomatic profession. The young Alexandre Barmine had been propelled directly into the service by an affair of the heart; but at least it was his own heart that had cried out.

Cousin, Cousine

A young, well-educated, highly-refined and rich Italian, Daniele Varè, was, in the decade preceding the First World War, contemplating his future when he was called upon by the brother of an old school friend who suddenly reappeared in Italy after a sojourn in British Central Africa. This young man, Sabbatini, had been acting as an overseer on a plantation belonging to a Scotsman at Blantyre. He had run the plantation while the Scotsman happily drank whisky in the sun—until it caused his premature death. Sabbatini had returned to Europe in order to meet the heirs of the unfortunate Scot, hoping to raise enough money to buy the plantation. Varè, who was keen on the idea of colonial adventure, supplied the necessary funds. The property was duly purchased and Varè undertook preparations to go out with Sabbatini to Africa; they were to take with them a group of young Italians who wished to try their luck in new surroundings.

Varè booked his passage from Naples to Mombasa and arranged to meet with Sabbatini in Milan at the Hotel Cavour before they sailed. Fortuitously, among the guests at the hotel was the Contessa delle Somaglia, a pleasant old lady who had frequently taken an interest in

Varè's doings; when she spotted him, she asked him up to her sitting room and asked if he had really given up his earlier idea of entering the diplomatic service. He replied that he had indeed abandoned the idea; he decided instead to make a life for himself as a colonial.

In the course of their conversation, it gradually became clear that the Contessa's real interest was not in Varè himself, but in that of her nephew, Ascanio, who, like Varè, had taken the examination for the diplomatic service, but had finished up among the "also ran". She thought that her nephew might be encouraged to try again if Varè did as well. But he had made up his mind: to Africa he would go.

Following the conversations with the Contessa, however, Sabbatini astonished Varè by asking if he really still meant to go out to Mombasa along with the others. When he replied that he did indeed, his young partner was obviously disappointed. The ship, it seems, was fully booked and no further accommodation was available. If Varè did not change his mind, there would be no room on board for anyone else. But why, Varè wanted to know, did Sabbatini suddenly need the extra place?

"The truth is, I was thinking of getting married."

"Do you mean that you want my cabin for your future wife?"

"That was the idea."

"And who is *die Betreffende*, as they say in German?"

"Well, so far, she doesn't exist."

Asked to provide some details concerning this non-existent woman who apparently would require the use of Varè's cabin, his friend explained that he had some cousins in Asti, and although he had not heard of them for some time, he remembered a little girl being there the last time that he had visited; she must now be seventeen or eighteen. His cousins seemed to him to be nice people, and he didn't think he could do better than marry one of them.

"Do you mean to tell me that you contemplate asking this girl, who probably does not know of your existence, to marry you offhand and to start with you for Central Africa by the first boat?" the astonished Varè asked.

"Yes."

Varè, impressed by this display of nerve, agreed that if the young cousin agreed to marry his friend he would concede his cabin to her:

"You are probably right that one requires a wife out there. But nobody would marry *me* on such short notice. I wish you good luck!"

Sabbatini immediately left for Asti, returning to Milan within three days to announce that everything had been settled. After offering his congratulations, Varè asked what exactly had happened when he met up with the cousins.

"Well," his young friend admitted, "it was a little difficult at first. You see, I arrived just in time for the father's funeral."

"Not a propitious moment, certainly. And then, what?"

Sabbatini explained that the cousins naturally assumed that he had come for the funeral and were deeply moved by this gesture of sympathy on his part. While they were on their way to the funeral, he took the opportunity to study the mourners carefully to see if he could determine which of them might be his possible fiancée.

"And you spotted her?"

"Yes."

"And, later on, you proposed?"

"Yes."

"Well, if you do not make a successful colonist, no one will. You are welcome to my cabin."

Sabbatini and his bride left for Mombasa and Blantyre. Varè never did go out. Following the suggestion of the Contessa, he and her nephew took the examination for the diplomatic service, in which both of them this time succeeded.

"And that," Varè explained years afterward, "is how I became a diplomat."

Source: Daniele Varè, *The Two Impostors*, pp. 69-71.

*   *   *

The entry of diplomats into the profession is, of course, a two-way street: both the individuals and the organizations that they serve have their motives. The qualities, talents and experience that are looked for in seeking out new blood for the diplomatic profession vary enormously, and organizations today often go to considerable effort and expense to find the people they are looking for: testing them, interviewing them, and investigating their background.

They also Serve...

Some of the qualities sought by the state vary with the circumstances of the situation. In the United States during the First World War, for instance, the British newspaper magnate, Lord Northcliffe, headed a mission on behalf of the Lloyd George government to determine the effectiveness of the British propaganda effort there. He reported that the French, Irish and German propaganda machines were much more effective than the British, and the impression was being conveyed that soldiers from the British Dominions and France were doing all the fighting, while the British were content to sit back, collect the money, and do little of the work.

The French in particular were making a concerted effort to get the American government to bring pressure to bear on the British to contribute more to the war effort in France—where, they maintained, the war had to be won. To this end the French circulated stories in the United States that the British had been slack in combing out their stay-at-homes, or *embusqués*, as the French called them. The French had even pointed scornfully to the large number of able-bodied British officers serving in various Missions in the US.

As a result, the new head of the British Military Mission in the US wondered if this background was responsible for the choice of military diplomatists chosen by his government to serve in Washington: "we were three jolly cripples. Wilson had been badly wounded twice, in the stomach and the head, and had to wear black glasses, and poor 'Kit' Cator shot through the lung, was a good imitation of a corpse...whilst I myself went about intermittently on crutches and could wear five wound stripes."

These diplomats must have been beyond reproach.

Source: Tom Bridges, *Alarms and Excursions*, pp. 207-8.

*   *   *

One of the aspects that is usually taken into account when deciding upon the appointment of ambassadors is how well their personal characteristics and experience is likely to be received by the people of the state to which they are appointed. It is illuminating to hear the kind of thinking that went on behind the scenes when James Bryce came to be appointed British Ambassador to the United States in 1906.

Verbosity and its Rewards

The King wished to appoint his good friend, Charles Hardinge, to the post—but the Foreign Secretary, Sir Edward Grey, regarded Hardinge as too valuable to be permitted to leave the Foreign Office itself, and refused to agree to the appointment. The King turned to Hardinge to ask for another suggestion.

Hardinge racked his brain all night to come up with a suitable alternative, and in the small hours of the morning finally had a brainwave: James Bryce, although within a year of the compulsory retirement age of seventy, would, Hardinge thought, be greatly appreciated in Washington, as he knew more of the history and Constitution of the United States than most Americans did. Perhaps equally important in Hardinge's estimation was that Bryce, "also had the quality of liking to make long and rather dull speeches on commonplace subjects which I knew to be a trait that would be popular with the American masses." The King "was enchanted at my suggestion..."

Source: Hardinge of Penshurst, *The Old Diplomacy*, pp. 131-32.

*　　　　*　　　　*

Wounds and dull speeches might appear to be rather surprising characteristics to be sought in diplomats, but the closer we get to the realities of diplomatic life, the harder it becomes to be surprised by anything.

Give 'em Hell, Bernie

What traits, one might wonder, led Woodrow Wilson to appoint the amateurish Bernard Baruch as American representative to the Reparations Commission when the peacemakers met at Versailles in 1919? Primary among them may well have been Baruch's reputation as a financier, but possibly Wilson, who had an inveterate distrust of career diplomats, was looking for something else as well.

One day, after Wilson had given an address before a plenary session of the Peace Conference at the Quai d'Orsay, he had one of his assistants find Baruch to tell him that he wished to see him. Baruch went over to where the President was conversing with a group of dignitaries. "Please wait for me, Baruch," Wilson said. He then took the financier and novice diplomat by the arm, walked out of the room and took him to the presidential limousine, giving instructions to his driver that they would be taking Baruch to his hotel.

"I hear a great many complaints about you," said the President to his worried appointee. "You must be doing a good job. You keep at it and don't worry. You'll stay on as long as I am President."

Source: Bernard M. Baruch, *The Making of the Reparation and Economic Sections of the Treaty*, p. 123.

*   *   *

In fact, it is impossible to predict what qualifications will be looked for in an ambassador—or what an ambassadorial audience might be expecting to find when one appears before it.

Thank you very much

A later British Ambassador to the United States, the Earl of Halifax, gave an after-dinner speech to a club in Milwaukee in the days before America's entry into the Second World War. When he had answered the last question, the proposer of the vote of thanks complimented him by saying, "Up to now there have always been some of us here who would have expected, when we met the British Ambassador, that we should find him too smart for us. After meeting Lord Halifax, we shan't think so any longer."

Source: The Earl of Halifax, *The Fulness of Days*, p. 267.

A Diplomat's Work is Never Done

Once admitted to the service, the diplomat discovers that a number of surprising tasks lay in wait: some of them delightful, some of them disgusting, and many of them boring.

Oh! To be Young

While diplomats are most frequently portrayed as white-headed, elderly statesmen, they can, in fact, be young—and behave in the way that the young will. One American diplomat, looking back after a lifetime in the diplomatic service, recalled how glorious it had been to live the life of a young diplomat in Constantinople in the years before the First World War. He recalled how he and his friend Jay, another youthful diplomat in the American embassy, experienced the pleasing sensation of being important and above the law; it seemed that they could do no wrong: "In perfect innocence we acted in the most high-handed way; once when a band of singing Greeks disturbed Jay's slumbers at Therapia, he put an end to their musical enthusiasm by firing a revolver over their heads and then having them all arrested."

Source: Lewis D. Einstein, *A Diplomat Looks Back*, p. 26.

*   *   *

The experiences of all young diplomats are not necessarily so pleasant. In fact, some of the discomforts that are encountered can be more than mere irritations, as the following description will show.

The Other East

A virile young Soviet officer found that after serving a mere two months as Consul in Karchi, Bokhara (where his predecessor had died of malaria), his health had almost been ruined. He suffered badly from abscesses—a common ailment among Europeans living in sub-tropical regions where the cold in autumn and winter can be very biting. "I used to dictate my orders and my mail lying in bed, my feet stretched out towards a sort of stove which stood in the middle of the room, and in which a gentle fire was maintained," he recalled. He conducted most of his official interviews in the same posture, as he found that he had to avoid standing up if he could possibly do so. "My left foot was so covered with open sores that I could not wear a boot on it, and had to go about with one foot in a boot and the other in a Turkish slipper."

In spite of adopting the local cure of considerable quantities of an aromatic and health-giving wine, he was not restored to good health until he was recalled to Europe.

Source: Alexandre Barmine, *Memoirs of a Soviet Diplomat: Twenty Years in the Service of the USSR*, p. 137.

*   *   *

The life that diplomats endure might be less romantic, and certainly less comfortable, than the one that they imagined for themselves before leaving home. While it might well be supposed that they lead a charmed life housed in luxurious surroundings in beautiful buildings in the best area in whatever city they happen to be in, this is not always the case. Consider, for instance, the conditions of life endured by a British Consul in northern Poland following the end of the Second World War.

Cold Comfort

While it was true that the Consul and his staff were lodged in a hotel, "luxurious" would hardly be an appropriate description. Their rooms were rarely heated; when the Consul confronted the hotel manager about this, it was explained to him that the hotel was deliberately kept short of coal because, in the basement of the hotel, the manager ran a cabaret-dancehall that was deemed by the communist authorities to be inimical to public morals.

To combat the cold, the occupants of the hotel used kerosene stoves in their rooms. The Consul slept in long woollen underwear, flannel pyjamas, an American Air Force sleeping-bag and any other bed-clothes that he could find. When he went to sleep at night, he placed his stove within reach of the bed and put a small saucepan of water on it. In the morning he lit the stove, waited in bed until the room warmed up a little, got up, and shaved with the hot water from the saucepan. Washing was difficult without a bath, and had to be done hastily in the cold, doing "about a quarter of one's person at a time" until someone discovered the existence of a bathroom that had been walled up. On those occasions when the Consul was fortunate enough to procure some coal to heat the water, he could actually have a bath in the tub, which "was also to be the place where confidential papers would be burnt in case of emergency."

Source: Eric Cleugh, *Without Let or Hindrance*, p. 153.

*　　　*　　　*

Many of the jobs that diplomats are required to perform are neither romantic nor adventurous, but perfunctory and tedious. In particular, the job of writing and revising speeches and reports is often one of endless tedium. The diaries of Charles Ritchie give a rich sense of the nature of such work.

Dealing with the Minister

"June 5, 1969

"Yet another Cabinet Minster—Pepin, the Minister of Trade and Commerce.... He is big and jovial, and looks like a cross between an Assyrian emperor and Groucho Marx.... A group of us went back to the Dorchester to work on his speech. It is a long time since I have put in such a session, yet how many hundreds of times I have done it and with so many different Ministers—battles of wits, will, prestige, over the inclusion of one civil servant's draft or the substitution of it for another; attempts by civil servants, gently, firmly, persistently, to eliminate the Minister's wilder, bolder—or just more vote-getting—passages in the text. Block that metaphor! Drop that joke! A final, exhausted tug-of-war over the elimination of the word "despite" in paragraph 4."

Source: Charles Ritchie. *Storm Signals: More Undiplomatic Diaries, 1962-71*, pp. 132-33.

*   *   *

*A*nother Canadian, Douglas LePan, gives an amusing account of what it is like to deal with the problem of getting a speech read properly. At the time LePan was principal advisor to the Canadian delegate at a 1950 meeting in Sydney of the Commonwealth Consultative Committee for South and South-East Asia. The delegate himself was one Robert Mayhew, the Canadian Minister of Fisheries.

Well Read

"At the time I am writing of, [Mayhew] was in his seventieth year and had the gaunt, stringy neck and rather watery, unfocussed eyes of an old man. He was liked and respected both in Cabinet and in the House of Commons. But he was a terrible speaker and had had practically no experience in international negotiations. To guide him through the rough waters of the meeting at Sydney was difficult in the extreme, and I had to advise him with more decisiveness and less defence than would normally be becoming a civil servant....

"Perhaps one illustration of my difficulties will be enough. I was rather pleased with the speech I had prepared for Mr. Mayhew to give at the first plenary session, which was to be open to the press. It said what needed to be said, and, into the bargain, it sounded like Bob Mayhew rather than like any of his advisers. When he delivered it, though, I was dumbfounded. He paid no attention to the punctuation, running on from the end of one sentence to the middle of the next before coming to a full stop. For all the world, it was like Peter Quince speaking the prologue to the play-within-the-play in *A Midsummer Night's Dream*. But what was to be done? With a thruster like Percy Spender presiding over the conference and with many in Ottawa on alert to see that we didn't exceed our instructions, it was no laughing matter. The first expedient I tried was to have everything triple-spaced for him. That didn't work. Then I tried leaving large spaces between sentences. That didn't work, either. Finally, I had every sentence typed as a single paragraph. Only then did the sentences come out more or less as they had been drafted...."

Source: Douglas LePan, *Bright Glass of Memory*, pp. 188-89.

* * *

Other diplomatic tasks can be just as trying. Young members of staff frequently find themselves in the position of acting as secretary, handyman, or governess to their elders. Diplomats, who traditionally came from well-to-do backgrounds were accustomed to being looked after and, until the twentieth century, anyone pursuing a career in diplomacy was expected to enjoy the luxury of a private income, with the result that many of them knew little about managing their own affairs.

Diamonds are Forever

One story seems to summarize quite neatly this attitude of an older generation of diplomatists, who would gradually disappear from the scene over the course of the twentieth century, to be replaced by a more professional, and circumspect, approach to the matter of private finances.

The young Charles Hardinge, employed as the private secretary to Lord Dufferin during Dufferin's time as ambassador at Constantinople, discovered that he had a rather different attitude to financial affairs. Dufferin used to complain of the heavy quarterly bills for which he was responsible, and the younger man, anxious to please, made great efforts to reduce expenses—with the result that he soon reduced the quarterly bill by £500.

Dufferin expressed his warmest gratitude for the saving that he had accomplished, but a few days after receiving this praise, Hardinge was handed a new bill for £500. He approached the Ambassador to ask what this was for, whereupon he was told that it was a diamond bracelet for Lady Dufferin. When Hardinge began to protest, Dufferin simply asked, "Did you not say you had saved for me £500?

Source: Hardinge of Penshurst, *The Old Diplomacy*, pp. 16-17.

*　　　　　*　　　　　*

Learning to look after their elders is but one of the many jobs awaiting the unsuspecting young. They soon discover that only a few diplomats actually engage in the exciting business of high politics, and many of them, especially in their early careers, find themselves dealing with situations that, however delicate they may be, and however important to the individuals involved, could most appropriately be described as trivial.

Grievances and Governesses

One such situation concerned a junior British official at Sinaia in Rumania before the First World War. When he arrived in Rumania, the young John Gregory was anxious to probe the difficult and complicated puzzle of Rumania's relations with the Triple Alliance of Germany, Austria-Hungary and Italy. But he soon discovered that his daily energies had to be diverted to a task that could not, by any conceivable stretch of the imagination, by defined as "political". It fell to him to investigate the grievances of English women who had come to Rumania to serve as governesses, and, if their grievances proved well-founded, to repatriate them to the British Isles. Before long he was seeing governesses in his sleep.

"They appeared by the hundred: from where I have no idea. When I had disposed of one crop, another bobbed up. Wherever I looked I saw governesses. There were days when they appeared to be sitting, like so many motionless elementals, on every seat of the hall of the hotel (where I lived), and on every seat of the hotel garden."

And they always had the same sad story to tell: of being lured from England under false pretences; that the family who had lured them out had turned out to be criminals, perhaps murderers; that they were not being paid; that their living conditions were intolerable, etc. Listening to these repetitious tales began to grind poor Gregory down, and yet he had to console the aggrieved women and enter into a prolonged, acrimonious and ineffective correspondence with their employers. He usually ended up repatriating the unfortunate women.

The young diplomat began to grow terrified as he foresaw a future devoted to nothing but listening to these tedious tales and writing meaningless letters, when he received, for a change, a visit from the employer of one of the governesses, who at least had a somewhat different tale to tell.

The employer was an elderly, peppery and rather decrepit Rumanian general. And this time it was he who had the grievance, the result of which was to modify young Gregory's entire view of the whole governess business. The poor old general came to complain that his governess was mistreating him: "She had first kicked him down his own stairs, and then thrown him on his own sofa and belaboured him with his own walking stick." Although the general was too incoherently irate to explain what it was he was after, he appeared to be demanding some kind of redress, compensation or protection. Gregory was unable to offer him anything. But the experience of the general did have the effect of changing Gregory's tone with the "helpless" governesses: "I gave up repatriating them and sent them away with advice which, if they ever acted on it, probably landed them in a Rumanian prison."

Source: John Gregory, *On the Edge of Diplomacy: Rambles and Reflections, 1902-1928*, pp. 58-60.

*   *   *

The young Gregory's experience with the governesses in Rumania may have been tedious, but at least it was not publicly embarrassing. Even elder statesmen occasionally find that diplomacy, in spite of its apparently rigid code of protocol and decorum, occasionally lends itself to some rather bizarre episodes.

Proudly Presenting: "Mr. & Mrs. America"

Few episodes can have been more bizarre than the appearance of "Mr. and Mrs. America" at the embassy of the United States in Tokyo during the summer of 1935. This "couple" consisted of two life-size dolls, sent over to Japan by the Mayor of New York on a good-will mission, where they were eventually received by Joseph Grew, the American Ambassador.

The suggestion for the "mission" had apparently come from the Board of Tourist Industry of the Japanese Railways. Mayor LaGuardia had taken up the idea and dispatched the dolls from New York—following an appropriate ceremony and much publicity—on board a Japanese liner, where they were given the "suite de luxe". When they arrived in Japan, they were immediately a great popular success, being taken all over the country by train, bus, airplane, ferry and every other available means of transportation. So popular were the dolls that when the Ambassador was informed that they would be calling on the embassy, he felt that he could not refuse to receive them without giving offence to the organizers and without creating an unpleasant impression amongst the Japanese.

Thus it was that the American Ambassador and his wife found themselves on the terrace of the embassy giving tea to a couple of life-size dolls in front of the assembled staff and reporters. The reception was a popular success, "although Mrs. America's arm dropped off as she entered." It was quickly re-attached, and the dolls were seated and given ice tea, "while we shook hands with them in front of a battery of press cameras."

Source: Joseph C. Grew, *Ten Years in Japan*, pp. 156-57.

*　　　　*　　　　*

Diplomats abroad frequently find themselves, as was the experience of Ambassador Grew, with having to live up to the expectations of those peoples amongst whom they live. Conversely, diplomats at home, working within their foreign office or department of state, may find themselves in equally delicate situations, as they are forced to live up to (or down to) the expectations (or desires) of their own citizens.

Devices and Desires

Such was the case in Britain when an important editor of the *Pall Mall Gazette* newspaper stirred up a campaign against the invidious traffic in "white slaves" This editor had established a connection with the British Foreign Office while pursuing the case of a particular young girl who was used by him as an experiment to illustrate the ease and impunity with which such seductions could be effected. One of the agents enlisted by the editor in this cause, professing to be a champion of all the virtues, and failing to obtain direct access to the Prime Minister, came to the Foreign Office seeking assistance.

The agent was introduced to one of the Under-Secretary's Private Secretaries, Arthur Hardinge, to whom he explained that many English girls were kidnapped and taken to brothels on the Continent. What the agent proposed was that he himself should undertake to visit these brothels, "disguised," he explained to Hardinge, "as a debauchee." Hardinge thought, in looking the gentleman over, that he might impersonate with ease the part that he desired to play.

What he wanted from Hardinge was a series of letters to Britain's ambassadors and ministers resident in those cities of Europe "in which profligacy of every kind was most rampant." Perhaps, he suggested, these representatives of the Crown might place at his disposal some youthful junior member of the diplomatic service, "to take him round these shocking scenes of vice." Hardinge advised the ingenious crusader that, while he himself lacked the authority to provide such introductions on his own initiative, perhaps he might approach the Under-Secretary, the flinty and upright Sir Philip Currie. "Is he," inquired the agent, "at heart a supporter of our moral crusade?" Hardinge confidently replied that he did not doubt that Sir Philip would sympathize with any moral object; and, so saying, showed him to the door that led to the Under-Secretary's office.

A few minutes later, Hardinge heard this same door bang violently, quickly followed by the sound of footsteps retreating down the hall. A servant then appeared in Hardinge's office to announce that Sir Philip wished to see him at once.

Why, the furious Under-Secretary asked, had Hardinge sent such a scoundrel to see him, and what had led him to suggest that he might be personally sympathetic with the aims of such a disreputable blackguard?

"I replied that I had merely suggested, not, I trusted, incorrectly, that any moral or virtuous undertaking could not fail to enlist his warm support, but that if I was mistaken, it seemed better that the agent's explorations should be discouraged by the highest authority, rather than by a mere junior official like myself."

Hardinge never did hear what actually transpired on the Continent, but he did vaguely recall that, in England, the agent's detective work "involved him in police court proceedings."

Source: Arthur Hardinge, *A Diplomatist in Europe*, pp. 83-84.

*   *   *

Not all of the unusual tasks that confront diplomatists are humorous. Particularly when serving abroad in cultures that seem exotic when compared with their own, diplomats are liable to be given some rather unpleasant tasks that they did not anticipate when joining the service. Certainly one vivid episode during the early career of the young Ernest Satow in Japan towards the end of the nineteenth century was unlikely to have been experienced at home in England.

Bearing Witness

An attack had been carried out against some foreigners in the town of Bizen, and the representatives of the Great Powers of Europe, including that of Great Britain, insisted that the guilty parties be properly punished. Chief among the guilty was one Taki Zenzaburô, a retainer of an important anti-European figure. Taki had apparently ordered soldiers under his command to fire on foreigners; he had subsequently been found guilty of this act, and the diplomatic representatives insisted that no clemency be shown. This meant that he was condemned to perform *harakiri*. The diplomats who had insisted on capital punishment were to be present at the ceremony, and Ernest Satow has left us with a description of the scene that they witnessed:

"We were guided to the Buddhist temple...at a quarter to ten. Strong guards were posted in the courtyard and in the ante-chambers. We were shown into a room, where we had to squat on the matted floor for about three-quarters of an hour; during this interval we were asked whether we had any questions to put to the condemned man, and also for a list of our names. At half-past ten we were conducted into the principal hall of the temple, and asked to sit down on the right hand side of the dais in front of the altar. Then the seven Japanese witnesses...took their places. After we had sat quietly thus for about ten minutes footsteps were heard approaching along the verandah. The condemned man, a tall Japanese of gentleman-like bearing and aspect, entered on the left side, accompanied by his *kai-shaku* or best men, and followed by two others, apparently holding the same office. Taki was dressed in blue *kami-shimo* of hempen cloth; the *kai-shaku* wore war surcoats (*jimbaori*). Coming before the Japanese witnesses they prostrated themselves, the bow being returned, and then the same ceremony was exchanged with us. Then the condemned man was led to a red sheet of felt-cloth laid on the dais before the altar; on this he squatted, after performing two bows, one at a distance, the other close to the altar. With the calmest deliberation he took his seat on the red felt, choosing the position which would afford him the greatest convenience for falling forward. A man dressed in black with a light grey hempen mantle then brought in the dirk wrapped in paper on a small unpainted wooden stand, and with a bow placed it in front of him. He took it up in both hands, raised it to his forehead and laid it down again with a bow. This is the ordinary Japanese gesture of thankful reception of a gift. Then in a distinct voice, very much broken, not by fear or emotion, but as it seemed reluctance to acknowledge an act of which he was ashamed—declared that he alone was the person who on the fourth of February had outrageously at Kôbé ordered fire to be opened on foreigners as they were trying to escape, that for having committed this offence he was going to rip up his bowels, and requested all present to be witnesses. He next divested himself of his upper garments by withdrawing his arms from the sleeves, the long ends of which he tucked under his legs to prevent his body from falling backward. The body was thus quite naked to below the navel. He then took the dirk in his right hand, grasping it just close to the point, and after stroking down the front of his chest and belly inserted the point as far down as possible and drew it across to the right side, the position of his clothes still fastened by the girth preventing our seeing the wound. Having done this he with great deliberation bent his body forward, throwing his head back so as to render the neck a fair object for the sword. The one *kai-shaku* who had accompanied him...had been crouching on his left hand a little behind him with drawn sword poised in the air from the moment the operation commenced. He now sprang up suddenly and delivered a blow the sound of which was like thunder. The head dropped down on to the matted floor, and the body lurching forward fell prostrate over it, the blood from the arteries pouring out and forming a pool. When the blood vessels had spent themselves all was over. The little wooden stand and the dirk were removed. Itô came forward with a bow, asking had we been witnesses; we replied that we had. He was followed by Nakashima, who also made a bow. A few minutes elapsed, and we were asked were we ready to leave. We rose and went out, passing in front of the corpse and through the Japanese witnesses. It was twelve o'clock when we got back to the consulate, where we found Sir Harry waiting up to receive our report.

The newspaper reports which reached England of this execution, and of the subsequent execution by *harakiri* of eleven Tosa men at Sakai gave a very distorted view of the facts. Charles Rickerby who was the owner and editor of "The Japan Times" of Yokohama was responsible for the attempts to mislead public opinion in both instances. He invented an account of the proceedings witnessed by Mitford and myself which was entirely false, and wound up by saying that it was disgraceful for Christians to have attended the execution, and that he hoped the Japanese, if they took revenge for this "judicial murder" would assassinate gentlemen of the foreign Legations rather than anyone else. As for being ashamed of having been present at a *harakiri* on the ground that it was a disgusting exhibition, I was proud to feel that I had not shrunk from witnessing a punishment which I did my best to bring about. It was no disgusting exhibition, but a most decent and decorous ceremony, and far more respectable than what our own Countrymen were in the habit of producing for the entertainment of the public in the front of Newgate prison.

Source: Ernest Satow, *A Diplomat in Japan*, pp. 345-47.

*   *   *

Diplomats who fail to understand the customs and values that determine the behaviour of those to whom they are appointed are not likely to get far in pursuing the interests of the state they represent. The young Satow soon developed both a respect and an understanding of the ways of the Orient, which would make him an effective diplomat. Understanding such ways does not necessarily mean submitting to them, however.

Who Goes Where

One Russian Minister to Persia in the era before the First World War discovered that his neighbour was to become the Grand Vizier. When the man came to be appointed to this high position one consequence was that the highway in front of his house became clogged with carriages, horses and servants, leaving hardly any passage for others using the road. The Grand Vizier himself began to behave in an arrogant way, leading to many grumbles amongst members of the European colony.

One day a junior official of the Russian Legation set out for a horseback ride, only to discover that the road in front of the house of the now-grand personage was totally blocked by carriages and the staff of visiting dignitaries. When he asked to be let through, his request was refused and he had to turn back. The Chargé d'Affaires of the Legation, Shcheglov, lodged a protest with the Grand Vizier, but when an unsatisfactory reply was received he decided to take drastic steps to counter the breech of behaviour.

Now it so happened that the road which wound past this house made a wide detour around the extensive property of the Russian

Legation before it joined the main highway. There was, however, a useful shortcut that cut across the grounds of the Legation, which the Russians kept open for public use. This furnished Shcheglov with an important advantage in his contest with the Grand Vizier. He ordered wooden barriers to be placed at both ends of the shortcut, and had the blockade manned by soldiers from the Legation guard. The soldiers were instructed that they were not to allow any Persians through the grounds, although Europeans would be free to use the shortcut. "And the Turks?" asked the Persian sergeant who would be in charge of the blockade. "Let them pass." The sergeant grinned and saluted. To allow the Turks through but not the Persians would be a real slap in the face.

The next morning, as usual, peasants from the surrounding villages came along the road and made their way to the shortcut, carrying the milk, poultry and vegetables that were destined for the market in Teheran. They were stopped and turned back. Men on horseback and in carriages arrived later, were stopped, and after heated arguments, were forced to turn back. In contrast, a carriage from the Turkish embassy was allowed to pass through the barrier, with military honours.

Just before noon, the Grand Vizier himself appeared, driving in state to the city. The guards from the Russian Legation formed a line across the barrier and refused to allow him through; the coach was forced to turn back. The news of this rebuff quickly spread to the capital. By the afternoon, the road was deserted as everyone, Europeans included, began to take the long detour. The official who precipitated the incident later recalled that, "we sat tight in our legation as if we were besieged. It was like a declaration of hostilities between our castle and the stronghold of our neighbour, a feudal war of the Middle Ages."

The siege lasted for two days, until the Shah was informed of what had occurred; he declared that no one had the right to obstruct the public roads, which were under his protection. A face-saving device was invented to bring the situation to a close: on the third day a Persian dignitary appeared at the Legation, bringing with him the message that the person who had been guilty of blocking the road in front of the Grand Vizier's house had been apprehended and sentenced to a severe flogging. Shcheglov tactfully pardoned the offender and asked that his sentence be remitted. The barriers were removed and no further complaints were heard about impertinent servants blocking the highway.

Source: Andrew D. Kalmykow, *Memoirs of a Russian Diplomat: Outposts of the Empire, 1893-1917*, pp. 90-91.

* * *

One challenge shared by all diplomats serving on missions abroad is that of understanding, and learning to work their way through, the different procedures by which foreign governments operate. Although the United States might appear to be somewhat less exotic than Persia, Europeans have always found that the American constitutional system presented them with some unusual, and mostly frustrating, challenges.

The American Way

A Swedish mission was sent to the United States in July, 1940 to purchase armaments to assist them in making a better defense of their neutrality while war was raging in Europe. The delegation was led by King Gustav's son, Prince Bertil, and included the former Swedish Foreign Minister, Gunnar Hägglöf, as well as Admiral Wijmark, whose principal aim was to purchase a cruiser for service in the Baltic. Soon after their arrival in Washington, they arranged to have an audience with President Roosevelt, who received them with his customary good humour and lack of formality.

Roosevelt listened thoughtfully while the Prince described the nature of their mission. The President was obviously eager to help, making arrangements himself by telephone for the Swedes to purchase some airplane engines. He followed this with a long monologue on the world situation, which depressed him deeply, as he was convinced that France would not be able to stand up for long against Germany. Shaking himself out of this despairing mood, he recovered his smile and asked, "Well, Prince, is there anything else I can do for you?"

The Prince, after some slight hesitation replied, "Yes, we are interested in a cruiser."

"A cruiser," Roosevelt exclaimed with delight, glancing at the pictures of ships that decorated his library. "What sort of a cruiser?" he asked.

The Prince described the naval situation in the Baltic, and proposed that a heavy cruiser was what they really needed.

Roosevelt couldn't restrain himself from interrupting: "Yes, I know," he said. "The Germans have two pocket battleships with 28-cm guns and also the heavy cruisers *Hipper, Seydlitz* and *Prince Eugen*. They are armed with 20-cm guns. Now let's see. What would you need?" He asked his assistant, General "Pa" Watson, to get down his copy of *Jane's Fighting Ships* from the shelf.

While the General was fetching the book, Roosevelt went on to tell his Swedish visitors that, "I've given away cruisers once before.... When I was Assistant Secretary of the Navy in 1913 I got President Wilson to agree to give two cruisers to Greece. I'm inclined to believe that otherwise war would have broken out between Greece and Turkey." Having been handed the book, he then began looking through the pictures while discussing gun turrets, speeds, fuel consumption, etc., topics that fascinated him so much that his visitors began to feel that he could go on about them forever.

Suddenly the President stopped and exclaimed: "This is the one! This is precisely what would suit you!" And he put in front of the Swedes a picture of the cruiser *Pensacola*, which was ten years old, 9000 tons, armed with ten 20-cm guns and capable of doing 32 knots.

Prince Bertil thought that the President's description of the ship sounded wonderful. "But how do we acquire her?" he wanted to know.

Now the fun began. "That's quite another story." Roosevelt became pensive. "Personally I would like Sweden to have her. She might help to keep the peace in the Baltic. But I'm only the President of this country," he said with a laugh. Then he went on to explain to his visitors that the Congress would have to give its permission before he could give them the cruiser.

"It isn't going to be easy," he warned them. "But it might be amusing to have a try. Let me see.... Have you spoken to Cordell Hull?"

They replied that they had not. He told them that they would have to begin their quest by approaching his Secretary of State. "I don't know what he will say. I really never know with him. But it is necessary to get his support. It is up to you to talk to him."

A few days later, the Swedish delegation were shown into the Secretary of State's office in the old State Department building. Hull was seated at an immense desk which was entirely covered in papers, files and books—except for a tiny square immediately in front of him, on which he rested his long, thin hands. He slowly rose to greet the Prince, gently asking him some questions about Sweden and Finland—while hardly appearing to pay attention to the answers. He then entered into a long monologue on peace and disarmament, assuring his visitors that his main interest was peace, a democratic peace without conquests, a peace founded in the spirit of brotherhood. Disarmament, he insisted, was necessary not only in military matters, but in customs and tariffs as well, if peace were to be secured; and here the monologue stopped for a moment while he silently brooded on the grim mistakes made at the World Economic Conference of 1933.

Prince Bertil seized the opportunity to raise the matter they had called on him to discuss: "We would very much like to discuss the desire of the Swedish Government to acquire a cruiser," he said, as firmly as he could.

"I beg your pardon?" Mr. Hull shook himself. "A cruiser?" He appeared to be surprised and reproachful. Things did not look good for the boys from Sweden.

Prince Bertil attempted to explain the military situation in Scandinavia and Sweden's naval shortcomings. Hull showed no interest. The Prince then tried to point out that the President was willing to support their request—but Hull simply sat staring at the ceiling. Finally, the Prince assured him that their request was entirely for the sake of peace: "I sincerely believe that the addition of a heavy cruiser to the Swedish Navy would substantially help the peace in the Baltic."

This did the trick. Hull at last began to show some interest. He stared intently at the Prince, leaned back in his chair and said carefully,

"Yes, Prince, if it's a question of peace I am with you. If the cruiser can secure peace in the Baltic I am ready to give my assent."

The interview was over. As the Swedes were leaving the room, Hull raised both hands in the air, saying, "God bless you, folks."

The excited delegation informed the President that the Secretary of State had agreed to Sweden's request for an American cruiser. But they found out that their quest had only begun.

Roosevelt told them that they would have to get the support of Senator Pittman of Nevada, the chairman of the Foreign Affairs Committee. Pittman had first been elected to the Senate in 1913, and eventually became the longest-serving Senator. His appointment to the chair of this committee did not attest to any specialized knowledge or interest; he had never actually been outside of the United States.

The Swedes took Pittman out to dinner, where he quickly proved to be an amiable character. After a pleasant dinner, he sat quietly with them in a corner, telling amusing stories in a rich Southern drawl while refilling his large glass of neat whiskey—which he would then empty in a single draught.

When the Prince finally began to speak to him about the cruiser, the Senator began to look grave. He asked for details. The Prince elaborated once again on the strategic situation in Scandinavia, the nature of the Baltic waters, etc. The Senator asked about Sweden's political system, and was pleased to learn that it was a democracy. He was, he assured his hosts, a Democrat; he had no sympathy with the Nazis, and less for the Soviets; he sincerely pitied the Swedes for being placed in such a difficult corner of the world.

The Prince pointed out that the proposed transfer of the cruiser to Sweden had the support of the President. This made no impression on the Senator. He then pointed out that Secretary Hull had also agreed to help. At this, Pittman suddenly became alert and asked if he had heard correctly; assured that he had, the Senator declared that he was ready to give his support; he immediately relaxed once again, and began to entertain his circle of visitors with more anecdotes—which no one found more amusing than he did himself.

Relieved, the Swedes reported to the President that they had cleared this hurdle. Roosevelt was impressed: "That's more than I could ever have got from Pittman," he said.

But the next hurdle would be an even more challenging one. "Now you will have to speak to the Republican leader in the Committee for Foreign Affairs, Senator Vandenberg. If you can persuade him to support your proposal, you can take over my job as President."

Vandenberg, widely regarded as the leading proponent of American isolationism, was a strict believer in the sanctity of the US neutrality legislation that had been adopted over the previous decade. But surprisingly, after listening to Prince Bertil and after putting some questions to him, he announced that he "wouldn't oppose the proposal so long as nobody else opposed it."

The Swedes began to feel understandably triumphant. They were very close to achieving their objective. Every day Admiral Wijkmark grew more devoted to the project, discussing his plans for *Pensacola* with the rest of the delegation, making lists of the personnel needed to man the ship, concerning himself with details of the ship's qualities and defects. The Swedes reported their triumph with Vandenberg to the President.

Roosevelt was incredulous. "Did Vandenberg really say this?" he asked. "Well, who knows? Everything is possible. Perhaps you will get your cruiser at last." He then threw his head back and began laughing heartily. The final and most difficult part still remained. The Swedes would have to approach Senator Hiram Johnson of California. "I can't help you in any way."

The delegation had difficulty even locating the seventy-five-year-old Senator, who lived by himself in a secluded bungalow. A meeting was finally arranged between him and the Prince however, and Bertil afterwards reported back to the delegation at the Hotel Mayflower.

"The bubble has burst at last," he later reported to them. It had been impossible to make any progress with Johnson. As soon as the Prince mentioned "cruiser", the aged Senator sat up in his chair and snapped, "Well, Prince, I'm bound to say it at once: I am dead against it." And that was that.

A disheartened Prince went to inform President Roosevelt of the news, who simply smiled and sighed, "yes, yes...you can see for yourselves how it is to be President of the United States." He sat silently for a while and then, in a deeply serious voice, said, "You see it takes a long, long time to bring the past up to the present."

Source: Gunnar Hägglöf, *Diplomat: Memoirs of a Swedish Envoy*, pp. 130-37

*　　　　*　　　　*

Not everyone faced such difficulties in making their way through the exotic jungle of the American political system; some found that Roosevelt himself was the problem.

All Presidents, Great and Small

Paul-Henri Spaak, the Foreign Minister of Belgium's government-in-exile in 1941 travelled to the United States for the first time before the US had joined the war. Although the reason for his visit was to attend a meeting of the International Labor Organization, he took the opportunity to meet with Roosevelt to explain to him the food situation in Belgium, which was very bad under the German occupation.

Spaak entered the Oval Office with some awe, but prepared to be charmed. He saw Roosevelt as the author of the New Deal, as a democrat who had dedicated himself to economic and social improvement; in fact, he regarded Roosevelt as something of a guide and mentor, as he had faithfully read his speeches in the pre-war years. He intended to take the opportunity of the meeting to make it clear to the President how much he admired him and his political ideals.

The reception that Spaak received from Roosevelt was deeply disappointing. The Belgian carefully explained the difficulties of the food situation in Belgium, exerting all his powers of persuasion in order to interest the President in the fate of his compatriots. But Roosevelt listened to him impassively, and when Spaak had ended his plea, "he declared coldly, without betraying the slightest sign of human warmth or compassion, that nothing could be done." The lack of interest or concern Spaak found hard enough to bear, but some of Roosevelt's comments angered him: "the trials through which Belgium was passing were not so tragic," Roosevelt declared. "Germany had gone through much the same experience after the First World War and had yet produced a generation that was physically fit..." The proof of this could be seen in the way the Germans were now fighting.

Spaak was dumbfounded. "There was no common ground between us, no meeting of the minds. I left the room which I had entered so confidently, so ready to show my admiration, in a mood of sadness and disappointment."

The Minister-in-exile did have a second opportunity to see Roosevelt in action before he returned to Europe, at an official reception the President was giving for the delegates to the conference. "We filed past him one by one. He shook each of us by both hands affectionately, smiled, and had a few friendly words for everyone." Spaak saw that Roosevelt succeeded in making each of the delegates feel as if he were an honoured guest, as a dear friend whom he was meeting once again after a long absence, but, "this artificial display of affection was almost more painful to bear than his cruel indifference of a few days before." Spaak's memory of his former hero was forever tinged with the disappointed frustration of having met him.

The next time he appeared at the White House, in April 1945, it was to be introduced to Harry Truman, a few days after Roosevelt's funeral. This time Spaak was forewarned that he was not to be admitted into the presence of a great man, and, as he entered the Oval Office, he was not overawed as he had been on the first occasion. This meeting too left a lasting impression. Truman, he remembered, "did not try to impress me; on the contrary, with touching sincerity he spoke to me of his anxiety about the responsibilities which he had just undertaken, and made no attempt to hide his feeling of not being altogether ready for the part he was expected to play." Although Truman lacked Roosevelt's brilliance and his charm, Spaak was struck by his modesty and his determination to do his duty without ostentation. He was thoroughly, and quite unexpectedly, captivated by the unassuming little man, of whom he had heard practically nothing in advance.

Source: Paul-Henri Spaak, *The Continuing Battle: Memoirs of a European, 1936-1966*, pp. 97-100.

*   *   *

*If individual personalities and governing systems can seem strange
to foreigners, so can the people themselves. And in an era of mass
culture it is perhaps not surprising that diplomats frequently find
themselves placed in the position of having to perform in front of
people from whom they would previously have been hidden from
view. Occasionally, such experiences may actually turn out to be
both memorable and happy.*

The Diplomat and the Crowd

On May 9, 1945, one day after V-E Day in the west, the Soviet
government announced to the Russian people that the war in Europe
was over. The news spread quickly throughout Moscow in the early
morning hours of the 10th, and by daybreak a holiday mood had
gripped the city. By ten o'clock a group of joyous students were
marching through the streets, singing and carrying banners; when
they reached the American embassy—next to which was the National
Hotel, where many Allied flags were flying—they burst into cheers.
They stopped in front of the Stars and Stripes and began to demonstrate their feelings of friendship for the United States and the Allies.

The square on which the embassy and the hotel were situated was
a huge one, and could have held 200,000 people; thousands soon
began to join the students gathered in front of the flags. The diplomats
were naturally pleased and moved by the cheering and waving, but
hardly knew how to respond. "If any of us ventured out into the street,
he was immediately seized, tossed enthusiastically into the air, and
passed on friendly hands over the heads of the crowd, to be lost,
eventually, in a confused orgy of good feeling somewhere on its outer
fringes." Unprepared to face this prospect, most of the staff came
onto the balconies where they stood waving back to the crowd.

George Kennan, who was temporarily in charge of the embassy
during the absence of the Ambassador, sent one of the staff over the
roof and into the hotel to fetch a Soviet flag, which was then hung
alongside the American. This produced roars of approval, but it still
seemed an inadequate response to these spontaneous demonstrations
of friendship. He decided that he had to say at least a few words of
appreciation. Going down to the first floor, he climbed out onto the
pedestal of one of the great columns that lined the building. Alongside

him, for a reason he could not later recall, came a sergeant of the military mission, who was in uniform. Their appearance created renewed enthusiasm on the part of the crowd, who pushed over the barrier that lined the sidewalk and moved onto the grass at the foot of the building, surrounding the pedestal. Kennan shouted out to them in Russian, "Congratulations on the day of victory. All honor to the Soviet allies."

The crowd, now roaring with appreciation, hoisted up a Soviet soldier on their hands until he was able to reach the pedestal. "He pulled himself up into our company, kissed and embraced the startled sergeant, and pulled him relentlessly down to the waiting arms of the crowd. There, bobbing helplessly over a sea of hands, he rapidly receded from view." Kennan succeeded in escaping back into the building, but the sergeant, who was actually a preacher in civilian life, was not seen again until the following day.

The crowd remained all day, and then into the evening, waving and cheering, a sight that must have dismayed the Soviet government, which had been denouncing the government of the United States as a bourgeois power for two decades. The local authorities tried to get the crowd to move on, but to no avail; they erected a bandstand and put a brass band in to play on the other side of the square, but the crowd refused to budge. The spontaneous outburst of enthusiasm was almost embarrassing to the diplomatic staff. "We had no desire to be the sources of such trouble on a day of common rejoicing. We had done nothing, God knows, to invite the demonstration, or to encourage its prolongation, once it had started. But we were even more helpless than the authorities."

Source: George F. Kennan, *Memoirs, 1925-1950*, pp. 240-42.

*   *   *

*P*erhaps it was this unpredictable and spontaneous outpouring of emotion on the part of the Russian people that led the Soviet authorities to put more effort into organizing "the crowd" in the future. The Suez campaign of 1956 sparked off a series of massive demonstrations in Moscow, held in front of the buildings of the *western embassies, and which were to become a regular feature of the "public diplomacy" conducted by the Soviet Union.*

The Well-Tempered Crowd

The members of the British embassy staff in 1956 one day found the courtyard of their grounds filled with demonstrating Russians. The demonstrators succeeded in cutting off one building from the other; they climbed onto the roof, where they posted offensive posters on the windows of the offices (and of the Ambassador's drawing room); and they managed to make the staff virtual prisoners in the building for most of the day.

In spite of the venomous words on their posters, however, the demonstrators all appeared to be young, attractive people who were in good humour. They seemed to be having a very pleasant time walking around the gardens and grounds, and behaved more as if they were on holiday than engaging in a serious political protest. In fact, there was little likelihood of any damage being done because the protest did not reflect a spontaneous upsurge of outraged feelings; on the contrary, it was punctiliously organized. There seemed to be such little chance of danger that the Ambassador decided to send one member of his staff to approach the appropriate Soviet official to lodge an official protest.

So, Cecil Parrott was sent through the crowd to look for the embassy's chauffeur. He found the people respectful and willing to allow him to pass through without difficulty. He was unable to locate the chauffeur, but in passing through the garden, he did spot a general of the militia—a rare sight in Moscow. Returning to the sanctuary of the embassy, Parrott suggested that the Ambassador might like to call the general in to ask him how long the siege was to last.

The Ambassador agreed. "When are these disgraceful proceedings going to end?" he indignantly asked. The general stiffened like a ramrod, clicked his heels, saluted and replied: "At a quarter to two, your Excellency."

Parrott felt sorry for the poor old general, who had been straight-forward and honest, and who would undoubtedly have to pay a price to his masters for being so forthright. Nevertheless, he was obliged, when making his protest, to quote the general's words as proof that the demonstrations, far from being spontaneous, had actually been officially planned and sponsored, "and I felt a cad in doing so. Indeed, I hate to think of that nice old man, more like a Zoshchenko character than a commissar, being possibly torn from the bosom of his family and shunted off to Siberia."

Source: Cecil C. Parrott, *The Serpent and the Nightingale*, pp. 76-77.

*   *   *

Not all crowds are so well behaved, or so well organized. This has been noted a number of times in the midst of one of the recurring phenomena of diplomacy in the twentieth century: the diplomatic tour. The tour might be undertaken by a head of state, a head of government, a foreign minister, or even a professional diplomat. The purposes of the trip may vary as widely as the itinerary; and so may the results. The trip may go precisely according to plan, or it may turn into a nightmare.

Nixon's Nightmare

"Nightmare" seems an appropriate description for what happened when, in the 1950s, the Vice-President of the United States, Richard Nixon, set out on a tour of almost every state in South America; only Brazil and Chile were to be passed by. Nixon, who assumed that the trip would be uneventful, advised several reporters not to bother coming with him; and in the early part of the trip, through Uruguay, Argentina, Paraguay and Bolivia, this assumption seemed to be valid.

The first hint that there was going to be trouble came at the Nixons' hotel in Lima, Peru, where a small crowd of demonstrators had gathered to heckle him. This raised the question of the next day's itinerary, in which the Vice-President was scheduled to visit San Marcos University; both the rector of the university and the chief of police let it be known that they would prefer the visit to be cancelled, but neither was prepared to take public responsibility for the cancellation, and Nixon was prepared to back out of the engagement only if they took that step. He had still not decided what to do about the visit by the time he went to bed that night, while the crowd outside the hotel was growing larger and chanting anti-American and anti-Nixon slogans.

The next day, after laying a wreath at the statue of San Martin, the liberator of Peru, Nixon made the decision to go ahead with the visit as planned. While he and his entourage were still some distance from the gates of the university, they could hear thousands of demonstrators chanting, *"Fuera Nixon! Fuera Nixon!"*—"Go Home Nixon!". Sometimes the chant became *"Muera Nixon! Muera Nixon!"*—"Death to Nixon!" Nixon took two of his aides and walked towards the crowd, shouting that he wished to speak to them, and asking why they were afraid of the truth. The crowd answered by throwing rocks at the three Americans, hitting one of them in the face and breaking a tooth. The visitors retreated to their cars, where Nixon stood up in his convertible and shouted at the crowd that they were cowards.

Nixon and his escorts went on to the Catholic University, where a receptive audience gave him a warm greeting; but they decided to make a speedy exit when word arrived that the demonstrators from San Marcos were headed in their direction. When the Americans reached their hotel, however, many of the demonstrators were already waiting. Rather than risk a confrontation with the crowd at the front entrance, Nixon decided that they would park a short distance away and enter the hotel by foot. By the time that the crowd realized what was happening, his team was able to form a wedge and force their way through and into the hotel—but not before one of the demonstrators managed to spit in the Vice-President's face.

As unpleasant as this episode was, things promised to get worse when, while in Bogotá, word reached the touring Americans that the Central Intelligence Agency had advised the Secret Service in Washington that there was a plot to assassinate Nixon during his visit to Venezuela. Even as the plane landed at Maiquetía Airport outside of Caracas, and even though the landing strip had been cleared of everyone except the official welcoming party, the travelling Americans could hear the chanting of demonstrators, who were pressed up against the fences along the edge of the runways or standing on the roof of the terminal building. As the official greetings took place, the chief of Venezuelan security assured Nixon that the crowd was harmless: "they are just kids."

The group had almost reached the terminal building when the band began to play the Venezuelan national anthem once again. They stopped to stand at attention, when it seemed as if it had begun to rain, until they realized that the crowd on the roof of the terminal was showering them with spit, which fell on their faces and in their hair. Nixon saw his wife's suit grow dark with tobacco-brown splotches. The pelting continued for some time, until they were able to get into their cars.

As the cars neared Caracas, the spit turned into a barrage of rocks, as mobs emerged from the side streets and alleys along the route. When they were about four blocks away from their destination, the Panteón Nacional, they found their route blocked with parked cars, and they were forced to stop. Hundreds of people began running in their direction. The Venezuelan motorcycle escort evaporated. The only remaining defenders of the visitors were twelve Secret Service agents. But there was no defence against the rocks, one of which hit the window of Nixon's car, spraying the occupants with tiny slivers and wounding the Venezuelan Foreign Minister in the eye; he started to bleed heavily, while moaning: "This is terrible. This is terrible."

One man approached the car with an iron pipe and began smashing at the window, sending more slivers in all directions and cutting several of the Americans. Nixon suddenly felt some relief when the car began moving again—until he realized that the movement was caused by the crowd rocking it back and forth. He remembered that such crowds sometimes turned cars over and set them on fire. He had begun to fear for his life when one of his aides pulled out a revolver and shouted, "Let's get some of these sons of bitches." Cooler heads prevailed however, and a short time later the cars were able to get away from the mob.

Nixon refused to continue with his scheduled itinerary and went straight to the embassy, where he heard that Eisenhower had dispatched two companies of airborne infantry and two companies of Marines to the Caribbean in order to be, "in a position to cooperate with the Venezuelan government if assistance is required." Communications with Washington had apparently been cut off after the report had been sent that the local security system had broken down and that the Nixon group was under siege. The ruling military *junta* were clearly embarrassed by the demonstrations; they begged the Vice-President to go ahead with the luncheon that had been planned for the next day, promising him that there would be no trouble, and that he would be delivered safely to the airport immediately afterward. Nixon reluctantly agreed, uncertain that they could live up to their promises. But they proved as good as their word.

When the Venezuelans called for him at the embassy the next day, "it looked as if they had come to declare war rather than take me to lunch. The courtyard was filled with tanks and jeeps and armored cars. There were twelve truckloads of troops flanking our limousines." Even the caterer had been replaced to prevent the food being tampered with. The trip out to the airport following the lunch was quite different than that of the previous day. The limousine in which Nixon rode "was an arsenal on wheels. The floor was piled with submachine guns, revolvers, rifles, tear gas canisters, and ammunition clips; there was hardly room for our feet." He was taken along the same route that had been used the day before—but this time the streets were almost empty, except for the armed soldiers who were patrolling them. "The few civilians I saw were holding handkerchiefs to their faces. At first I thought this was a protest sign, but when I saw the police wearing gas masks I realized that the whole area had been tear-gassed." When they arrived at the airport, "it was like a ghost town." There was no more trouble.

The risk that was run on this diplomatic tour was not without its rewards; for weeks after their return from South America the Nixons could go nowhere in public without people standing up to applaud. And, for the first time, Nixon pulled even with Kennedy in the presidential polls.

Source: Richard M. Nixon, *RN: The Memoirs of Richard Nixon*, pp. 187-93.

*　　　　*　　　　*

*D*angers lurk whenever diplomats enter the public arena, and the consequences are always difficult to predict.

Egg on the Face — of Whom?

When the Earl of Halifax, in his capacity as British Ambassador to the United States, was touring the Midwest in the summer of 1941, he found "isolationism" there to be just as deeply-entrenched as he had been warned. But an interesting little episode gave things a nudge in the other direction.

When Halifax, as part of his tour, called on the Roman Catholic Archbishop in Detroit, he was waylaid by a party of picketers; a number of elderly ladies had, in fact, positioned themselves outside the Archbishop's door, awaiting the Ambassador's arrival. When he appeared, the ladies began shouting out their criticisms of the British for attempting to drag American boys into the front lines along with them.

The ladies underlined their verbal assault by throwing eggs and tomatoes at the helpless diplomat; even the American policemen assigned to see to his security felt that this was not a case for drawing their revolvers out of their holsters. So the diplomatic entourage had to stand and take their punishment while they waited for the Archbishop's maid to open the door. When she finally did appear, Halifax was able to clean the debris of egg and tomato from his coat.

Many Americans found this discourteous treatment to be shameful, and, ironically, it served to provide the Ambassador with a more sympathetic audience in the future. Halifax aided his own cause when the American press widely reported his singular remark when he was asked to comment on the affair, that "the United States was a very lucky country to have eggs and tomatoes to throw around, when in England we only got one egg a month."

Source: Earl of Halifax, *The Fulness of Days*, pp. 285-86.

*　　　　　*　　　　　*

All diplomats know that one of the requirements of working within a system of bureaucracy is to produce that which the bureau requires. This consists of a number of things, but the essential ingredient is paperwork. Paper is used to convey information, to correct misapprehensions and to establish a record. But it can also be used to provide evidence of activity, as the following story suggests.

How Reports get Written

Not long after being appointed Ambassador to New Delhi, John Kenneth Galbraith received a call from the Polish Ambassador. The Pole, a bulky man with heavy glasses and a swarthy face, had a reputation for being nasty—but in calling on Galbraith he was attempting to be helpful. The important thing, he informed the new boy, was to find material that justified a telegram home. Why? Because it showed that the diplomat was hard at work: "it reminds the Foreign Office of his existence; and it establishes the value of his post."

The difficulty, the astute Pole pointed out, was finding such appropriate material. For instance, when Galbraith had recently come down from Kashmir to meet with Ambassador Harriman and the Prime Minister of India, that suggested something pretty important, and worthy of a telegram. Galbraith himself might find that any news gleaned from embassies east of the iron curtain provided the "good" material that Washington expected him to provide. Was the Polish Ambassador proposing a *quid pro quo*? He encouraged Galbraith to be generous with his information: "In conversation with the American Ambassador, I learned..." made, he said, "a fine beginning for another ambassador's cable."

Source: John Kenneth Galbraith, *Ambassador's Journal: A Personal Account of the Kennedy Years*, p. 116.

*　　　　*　　　　*

Work keeps diplomats away from home and familiar people for extended periods of time; an absence felt most strongly around holiday time. While stationed as the Canadian ambassador in Bonn, Charles Ritchie travelled to Paris to meet a Canadian delegation shortly before Christmas...

Homesickness

"December 20, 1954

"I am here for [Secretary of State for External Affairs] Mike Pearson's visit, spending my time with the Canadian delegation. Rye whisky in the hotel sitting-room, then a straggle of the delegation, a couple of secretaries, and a tame journalist; we all drift out to some unlikely restaurant or night-club for the evening. All day is spent wandering around hotel corridors, waiting for the Minister to come in or go out, waiting for the typing to be finished, knocking at doors with Draft 3 of the speech in one's hand. Where *is* the Minister? Out buying a present for his wife? A good dose of Canadians. When I went to the plane to see them off I felt like I'd like to stay [on the plane] and arrive home for Christmas.... I thought what hell it would be to be an exile, to see a plane leaving for Canada and to know that I could never go back."

Source: Charles Ritchie. *Diplomatic Passport: More Undiplomatic Diaries, 1946-62*, p. 85.

Madness in Their Methods?

It is widely assumed that the time-honoured definition of a diplomat as someone who "is sent abroad to lie for his country" is an accurate one. Like most maxims, however, the truth that it tells is only a half-truth. The following anecdote from diplomat and diarist Charles Ritchie is a classic example of how it is not always necessary to tell the whole truth. In this tale, Ritchie is being pressured to line up co-sponsors for a Canadian resolution at the UN in 1960.

Diplomacy Unbuttoned

"Mr. Ambassador, there is an urgent call for you from the Minister of External Affairs in Ottawa. Would you care to take it now? He is waiting on the line." "Waiting on the line"—that will never do. With hurried apology to my colleagues, with controlled speed—one does not run but moves quietly to the voice of the master—"Hello, Charles. How are things down there? Got everything lined up for our resolution? Who's supporting—how many co-sponsors?" "What? only nine countries? We'll have to do better than that. What about Australia? No, darn it, we didn't vote for *their* resolution. India?" "So they want to make it more like an Indian Resolution, do they? Charles, you'll have to get more co-sponsors quickly. I want to make an announcement in the House of Commons tomorrow. Twist a few arms—I know you can do it. Good luck, and let me have the additional names later in the day." It is all very well, but where is one to find these "additional names"? I have already canvassed all those delegations which are in sympathy with our resolution. I have already incorporated some of their amendments into our text as bait for their support. I wish the Minister was here to twist a few arms himself. No doubt he could do it; he is a practised politician and experienced vote-getter. All day I go from pillar to post seeking out even the most unlikely allies and by late afternoon I am still one short of a total of twelve co-sponsors. But I have reached the end of the line. No one else is interested in the Canadian resolution. I go to the lavatory and, standing at the urinal next to me, buttoning up his trousers, is the Ambassador of Haiti. I barely know the man—our relations with Haiti are minimal. The Duvalier regime is not popular at the United Nations. "Excellency," I say to him in my most polished French, "may I have a word with you?" He looks surprised, almost affronted, at this approach to him in this place. I draw him into the washroom. I do not attempt to explain the merits of our resolution; I simply say, "I am offering Your Excellency a unique opportunity to associate your country with a great initiative for the cause of peace." I venture the suggestion that President Duvalier could not fail to approve. I point out that as the list of co-sponsors appears alphabetically, Haiti would rank high on the printed list, above other important nations. The Ambassador, a small, stout, elephant-coloured man, pauses and stares at me through thick horn-rimmed glasses, and then, "Excellency, I shall have to consult my government." "I fear," I reply, "that the list closes this evening. Would it be possible to have an answer before midnight tonight?" The Ambassador bows and emerges from the washroom. At 11:30 he telephones me—Haiti accepts. I have achieved twelve co-sponsors.

Source: Charles Ritchie, *Diplomatic Passport: More Undiplomatic Diaries, 1946-62*, pp. 182-83.

*   *   *

Lies and half-truths are certainly told, but it is not always appropriate to tell them—in which case different tactics may be adopted.

Telling the Truth for One's Country

One young diplomat learned that there is more than one way to skin a cat early on in his career. When Charles Hardinge was sent to the British embassy at Constantinople to work under the Ambassador,

Lord Dufferin, he discovered that he was able to learn a great deal of the science of diplomacy by watching and listening to the older man. One day, for instance, in the midst of a crisis over Egypt, Dufferin sent the young man with a message to the Russian Ambassador. Hardinge, expecting to engage in some delicate and challenging diplomacy, asked what he was to do if the Russian asked him questions. The advice of his mentor was disarmingly simple and instructive: "Tell him the truth. He will not believe you."

Source: Charles Hardinge, *The Old Diplomacy*, p. 13.

*   *   *

Senior diplomats are usually prepared to offer advice to their juniors; training the young is but one of their duties. But governments who send their diplomats off to foreign lands to accomplish certain tasks are not necessarily content to rely on the advice and instructions that they provide. At times, they seem to believe that more direct incentives may be necessary in order to ensure that their wishes are carried out.

Performance Incentives

Hugh Wilson was one of those American diplomatists assisting the American delegation at the Peace Conference in Paris in 1919. He divided his time between the Hotel Crillon and the Legation in Berne, Switzerland, where he was serving as the Chargé. He discovered that supplicants were constantly showing up at his office in Berne, trying to arrange a meeting with the great President Wilson. Many of these simple people believed that five minutes of conversation with the President would solve their problems, and hundreds of them showed up, hoping to arrange a meeting in Paris, or at least have a statement and a petition presented to him.

Hugh Wilson particularly recalled a short gentleman in a silk hat and a black frock coat, with round ruddy cheeks, a beaming smile and glistening black hair. The visitor announced that he was a Prince of Daghestan. It seems that the new rulers of the self-proclaimed republic of Daghestan had commissioned him to call on the President to lay before him their wish to retain their independence, and their fears that they might be incorporated within the Soviet Union. The Chargé carefully explained to him that his application for a visa would have to be sent to the French authorities in Paris, and that he would have to remain in Berne for some days while he waited for a reply. At this point the Prince of Daghestan rose from his chair, shook hands, and accompanied Wilson to the door.

When Wilson opened the door for his visitor, he was confronted by a huge figure standing on the threshold: an enormous man stood with folded arms, clothed in baggy trousers, soft leather boots and a leopard skin; he also wore at his waist a dangerous-looking curved scimitar. The Prince said something to the man in a language that Wilson did not understand; the man then turned to him and bowed deeply.

Wilson said to the Prince, "Do you mind my asking whether this rather formidable person is a bodyguard, or a valet, or both?"

The Prince replied that the man performed a mixture of both roles. "You see, my Government realizes that when its representatives go abroad into great cities, they have had little experience with the temptations of civilization, so we have the habit of detailing a simple peasant of unquestioned loyalty to accompany them and be responsible for their behavior abroad."

This must have been a considerable inducement to proper behavior. But the Prince further explained that his colleague had another duty to perform as well, that he was, in a sense, responsible for the success of the Prince's mission.

"How do you mean?" the naive American asked.

"Well, it is very simple. He knows that my mission is to see the President of the United States in Paris. If I fail in my mission he knows what his duty is and he will perform it."

"With the scimitar?" Wilson asked.

"Yes," the Prince replied.

Unfortunately, so frantic was the transaction of business in the following months that Wilson never heard whether the Prince actually made it to Paris—and if not, whether his countryman did his duty with the scimitar.

Source: Hugh Wilson, *Diplomat between Wars*, pp. 70-72.

$$*\qquad\qquad *\qquad\qquad *$$

*A*dvice or threats: it is difficult to know upon what basis the *advancement of a young diplomat can be assured. Sometimes, it seems as if a successful career in diplomacy is simply in the laps of the gods.*

A Career Goes to the Dogs

Dimitrii Abrikossow, a young member of the Foreign Office staff in St. Petersburg before the First World War, happened to share an apartment with a curate, who one day expressed the wish that they should have a dog to keep them company. Fortuitously, a short time later Abrikossow was offered a magnificent borzoi, which looked golden in the sunshine, and which had wonderfully expressive black eyes. As the young diplomatist was in the habit of returning to his apartment for lunch each day, he began taking the dog with him to the Foreign Office, where he would leave it at the foot of the staircase, chained to the railing. Everyone passing the dog would stop to admire it and ask to whom it belonged.

Now, Abrikossow had grown more and more discontented with his Foreign Office existence in St. Petersburg. He had entered the diplomatic service because he wished to see the world and to partic-ipate in the adventure of international politics. Instead, he found himself leading the life of a bored bureaucrat, spending most of his time checking the details of those Russians who had had the misfortune to die while they were outside the country. He was desperate to leave the confining atmosphere of the Foreign Office, but could see no way out.

The dog came to his rescue. One day, without warning, the Chief of Personnel—an elegant man who wore the court uniform with one spur attached to one boot—called Abrikossow into his office and, after complimenting him on his magnificent dog, asked him what he would say to an offer to go to London. The Russian Ambassador there had asked for an increase in staff, and had stipulated that the clerk to be sent must be a good worker with sufficient means to lead a life befitting a member of the embassy. It seemed that promising candidates were difficult to find, most lacking either the industriousness or the financial means. But Abrikossow, who had become known around the Office as "the man with the magnificent dog" appeared to be a likely possibility because, as the Chief of Personnel put it to him, a man who owned such a dog could not be poor. And besides, anyone prepared to devote his days dealing in the details of dead Russians abroad must be industrious as well.

Abrikossow was duly sent off to London, where he was initiated into a long career in diplomacy.

Source: Dimitrii Abrikossow, *Revelations of a Russian Diplomat*, pp. 92-93.

*   *   *

The gods of fate are not always kind, and when they fail to do their job, the mortals in charge are forced to deal with the consequences.

Another Career Goes Nowhere

One of the tasks of the Private Secretary to the British Foreign Secretary was to deal with the career aspirations of those in the service. One such Private Secretary was the dignified, immaculately-attired and unapproachable Henry Foley, who was one day called upon by a desperate consul. The consul, it seems, was monomaniac-ally determined that he should be given a particular post in the service. When Foley informed him that he could not have it, the poor man drew a revolver from his pocket and blew his brains out, right there in the office.

Foley rang his bell to summon one of his clerks who was told to deal with the mess. Maintaining an impassive silence, the clerk proceeded to mop up the blood on the carpet—with official blotting paper.

Source: John Gregory, *On the Edge of Diplomacy: Rambles and Reflections, 1902-1928*, pp. 22-23.

*   *   *

Success in diplomacy, whether it be making one's way through the ranks or in negotiating successfully with foreigners, may appear to some to be determined by fate, but others prefer to take destiny into their own hands.

Rowboat Diplomacy

There is, for instance, the story of the American consul at Smyrna, a Colonel Madden, a veteran of the Civil War who wore his military decorations in recognition of the courage that he had demonstrated on the field of battle. His diplomatic method frequently transferred the behavior of the battlefield to the offices of state, which, not surprisingly, led to some rather unconventional scenes.

Once, when the Turks had locked up an Armenian who happened to be an American citizen, Madden protested and demanded his immediate release. The Turks refused on the ground that the individual had formerly been an Ottoman subject and that their government did not recognize the right of their nationals to change their subjection. Madden thereupon took an axe, went to the prison, smashed the doors open and released the man.

Another time the Turks had seized some American goods and locked them up in the customs house, refusing to give them up until some taxes were paid on them. Madden, refusing to pay taxes that he regarded as illegal, got hold of a rowboat, mounted a cannon in the prow, pulled out in front of the customs house and sent word to the Governor that, if the goods were not released within minutes, he would open fire. The goods were handed over instantly.

Source: George Horton, *Recollections Grave and Gay: The Story of a Mediterranean Consul*, pp. 93-94

*　　　*　　　*

One advantage of the direct approach must surely be that one can at least work off some of the frustrations created by the usual necessity of diplomatic restraint. But revenge can be sweet, no matter what method is used to accomplish it, and no matter how small the victory itself might be.

Speedboat Diplomacy

The British Air Attaché in Finland in the days before the Second World War, "Freddie" West, lived on a small island near Helsinki. He used to commute to his office each day by boat, a beautiful Finnish speedboat with a powerful outboard motor. It just so happened that the German Military Attaché lived nearby on another island, and he too had a boat in which he used to commute to work. At its stern he proudly displayed an oversized Swastika flag.

West regularly enjoyed himself on the way in to work by allowing the German to chug past him and then, carefully judging his distance, overtake him in a narrow channel which they both had to navigate. West's boat would create a tremendous wake at high speed and the German boat would come perilously close to capsizing "while most undiplomatic language in guttural German wafted across the water amidst the cough and splutter of my outboard motor."

Source: P.R. Reid, *Winged Diplomat: The Life Story of Air Commodore "Freddie" West*, p. 136.

*　　　*　　　*

There are, of course, less forceful methods of taking revenge. The practical necessities of politics sometimes compel diplomats to do things that they find distasteful or unpleasant. When they feel that they have been pushed unnecessarily into such an awkward position they are quite likely to remember it and extract a payment for it later on. Moreover, schooled as they are in the secrecy that is usually required of the diplomatic arts, the pleasure that they derive from

*extracting payment at a later date may be known only to themselves.
To many diplomats, quiet retribution may be the keenest pleasure
of all. Consider, for instance, the triangular relationship between
a banker, a diplomat and Mediterranean politics.*

Revenge is Sweet

In 1908 the British Foreign Office decided that it was important for
their interests to strengthen the Bank of Morocco, and that this could
be done only by obtaining a substantial sum of money to be loaned
to the bank. The Foreign Secretary, Sir Edward Grey, approached
one of the leading bankers in Britain, Sir Ernest Cassel, with the
suggestion that he loan half a million pounds to the Moroccan bank.

The banker readily assented to the proposition, but under one
condition: that he should be made a G.C.B. (Knight Grand Cross of
the Bath). Grey calmly accepted the condition; although it was not in
his power to grant such an honour, he would place the idea before the
Prime Minister. The Permanent Under-Secretary, Charles Hardinge,
who was present at the interview with Cassel, regarded such a
condition to be bad form indeed. The banker got his G.C.B., but
Hardinge was determined to get even for Cassel's lack of unselfish
patriotism—an aim that he managed to keep strictly to himself.

Some time later, when Cassel wished to create the National Bank
of Turkey, he offered Hardinge, who had a considerable reputation
in that country, the appointment as head of the bank there, with a
salary of three to four thousand pounds a year. Hardinge declined the
offer, but, when Cassel asked him to suggest a suitable candidate, he
volunteered the name of Sir H. Babington Smith. Before long Babington Smith called on Hardinge to seek his advice on some matters
connected with the appointment, and particularly on the subject of
salary. "Upon that point I strongly recommended him to refuse to
accept the appointment with a salary of less than £10,000 a year."

Babington Smith later described to Hardinge the interview that took
place in Cassel's bedroom, where the financier was laid up with a
chill. After a long discussion of the proposed operations of the bank,
Babington Smith inquired as to salary. "He was offered £3,000 a year
with certain extras. He declined the post and on being asked what

salary he desired, he claimed not less than £10,000 a year and left the room." Hardinge must have been delighted when Babington Smith told him that as he walked out of the bedroom, "Cassel's face was a picture of astonishment..." Within twenty-four hours the salary demand had been met, and Babington Smith accepted the post, which he went on to hold until the outbreak of war with Turkey.

"This little transaction gave me great pleasure as a set-off to Cassel's G.C.B.," Hardinge later recollected.

Source: Hardinge of Penshurst, *The Old Diplomacy*, pp. 164-65.

*　　　*　　　*

The quid pro quo, the "tit-for-tat" is one of the most commonly repeated themes in diplomacy, and diplomats often find that their smallest victories are the sweetest. Some of their manoeuvres are not necessarily designed to accomplish the realization of geopolitical ambitions. Sometimes tactics are employed to safeguard privileges that have become customary, or to insist upon equality of treatment between their respective representatives.

Parking-Lot Diplomacy

Shortly after Alexander Haig had been appointed Secretary of State by Ronald Reagan, he began to receive the customary formal calls of welcome from the envoys of the states represented at Washington, which included the Soviet Ambassador, Anatoliy Dobrynin, at that time the dean of the diplomatic corps. Dobrynin enjoyed, by virtue of his status and reputation, a number of special privileges in Washington. Whereas the other 150 ambassadors accredited to the US government would, when calling in at the State Department, drive up to the main entrance on C Street, walk across the lobby, and ride up in a public elevator, Dobrynin alone had the privilege of driving into the basement garage and then riding a private elevator to the seventh floor, where the Secretary's office is located. The Soviet Ambassador was abruptly and unexpectedly denied these special privileges one day, but it was bureaucratic pique, not high politics, that led to the denial.

While Dobrynin enjoyed such special privileges in Washington as a direct phone line from his desk into the Secretary of State's switchboard, his counterpart in Moscow was kept in sterile isolation. The chief of the Soviet desk in the Bureau of European Affairs at the State Department, Robert German, applied to Assistant Secretary George Vest for permission to take away Dobrynin's parking privileges, in order to get the Soviets' attention.

Vest, without consulting the Secretary of State, approved of the idea. German informed the Soviet embassy of the decision. The day that Dobrynin was to call on Haig, his secretary telephoned Haig's office—where, as it happened, they knew nothing of the change in arrangements—to ask where the Ambassador could park. "Oh, in his usual place, I suppose," replied a clerk, in complete innocence.

Dobrynin accordingly proceeded into the garage, where German had stationed one of his officers in the event that there should be a test of wills over the matter. The limousine was halted, ordered to back out of the garage, and forced to proceed to the C Street entrance in the same manner as every other ambassador. A flustered and surprised Dobrynin was forced to step out of his car and into the thicket of microphones and cameras that awaited him.

Source: Alexander M. Haig, Jr. *Caveat: Realism, Reagan and Foreign Policy*, pp. 101-2.

*　　　　*　　　　*

One method of diplomacy that has become increasingly common-place is the summit conference. One feature which is supposed to contribute to the improvement of the international climate is the opportunity that such meetings offer for personal relationships to develop between heads of government.

Driving to Détente

A distinctive relationship certainly developed between Leonid Brezhnev and Richard Nixon, who met a number of times over the years. The American president was, it would seem, rather surprised to discover how "americanized" the Soviet president was. Once, while flying to California in *Air Force One*, the two leaders were given a spectacular view of the Grand Canyon; Brezhnev commented that he had seen something like this many times in cowboy movies.

"Yes," Nixon replied, "John Wayne."

Upon hearing this magical Hollywood name, Brezhnev, "jumped back from the window, hunched his shoulders, put his hands to his hips, and drew imaginary six-shooters from imaginary holsters."

At a meeting at the presidential retreat at Camp David however, Brezhnev's adventurous spirit turned out to be more than Nixon had bargained for. The Soviet president, who collected luxury cars, was presented with a dark blue Lincoln Continental, donated by the manufacturer to commemorate his visit to the United States. Brezhnev was delighted with his gift, which was upholstered in black velour and had "Special Good Wishes—Greetings" engraved on the dashboard.

Insisting that he be allowed to try it out immediately, Brezhnev climbed into the driver's seat and motioned to Nixon to join him on the passenger's side. The head of the Secret Service detail turned white as the two most powerful political leaders in the world took off along the narrow track that runs along the perimeter of Camp David. As Nixon sat there, he recalled that Brezhnev was accustomed only to driving down the special centre lane in Moscow, and was afraid to think what would happen if a Secret Service or Navy jeep suddenly turned a corner onto the one-lane road.

Brezhnev reached the top of a very steep slope, where a sign read "Slow: dangerous curve." There was a particularly sharp turn at the bottom of the hill, and Nixon knew that, even when he drove a golf cart along this route, he had to brake carefully in order to avoid going off the road. Brezhnev approached the slope going more than fifty miles an hour. He paid no attention to Nixon, who was calling out,

"Slow down, slow down." As they reached the bottom, there was a squeal of rubber as Brezhnev slammed on the brakes.

Astonishingly, he negotiated the turn successfully. He calmly turned to Nixon, and commented that, "This is a very fine automobile. It holds the road very well." Nixon diplomatically responded that the Soviet president was an excellent driver: "I would never have been able to make that turn at the speed at which we were travelling."

Source: Richard M. Nixon, *RN: The Memoirs of Richard Nixon*, pp. 880-81.

*   *   *

If unflappability is one characteristic expected of diplomats, impassivity is another that is frequently encountered. And one diplomatist who was particularly noted for maintaining an olympian detachment from the common affairs of men, and for showing little or no emotion when confronted with their petty problems and worries, was Woodrow Wilson.

The Sound of Silence

Constantin Dumba, Ambassador of Austria-Hungary to the United States during the First World War, recalled one of only two interviews he had the unusual privilege of obtaining with Wilson. Throughout the entire meeting Wilson sat without saying a word; he failed to ask even a question. The Ambassador left the meeting deeply discouraged. The subject that Dumba had wished to discuss with the President was that of the treatment of Austro-Hungarian prisoners of war in Russia. After the spring of 1915 several hundred thousand soldiers had been taken prisoner; although they were in their summer uniforms, they were shipped off to Eastern Siberia and spent the winter there. Recognizing that there was terrible destitution in these camps, a Relief Committee had been established in Tientsin, China. But the Russian authorities had refused access to the camps, and the Committee was unable to get clothing, medicines and bandages to the prisoners. Even the delegates and doctors of the American Red

Cross had been denied access. Dumba had approached Wilson in order to appeal to him to intervene personally with the Tsar, whose kind-heartedness was proverbial; the Ambassador was certain that the Tsar himself was being kept in ignorance of the deplorable conditions, and that a personal appeal from the President would have an immediate effect.

But Wilson, who had said nothing during the interview, had promised nothing. Weeks passed, and Dumba despaired of achieving any result, when he learned from the State Department that Wilson had, in fact, taken action. The President had written a personal letter to the Tsar and had sent it by courier to the Ambassador of the United States in St. Petersburg. He instructed the Ambassador to deliver the letter to the Tsar at an *ad hoc* audience, which he was to obtain without stating the reason for it. These measures had been carefully conceived by the President and his staff in order to prevent Sazanov, the Russian Foreign Minister, from intercepting the communication and somehow forestalling action. The American Ambassador reported that the Tsar had been indignant when he was informed of the condition of the prisoners, and that he had immediately issued the necessary orders by telegraph. American doctors left Tientsin unhindered, carrying furs, blankets, and medicines to the unfortunate prisoners.

Source: Constantin Dumba, *Memoirs of a Diplomat*, pp. 196-97.

*　　　　*　　　　*

*S*ilence is, of course, an impossible tactic to employ when in the *public forum, and diplomacy has increasingly become an object of public spectacle. Different settings call for different tactics, and it is refreshing to note that humour may still be employed to some effect, in spite of the changing circumstances.*

The Heat of Public Debate

On one occasion in the 1920s, the Council of the League of Nations was meeting in Geneva. The representatives on the Council had been sitting all morning and afternoon throughout a hot and sultry day in a room that was crowded with reporters and members of the public who had been attracted by the intensity of the debate that was in progress. The atmosphere in the room grew more and more oppressive as the discussion dragged on through the afternoon until at last the room was cleared in order that the Council, which had found itself unable to consent to the resolution that had been drafted by its *Rapporteur*, might arrive at an alternative resolution.

But the Council had now taken upon themselves the hopeless task of drafting a new document—and in a few minutes there were as many drafts before the Council as there were representatives. Austen Chamberlain, the British Secretary of State for Foreign Affairs who was sitting on the Council at the time, later recalled how, when everyone was exhausted and their nerves on edge, the witty and effervescent French Minister of Foreign Affairs, Aristide Briand, stepped in to save the day:

> I happened to have been the *Rapporteur* whose proposal had been rejected. I thought I had done my share and, leaving my colleagues to their task, I retired into the background to await the result of their united efforts. Presently I was joined by the representative of the Netherlands. "*Ouf!*" he exclaimed, "*c'est comme un accouchement dans une gare!*" and indeed the scene was one of not less embarrassment and confusion. Later we resumed our places at the table. The heat was oppressive. Only one member of the Council seemed insensible to it; he who never seemed warm enough had sat all day in a thick overcoat which at this moment he was wrapping more closely around him. "Look at our friend,' said Briand; 'I am sure that when he dies he will leave directions that he shall be cremated and, as they push the coffin into the furnace, you will hear his voice crying, "For God's sake, shut that door. There's an awful draught!"

The members of the Council—including the victim of the joke—shared a good laugh and they soon afterwards reached an agreement.

Source: Austen Chamberlain, *Down the Years*, pp. 182-83.

*　　　*　　　*

Diplomatic gatherings open to the public, then broadcast over radio, and now televised, have given rise to many new opportunities for diplomats to indicate their discontent or disapproval. One of the most common of such demonstrations has been the diplomatic walkout, in which an entire delegation indicates the displeasure of the state it represents by rising as a group and walking out of the forum of discussion.

A Diplomatic Walkout

An interesting variation on this theme occurred at the San Francisco conference to establish the United Nations. Not surprisingly, the diplomatic jousting between the United States and the Soviets was intense, with particularly bitter quarrels arising over procedures.

At one juncture, when the British delegate was making a statement immediately after the Soviet delegate, Gromyko, had been overruled by the chairman, Gromyko rose from his seat, looked around, and proceeded to walk up the centre aisle of the auditorium. He was soon followed by all the other delegates representing communist states, including one lady delegate from Czechoslovakia. Photographers began snapping pictures of the walkout, the television cameras began to roll, the other delegates stood up to watch the procession. The British delegate, although he could not be heard above the din created by the movement, continued to speak.

Gromyko eventually reached the end of the aisle, turned, and disappeared into the gentlemen's restroom; the male delegates from the communist states followed him in, but the lady was left on her own. Reporters raced for telephones to transmit the news; the British delegate ceased his address.

After some time, Gromyko re-emerged and proceeded down the aisle to his seat, with his sympathetic colleagues following in his wake, including the lady who, by this time, was blushing at the applause coming from the galleries.

Source: Dean Acheson, *Present at the Creation: My Years in the State Department*, p. 547.

*　　　*　　　*

Gromyko had undoubtedly not intended to lighten the atmosphere by means of his little trip to the men's room. But sometimes diplomats quite consciously use humour to good effect.

Disarming the Diplomats

When Maxim Litvinov appeared on behalf of the Soviet Union at the Disarmament Conference of 1932 he caused a small sensation by advocating a proposal that everybody should disarm, immediately and totally. This was a marvellous, and typical, Soviet propaganda stunt, but it was not calculated to impress the diplomats assembled there, especially those from Britain and France, with whom Litvinov was desperately attempting to improve relations in the face of the growing Nazi threat in Germany.

As none of the leading statesmen would bother replying to this transparently foolish proposal, two of the lesser lights decided to enter the fray. The first attacked the Soviet proposal as clearly impractical, carefully dissecting the plan in a way that made his refutation unanswerable. The next speaker was Salvador de Madariaga of Spain. As impressive as the first speaker's rhetorical display had been, the Spaniard felt that the situation called for something different, something beyond intellectual debate; a dramatic apologue, he thought, was what was needed.

He chose, therefore, to recount a story that he attributed "to a distinguished British Statesman" (meaning Winston Churchill, although it later turned out that the story went back at least to the eighteenth century):

> The animal kingdom, it seems, had decided to disarm, and thus its various representatives met in conference, each with its own plan of how this might be achieved: the bull, eyeing the eagle, advocated the clipping of wings down to a minimum size; the eagle, fixing the lion, proposed that all claws should be cut down; the lion staring at the elephant, demanded that all tusks should be filed off or extracted; and the elephant, winking at the bull, said something about horns; whereupon the bear came forward and demanded that

all weapons of every kind whatever should be done away with, so that nothing remained but a fraternal hug.

The room broke up in laughter, and even Litvinov himself could not refrain from joining in.

Source: Salvador de Madariaga, *Morning without Noon: Memoirs*, pp. 247-48.

The Art of Communication

The art of communication is, perhaps, the essence of the craft of diplomacy. Over the years, states have found a variety of methods by which they attempt to make their views known, and through which they attempt to influence the behaviour of others. The telegraph and the telephone have been frequently used in recent times in order to communicate urgent messages, but some of the more traditional forms of communication have continued to be used in the twentieth century. When a formal, precise record is felt to be desirable, the diplomatic "Note" has remained an important tool in the diplomat's bag, in spite of all the devices that modern technology has to offer. Such a communication is customarily handed to a foreign minister by an ambassador, or vice-versa. But this is not always as straight-forward as it might seem.

Note, Note, Who's Got the Note?

When the British government complained to the Soviets about their behaviour during the Zinoviev Letter affair, the Soviets responded with a Note, which was then deemed by the British Foreign Office to be inappropriate, and therefore unacceptable. A member of the Office, John Gregory, was assigned the task of, quite literally, returning the Note to the Soviet Ambassador.

Gregory, who had always been on good terms with Ambassador Rakowsky and thus did not anticipate any particular difficulty in carrying out his instructions, arrived at the Ambassador's house in Hampstead one evening. Rakowsky, wearing a dinner jacket because he was expecting guests, initiated a cordial conversation, asking where Gregory had taken his recent vacation. When it transpired that they had both been in the Tyrol, Rakowsky expressed his regret that they had not known this beforehand, or they might have had a pleasant dinner together, one in which it might have been possible to avoid discussing politics. After these pleasantries had been exchanged, Gregory attempted to broach the subject of the Note: "I don't want to appear fussy, but it isn't really, if you don't mind my saying so, exactly the kind of Note we care to receive from foreign Governments."

"But I am afraid," answered Rakowsky, "my instructions were to deliver it".

"I really am sorry to be a nuisance, but mine are to return it to you."

The two diplomats then returned to their memories of the Tyrol and the joys of vacation. Eventually, Gregory felt that he had no choice but to bring up again the subject he had been sent there to discuss. He had better, he said, leave the Note with the Ambassador; whereupon Rakowsky replied that he could not possibly take it back. A long pause followed.

Lighting up cigarettes, they discussed the subject of automobiles for some time; then Gregory once more returned to the charge. "Look here, you really mustn't be keeping your guests waiting any longer, and I must be getting back to my own dinner. What about that Note?"

"What about it?" Rakowsky asked, taking care to avoiding catching Gregory's eye.

Having reached another standstill, the two diplomats got up from their chairs and strolled around the study, when Gregory saw his opportunity. With Rakowsky's back turned for a moment, Gregory quickly drew the Note out of his pocket and placed it on the writing-table. But Rakowsky, having spotted the movement out of the corner of his eye, took up the Note from the table, and handed it back.

They lit up fresh cigarettes. Gregory took the Note out of his pocket again and quickly stuffed it into one of Rakowsky's. Rakowsky removed it from his pocket and pressed it back into Gregory's hand. And there they stood for a few moments, their hands locked together with the Note. Rakowsky managed to disengage himself, and the Note was back where it had begun.

Gregory sensed that his only chance was to place himself between Rakowsky and the door, leap forward and stick the Ambassador with the note, then leap backwards and bolt out the door. This he did, but Rakowsky was after him like lightning; Gregory ran for the hall, collided with some of the Ambassador's guests, leaped into his car and raced back home without the Note. He had triumphed at last!

That same evening, Rakowsky posted the note back to Gregory.

Source: John Gregory, *On the Edge of Diplomacy: Rambles and Reflections, 1902-1928*, pp. 224-27.

*   *   *

*P*assing *a diplomatic document on can be difficult in itself; but it can be even more difficult to keep things private and out of the public eye until all parties are agreed that the time for an announcement has come. Conferences are particularly notorious for creating the danger of leaked information; too many people gathered together in one place in order to discuss interesting and controversial topics almost inevitably leads to things becoming known that the diplomats would, for the most part, prefer to keep to themselves. This danger has been exacerbated in the modern age as a result of the popular press coming to regard it as its duty to secure, and publicize, any information that they are able to get.*

Going Public

An early example of this fact of modern diplomatic life occurred at the Congress of Berlin in 1878, where the Great Powers of Europe met to solve the "Eastern Question" in the aftermath of the Russo-Turkish War. *The Times* of London had an enterprising correspondent in Berlin, Sir Donald Mackenzie Wallace, who was determined to achieve the *coup* of giving the world its first public account of the results of the Congress. He managed not only to achieve, but to surpass this objective.

Wallace succeeded in striking a bargain with the representative of a small Balkan state: he arranged that they should exchange overcoats in the ante-room in which the plenipotentiaries hung their garments each morning before beginning the day's deliberations. Wallace was to place in the pocket of his Balkan pal's overcoat a large packet of five-pound notes; in exchange, the diplomat was to slip into Wallace's pocket the full and final text of the Treaty of Berlin.

The exchange was carried out precisely as it had been planned. Wallace immediately hopped a train to Brussels, knowing that the German Press Bureau would have delayed transmitting a telegram on such a vital piece of political news without its having first received the *imprimatur* of the Censor. He left Berlin in the middle of the day, and was safely in Brussels later that night. He did have some difficulty in persuading the telegraph officials there to send a message of such enormous length, and which cost a small fortune—but he eventually managed to overcome their doubts.

The next day the full text of the treaty appeared in a special edition of *The Times*—before the signatories of the treaty had actually penned their names to the final document in Berlin!

Source: Arthur Hardinge, *A Diplomatist in Europe*, pp. 168-69

*   *   *

*G*iven enterprising behaviour such as that demonstrated by The Times correspondent, diplomatists have learned to be keenly aware of the role played by the press, and more especially so when the negotiations they are pursuing are meant to be secret. They have found some intriguing ways of responding to the difficulties that this presents.

Staying Private

In 1940 a diplomatic mission from Sweden came to the United States in search of various kinds of assistance that might enable the Swedes to prepare for the danger posed by German expansion. The United States, of course, was not yet at war, and foreign diplomats in general were aware that an isolationist mood in the country made it difficult for US government officials to provide much in the way of assistance to foreign states if it appeared that such assistance might compromise their neutrality. The Swedes badly needed American dollars, which they might then use to purchase the military equipment they so desperately needed. The first step in the Swedish Foreign Minister's pursuit of the dollars was to approach the Export and Import Bank, where he was told that it was the head of the Reconstruction Finance Corporation who approved or disapproved of foreign requests for credits.

The head of this Corporation was Jesse Jones, a rich Texan who received the Swedish diplomat, "with all the expansive hospitality of an important man from Texas." After some time was devoted to admiring Jones' favourite toy, a model of the city of Houston, the Foreign Minister outlined Sweden's economic situation and its need to rearm, given the current situation in Europe. He found it difficult to concentrate on what he was saying, however, "as Jones had the intimidating habit of spitting right across the desk in the direction of a spittoon about a yard away. He always hit the target." In spite of the distraction, the Minister succeeded in convincing the Texan, who arranged another meeting for later in the week but cautioned the Swede that the loan request must be kept a strict secret.

When the Foreign Minister appeared for the next meeting, Jones received him, "his long legs resting again on his impressive desk". This time, however, two men were seated in a corner of the room; Jones did not introduce them, but leaned over to the Swede and whispered, "Repeat what you said last time, but in a loud voice so that the men in the corner can hear you." The diplomat was mystified by this procedure, but did as requested. When he had finished repeating his report, Jones sat up in his chair and declared with unusual formality, "Well, we will have to consider this very carefully." The two men seated in the corner got up from their chairs and left the room.

When the visitors had gone, Jones began to laugh loudly, explaining that the two men were journalists. The surprised Swede protested that Jones had specifically stipulated that there must be no publicity. "Yes, that's exactly why I asked the newspapermen to come. They have been allowed to listen to your report, but only under promise of secrecy. If I hadn't invited them, there would have been considerable risk of their making conjectures about your visits to me." Now certain that the arrangement granting credits to the Swedes would remain strictly private because of the promise that bound the journalists, Jones proceeded to authorize the credits on his own authority.

Source: Gunnar Hägglöff, *Diplomat: Memoirs of a Swedish Envoy*, pp. 129-30.

*   *   *

The press is not the only factor that must be taken into account when diplomats are communicating with one another. Their enemies may certainly be expected to try to uncover whatever information they can concerning their activities and policies, and states have long been in the business of spying in order to anticipate and forestall the diplomatic stratagems of their opponents. Sometimes they go even further, and keep an eye on their friends.

Allies...of a Kind

In the autumn of 1941, following an intensive propaganda campaign, Hitler delivered an important speech at the *Sportpalast*. Immediately following the speech, the Italian Ambassador in Berlin, Dino Alfieri, sent a long telegram to Rome in which he unequivocally stated that the speech had met with a decidedly frigid reception. He explained that Hitler had sought to excuse himself in the eyes of his people for failing to keep his promise of a swift victory, and for his inability to foretell how long the war would last. In the passage of the speech that dealt with Germany's allies, Alfieri reported, Hitler had barely mentioned Italy. The Ambassador had sent the telegram in the *Impero* code, the most secret one that was available to the embassy.

Soon afterwards, Alfieri paid one of his monthly visits to Ribbentrop, the German Minister of Foreign Affairs, who gave a long, formal description of the current political and military situation. Ribbentrop sent his interpreter-stenographer out of the room, explaining to Alfieri that he wished to speak confidentially and frankly to him.

"I am at your disposal," the Ambassador replied.

"We have been informed that after the Führer's recent speech a telegram was despatched from your embassy containing comments which were far from friendly and sympathetic in tone."

Ribbentrop's statement profoundly shocked Alfieri, who attempted to remain impassive while finding out how much the Germans actually knew. Implying that he wasn't necessarily aware of the telegram in question, he replied that a great many telegrams were sent from the embassy each day.

"But the one to which I refer bears your signature."

Alfieri concurred that, although this might well be the case, almost all telegrams leaving the embassy were signed by him; only the most important ones containing a political content were submitted to him for censorship.

"The telegram in question is an important one, and its contents are political. The Führer has seen it and is most displeased," Ribbentrop added, averting his gaze.

While the Foreign Minister spoke, Alfieri reflected on the gravity of the fact that a highly secret telegram had been deciphered, and that Ribbentrop would dare to reveal this to him. Rather than immediately uttering a vehement protest, he asked what this was all about; Ribbentrop then repeated verbatim the entire contents of the telegram. Alfieri looked him in the eye and said, calmly and frigidly: "The telegram was from me. I wrote it with my own hand. But now," he added, rising from his seat, "I ask you to explain why you have raised this matter." His indignation was by this time barely concealed.

Ribbentrop, apparently realizing that he had gone too far, also rose to his feet: "I beg you not to place a false construction on what was intended as a gesture of sincerity and friendship. Telegrams of this kind can detract from the usefulness of your mission."

But this attempt to appease the indignant Ambassador had the opposite effect. He again insisted that Ribbentrop explain why he had raised the matter. "The friendship and the alliance between our two countries need in no way restrict my freedom of judgment, which I reserve completely. I am responsible for my actions solely to my Government."

Ribbentrop attempted once more to explain things away, but Alfieri cut him short. "I think," he declared, "that nothing remains to be said."

Experts were called in to investigate the Cipher Department of the embassy, but they could find nothing. The *Impero* code was replaced by another. Nothing more was done; there was no sequel to the story. But the Italian Ambassador had received a fresh insight into the meaning of German friendship.

Source: Dino Alfieri, *Dictators Face to Face*, pp. 168-70.

*   *   *

Every method of communication carries its own special hazards, but the telegram, used for almost a century to carry the most urgent messages, was more hazardous than most, even without interception by "friendly" or unfriendly Powers.

The Trouble with Telegrams

A conference was held in Chicago during the Second World War in an attempt to work out the organization of international civil aviation when the war ended. The leading roles were played by the United States and Great Britain, who could not agree on a number of substantial issues. The British were particularly keen on the principle of "escalation" which would relate increases in the frequency of services offered by a country's airlines to the ratio of passengers carried to that of the seats offered. After the failure of considerable efforts reach an accommodation between this principle and the American position that the fewest possible restrictions should be placed on airline expansion, the chief British negotiator, Lord Swinton, appealed to London to be allowed to drop it.

He received his reply from the Minister for Aircraft Production, Max Beaverbrook, via telephone. When Swinton heard Beaverbrook's voice he said, "Max, go to hell: it's three o'clock in the morning here," and hung up the receiver.

The next day a telegram arrived from Beaverbrook that made a number of points, one of which was "You may abandon escalation". The British delegates were delighted by this surprising news and immediately rushed down to the meeting room to announce this decision, which was received with great enthusiasm by the assembled delegates.

Two hours later a "chaser" telegram arrived from Beaverbrook saying, "In my previous telegram, before 'abandon' insert 'not'." But it was too late. A British delegation does not go back on its word.

Source: Paul Gore-Booth, *With Great Truth and Respect*, p. 132.

*   *   *

The telephone, on the other hand, might reasonably be thought of as having removed most of the obstacles that stood in the way of clear communications between individuals and governments. This idea was certainly at the bottom of the installation of "hotlines" between heads of states and governments. While the most famous of these is the line between Moscow and Washington, many others do exist, including one between Ottawa and Washington.

Is Charlie There?

As Prime Minister, John Diefenbaker had liked to keep the Red Phone displayed prominently to impress visitors. His successor preferred to set a different tone; Lester 'Mike' Pearson hid the "hotline" to the President of the United States from view when elected to office in 1963. A little more than a year later he could no longer remember where it was so when it rang one afternoon during a consultation with External Affairs Minister Paul Martin, Pearson could not locate the phone.

"My God, Mike, don't you realize this could mean war?" Martin exclaimed as they scrambled frantically around the room.

Pearson's reply was entirely calm, "They can't start a war if we don't answer the phone."

The phone was finally located and when the Prime Minister answered, he heard a voice asking "Is Charlie there?" The caller was informed he had a wrong number.

Source: Peter C. Newman, *The Distemper of Our Times*, pp. 38-39.

*   *   *

Trouble could also occur with the hotline between Moscow and Beijing.

The Trouble with Telephones

In 1969, during one of the Sino-Soviet border confrontations, Premier Kosygin resorted to the telephone in order to contact the Chinese—something that the Kremlin had, according to Chou En-lai, not done previously. And this "improved" form of communication quickly presented its own problems.

When the Chinese operator answered the telephone, Kosygin announced himself and asked to speak to Chairman Mao. The operator crisply replied, "You are a revisionist, and therefore I will not connect you." The hapless Kosygin then asked if he might speak to Chou instead—but the operator gave him the same reply and broke the connection.

Source: Richard M. Nixon, *RN: The Memoirs of Richard Nixon*, p. 568.

*   *   *

The Russians were not the only ones to discover that the proletarians who operated the lines of communication could play a role in diplomacy—and this was even more obvious in the days of pre-digital electronic equipment. But some diplomatists proved more adroit in dealing with this situation than others.

Anyone Listening?

The shrewd and clever Pierre Laval once told the story of how, at a delicate moment in the relations between France and Germany, he had decided to speak directly to the German Chancellor, Dr. Brüning, on the telephone. He managed to contact his German counterpart easily enough, but he was unable to hear a word that Brüning said.

It did not occur to Laval to wonder why the connection was so bad; he immediately roared down the line: "If I cannot hear Dr. Brüning's next sentence as if he were in my room, there will be many expulsions from the service to-morrow morning in the *Official Journal.*"

Immediately after this announcement the line became perfectly clear, and Laval was able to hear every word that Brüning said.

Source: Salvador de Madariaga, *Morning without Noon: Memoirs,*
p. 231.

*　　　　*　　　　*

In the world of diplomacy there are many ways in which states are able to communicate with one another, some of which are a good deal more subtle than official Notes or telegraph messages. In fact, some forms by which diplomats communicate with one another are so subtle that it may not appear that anything is actually being said—except to those assiduous students of the craft of diplomacy who are constantly on the watch for any sign of changing attitudes or policies.

Ping-Pong in Peking

One of the most significant shifts in the alignment of world politics in the Cold War era began with the arrival of the Chinese table tennis team in Japan in April 1971 for the World Table Tennis Championships. On a day of rest in the competition, one of the young American competitors, Glen Cowan, approached the captain of the Chinese team, Chuang Tse-tung, looking for a ride on their bus to an outing they had planned to some pearl farms. Cowan was permitted to join them, and the next day decided to show his gratitude by presenting Chuang with a T-shirt; Chuang accepted the gift and presented a Chinese handkerchief, printed with Chinese scenes, in return.

The next day the Chinese stunned the Americans, who had had no official relations with the government of mainland China for more than two decades, by inviting the team to visit China. The manager of the US team quickly called the embassy in Tokyo to ask for advice. The China specialist there, William Cunningham, recommended that they accept the invitation as being in keeping with the general desire of the Nixon administration to improve relations with China. Henry Kissinger, who believed that "one of the most remarkable gifts of the Chinese is to make the meticulously planned appear spontaneous," saw the invitation as indicative of China's desire to match the American efforts at improving relations.

The visit of the table tennis team created an international sensation. Their arrival was described in a broadcast over Peking radio, and they were received in the Great Hall of the People by Chou En-lai, the Chinese Premier, who declared, "You have opened a new chapter in the relations of the American and Chinese people," and he was confident, he said "that this beginning again of our friendship will certainly meet with majority support of our two peoples."

When the stunned American athletes did not respond to this prodding remark, Chou asked: "Don't you agree with me?" The Americans burst into applause and invited the Chinese team to visit the US. The invitation was accepted immediately.

To Henry Kissinger, who tells this story in his memoirs, "the whole enterprise was vintage Chou En-lai." He interpreted the story as a brilliant form of communication with various levels of meaning. Most obviously, the invitation and the reception symbolized the Chinese desire to improve relations with the US, while "on a deeper level it reassured—more than any diplomatic communication through any channel—that the emissary who would now surely be invited would step on friendly soil. It was a signal to the White House that our initiatives had been noted."

Selecting the table tennis team as the medium for conveying the message also meant that the initiative avoided any jarring political overtones, as the team was about as politically neutral an entity as could possibly be found. "But it was also a subtle warning to us: If Chinese overtures were rebuffed, Peking could activate a people-to-people approach and seek to press its case in a public campaign"—as Hanoi had been doing with such great effect throughout the war in Vietnam.

Diplomacy conducted through the manipulation of symbols may be circuitous and subtle, but it is used frequently, and often to great effect. Not long after this adventure in ping-pong diplomacy the President of the United States visited China, and a revolution in international politics was underway.

Source: Henry Kissinger, *White House Years*, pp. 709-10.

*　　　　*　　　　*

In the game of subtle communications, it takes two to play. If one party is straightforward and blunt, it may be a mistake to read a variegated series of interpretations into their remarks; but once the two parties have implicitly agreed that their communications are going to be subtle and open to careful analysis, they have to learn to abide by the rules of this highly sophisticated game.

Running Dogs and Empty Cannons

Not long after the adventure in ping-pong diplomacy, Henry Kissinger found himself in Beijing to work out the details of the visit to China by Richard Nixon. As Kissinger, his entourage and his hosts made their way from the airport into the centre of the city, they travelled along roads that were closed to traffic and which were heavily guarded. Along the route, they passed signs that had been painted, mostly in Chinese but some in English, denouncing American imperialism. When they reached their rooms in the guest house that had been prepared for them, they found English-language propaganda bulletins that carried on the cover an appeal for the people of the world to "overthrow the American imperialists and their running dogs."

Kissinger decided to respond to this form of "communication" by instructing a member of his staff to return his pamphlet to a Chinese protocol officer—with the explanation that the pamphlet must have been left behind by a previous party. He then had the rest of the bulletins collected and returned to the Chinese without comment.

A new conversation was initiated in which few words were spoken. The day after the arrival of the American party the Acting Foreign Minister of China called for Kissinger at the guest house in order to escort him to a meeting with Chou En-lai. In the car along the route to the meeting in the Great Hall of the People, the Acting Minister explained that the government of each nation had its own methods of communicating with its people, and that, whereas the US government utilized television and radio, the Chinese government utilized wall posters. He then pointed, as an example, to a spot they were passing at that moment, where only yesterday there had been a poster castigating American imperialism; a new poster now announced in English: "Welcome Afro-Asian Ping-Pong Tournament." The Minister then advised the Americans to pay attention to how the Chinese government acted and to ignore its rhetoric; the anti-American propaganda, he explained, was "firing an empty cannon."

By the time he wrote his memoirs, Kissinger was still uncertain who was communicating to whom with the posters and the pamphlets. Had the offending signs been put up by Chou's opponents, and had Chou "then used my protest to get Mao to overrule them"? Or had the signs been erected "with Chou's approval to test the limits of our tolerance"? And of course there was always the possibility that "they had been put up long before and left by bureaucratic inertia." Whatever the case, the offending posters were not seen again, and from that point on Kissinger and his entourage were treated as honoured guests. Someone had certainly communicated something, somehow.

Source: Henry Kissinger, *White House Years*, pp. 776-79.

*   *   *

A time-honoured method of communicating by symbolic demonstration is through the giving of gifts. The gifts range enormously in both their value and significance; most are mere tokens, a minor and insignificant part of a ceremony which in itself may be merely perfunctory. Photographs of institutions visited, engraved scissors used to cut ceremonial ribbons, and hand-crafted objects produced by local artisans, collect in the suitcases of diplomatic travellers like stamps in a passport. But there are also gifts of more enduring value and political significance: paintings, crystal, silver, limousines, and airplanes are likely to testify to the pursuit of some political objective. Most often the gifts are graciously given and politely accepted. But not always.

It's a Gift

When Mrs. Indira Gandhi succeeded Shastri as Prime Minister of India following his heart attack in 1966, the United States Government was anxious to take the opportunity of the change in leadership to improve relations with India, which had been deteriorating in recent years. The American Ambassador at New Delhi, Chester Bowles, was pleasantly surprised therefore when, early in March of that year, he received a cable from Secretary of State Rusk informing him that President Johnson was interested in taking up a suggestion that Bowles had made in 1963 to create an "Indo-American Foundation".

The idea was that the Foundation would be financed by the huge reserves of rupees that the US had accumulated through the sale of wheat to India. Bowles had proposed an institution that would have an Indian President, an American deputy, a board of trustees composed equally of representatives from the two countries, and a staff that would consist largely of Indians.

The Foundation, which was to be located in India, would be structured along the same lines as the Rockefeller and Ford Foundations. An endowment of 300 million rupees would provide an annual income of 10 to 14 million, which would be used to finance university projects, scientific research, etc. The proposal, which had been enthusiastically received by those in the Indian government with whom

Bowles had conferred, and with whom he had drawn up an agreement in the winter of 1964, had ultimately been blocked in Washington.

By 1966 however, with Mrs. Gandhi about to visit Washington, President Johnson was looking for some dramatic gesture that he could make in order to demonstrate his goodwill; he had come across the Bowles proposal for the Foundation and was now eager to promote it. He was even more eager once Mrs. Gandhi arrived in May and he had met her: he was deeply impressed by her warm and confident manner and in the political astuteness she demonstrated in a lengthy private conversation with him.

Thus, at an official White House dinner to honour her, Johnson was able to sincerely declare his great pleasure in announcing that the US was prepared to support the creation of the Foundation. On the spur of the moment, he went even further and pulled another rabbit out of the hat by making a present to Mrs. Gandhi of the *Anton Brun*, which was President Truman's old yacht, *Williamsburg*. The ship had been rebuilt and equipped for deep-sea research, and the Indians were known to want a ship of this kind for offshore exploration in the Arabian Sea and the Bay of Bengal.

The final event in Mrs. Gandhi's visit to Washington was a cocktail party at the Indian embassy, which was to be followed by a smaller dinner party. According to protocol, the President had not been invited to dinner, but he came for cocktails and enjoyed himself so much that he asked if he could stay for dinner. There he gave a toast which, "delivered in his Texas drawl, was once again a glowing tribute to Mrs. Gandhi and her government and an assurance of everlasting friendship and understanding; indeed, the clouds seemed at long last to be drifting away."

When the Prime Minister returned to her own country, however, the clouds began to gather once again. Johnson's announcement of the Foundation had taken the Indian press, parliament and public by surprise. Even the economists and political scientists of Delhi University, many of them American-educated, attacked the proposal. The Left asserted that the Foundation was a clever attempt on the part of the US to subvert the Indian educational system. Mrs. Gandhi, in the face of widespread criticism, felt that she had little choice but to set the idea aside for the time being.

Mrs. Gandhi followed her trip to Washington by making a similar state visit to Moscow in July. At the end of her visit she and Premier Kosygin issued a joint press statement that called for an end to the US bombing of North Vietnam, and which also contained some vague allusions to the nefarious "imperialistic powers". Not surprisingly, these remarks, which were interpreted as attacks on the United States, incensed Washington, and demolished much of the goodwill that had so recently been created.

Even the gift of *Anton Brun* backfired. The vessel ought to have arrived in Bombay by September 1966. When September came and went, Ambassador Bowles cabled the State Department to ask what had caused the delay. He was told that Senator Wayne Morse had held up the gift. He then wrote to Morse, who assured him that he had no objection to it.

Another three months passed, and still the vessel was nowhere in sight. When Bowles again cabled Washington he was told this time that it had been discovered that *Anton Brun* would require new engines—but there was no way to pay for them. He then contacted the Secretary of the Navy, Paul Nitze, and this last hurdle was finally cleared. The gift could at last be delivered.

Four months later, Bowles asked again when they could expect to see *Anton Brun* in Bombay. The cabled response read: "Unfortunately the *Anton Brun* sank last week in New York Harbor while being launched from dry dock."

Source: Chester Bowles, *Promises to Keep: My Years in Public Life*, pp. 512-15.

*   *   *

*G*iving gifts of an appropriate nature—and appropriate value—can also pose difficulties

Blankets from Birmingham

When Margaret Sinclair married Pierre Trudeau, the Canadian Prime Minister's new wife was frequently dismayed by the cheapness of the gifts provided by the External Affairs Department for protocol purposes. On one occasion on a visit to Moscow she was showered with gifts ranging from an amber necklace to a bone china tea set. In return she was expected to present to the Prime Minister's daughter, "a meager plate silver maple leaf, costing probably no more than twenty-five dollars."

In embarrassment Mrs. Trudeau pretended instead that through an oversight the present she had intended to give had been left behind; on her return to Ottawa she arranged to have a mink stole dispatched to Moscow.

When the young Prime Minister's wife inquired into External Affairs' policy in the matter of gifts, it turned out there wasn't any. A cupboard had been stocked with a variety of items, most of which seemed to Mrs. Trudeau to be "worthless rubbish". Nor had care been taken to investigate the ancestry of the stock in the gift cupboard. She discovered that a Canadian delegation to London not long before had presented a blanket as a gift; it was not until the presentation that the officials realized that their 'distinctly Canadian' gift had been manufactured in Birmingham.

Source: Margaret Trudeau, *Beyond Reason*, pp. 130-31

*   *   *

The giving of a diplomatic gift is rarely a spontaneous act, but sometimes the negotiations behind the scenes are the most fascinating part of the entire affair.

Blessed are those that Give

The process by which one is initiated to the custom of diplomatic gift-giving may perhaps account for the behaviour of the individuals involved. This certainly appears to have been the case with Achmad Sukarno, Indonesia's first President, who made his initial visit abroad as head of state to the United States in 1956. There he enjoyed an unforgettable month, which included a trip to Hollywood, press references to him as "the George Washington of Indonesia", and an honorary doctorate from Columbia University. When he returned home, his airplane was filled with gifts, including refrigerators; the automobile that he had been given would arrive later.

The trip apparently whetted his appetite for future travels; in the years that followed, one government after another was asked to receive him as an official guest, along with the forty or so retainers who accompanied him. Coming from a head of state, any government would have had difficulty in refusing such a request—a difficulty that was made more acute in Sukarno's case by the desire on the part of the West to keep him in the anti-communist camp.

One day the Australian Ambassador in Djakarta, W.R. Crocker, was called on by one of Sukarno's assistants, to be told that the President had been invited to visit New Zealand and, as he would have to pass through Australia to get there, he assumed that the Australian government would also wish to invite him to be their guest. The assistant then went on to explain that the President expected to receive "suitable gifts" on such an occasion, as did the senior members of his entourage.

What, the Ambassador inquired, would suitable gifts consist of? Would, for instance, some kangaroos—the national animal of Australia—be appropriate? They would, he suggested, fit well into the presidential palace gardens. The President's assistant testily replied that the gifts "should be costly, not just symbolic". The Ambassador asked if he might be given a more definite indication of what sort of gifts would be appropriate.

The presidential assistant returned two days later with his list. For Sukarno's Prime Minister, a dining table "of costly wood," a French tapestry or a valuable old Chinese vase would be suitable; the Foreign Minister ought to be presented with a set of books, such as a set of encyclopedias. For President Sukarno himself, "a big Italian or French chandelier" could be considered, but the most suitable gift would be a marshal's baton made out of "the best wood and inlaid with gold and jewels, or one big jewel, or, better, a cluster of jewels, for each of his five marshal's stars." Moreover, as the President was now engaged in building up his library and art collection, he ought also to be presented with a set of valuable books or a painting.

Alas, the visit was postponed indefinitely, and the gifts never did make their way to the presidential library, art gallery, dining room or treasure chest.

Source: W.R. Crocker, *Australian Ambassador: International Relations at first hand*, pp. 11-13.

*   *   *

One of the most enduring images of the Second World War is that of Winston Churchill gnawing on a cigar, or with one in hand. Few would suspect, however, that his love of cigars gave rise to a diplomatic incident.

The Duties of Office

Late in 1940, although the Battle of Britain had been won, the Battle of the Atlantic continued to rage. Many supply ships were being lost, and a rigorous system of rationing was imposed in Britain. Imported luxuries were practically nonexistent, as only essential items were allowed into the country. The Prime Minister was perhaps the only one who regarded cigars as an essential item; and by this time, smoking ten to fifteen a day and generously giving many away, he had consumed his entire prewar supply. Friends and admirers did send him some on occasion, but the demand far exceeded the supply.

The situation was becoming desperate when one day the Cuban Minister of the Legation in London appeared at 10 Downing Street with a huge cedar cabinet. To Churchill's delight, the Minister informed him that the cabinet contained five thousand of the very best Havana cigars—a token of admiration from the government and the people of Cuba. The Prime Minister was relieved and overjoyed; but not for long.

The next day an official from His Majesty's Customs and Excise called with the information that the Prime Minister owed £10,000 in Customs duty and Purchase Tax. This amount was exactly equivalent to the Prime Minister's annual salary. Churchill's personal assistant, John Colville, suggested that the cigars were a kind of necessity, as the British public would certainly be disappointed to see Churchill without one, but the official remained "granite-faced and adamant." Only the King, he insisted, was exempt from Customs duty.

When Colville broke the sad news to Churchill, he was simply instructed that, "It is up to you to find a satisfactory solution."

Colville, who had been seconded to the Prime Minister's staff from the Foreign Office, turned to the Office for a solution. He spoke to the Foreign Secretary's Private Secretary, explaining that the Prime Minister would obviously have to return the cigars and refuse to accept the gift. He pointed out that although this would quite likely lead to a total breakdown of goodwill between the British Empire and Cuba, "one must, of course, have one's priorities." Did he not recall, however, having seen in the Foreign Office telegrams, "a report that the American Government were perturbed about the possible use of Cuban bases by German U-Boats?" But then America was not even a belligerent in the war, and if the British government did not care about the loss of Cuba's goodwill, why should they concern themselves with American opinion?

Later that same day, a letter was despatched from the Foreign Office informing the Lord Commissioners of the Treasury that it was of vital political importance that no offence be given to the Cuban government in the matter of their gift to the Prime Minister. Colville remembers that the episode reached a happy dénoument: "The Lord Commissioners gave way with good grace; the requisite instructions were sent to the Customs: Churchill kept his cigars; and I kept my job." In each succeeding year until the war ended a beautiful cedar box was delivered to Churchill by the Cuban Minister—and every year it was admitted duty free.

Source: John R. Colville, *Footprints in Time*, pp. 105-6.

* * *

All diplomats, great and small, discover that they need to be cautious where gifts are concerned—both in the giving and in the receiving of them.

Going to the Dogs

When a young Charles Hardinge, who would one day become Permanent Under-Secretary of State in the British Foreign Office, was beginning his career in diplomacy, he joined the embassy in Constantinople as a very junior member. He was determined to see the country and familiarize himself with its customs and its people. He discovered, among other things, how unwise it could be to praise anything possessed by a Turk.

One night, staying in the house of a Turkish official, he happened to comment how much he admired the official's two beautiful Anatolian greyhounds. The Turk immediately said *"Sizin"*, meaning "They are yours."

Hardinge's Turkish servant was deeply upset, explaining that they would now be forced to take the dogs, who would have to accompany them on the remainder of their journey through the countryside. If they did not take the dogs, the official would be deeply offended. Hardinge assured his servant that he had no intention of hampering his movements by taking along two dogs that he did not even wish to have. They agreed that the tactful thing to do would be to resume their trip early the next morning, before the official had arisen. This they did successfully, without embarrassing the official, and without encumbering themselves; they felt they were to be congratulated on this well-executed and tactful escape.

But young Hardinge discovered that it was not to be as easy as this: "Three months later a Turk turned up at the embassy leading the two dogs which I had to accept and which placed me also under the obligation of sending the official a handsome present and of rewarding the man who had brought the dogs." Had he arisen to his later status, such an encumbrance as this unwelcome gift may not have been an insurmountable problem. Hardinge was, however, but a very junior member of the staff. "I did not have the dogs very long before they raided the kitchen of Sir Hugh Wyndham, First Secretary of the embassy, and carried off a leg of mutton which was being cooked for his luncheon, and he insisted on my getting rid of them."

From this point forward, Hardinge learned to be more restrained in issuing casual praise when travelling in unknown lands and when working with unknown foreigners.

Source: Hardinge of Penshurst, *The Old Diplomacy*, p. 21.

*   *   *

It is almost certainly due to familiarity with situations such as the one described by Charles Hardinge that diplomats learn to be cautious in expressing themselves. This does not mean that they remain silent, however, as most of them soon discover the art of the double entendre.

The Unpleasantness in Cairo

Lord Killearn, British Ambassador to Egypt during the Second World War, happened to mention to a prominent Egyptian, Ahmed Maher (who was later to become Prime Minister) that he was going away for six weeks leave. He expressed his hope that nothing unpleasant would happen during that time, at which point the Egyptian assured him that, "Nothing unpleasant ever happens when you are away." A *double entendre* worthy of the most distinguished diplomats.

*   *   *

Some diplomats go further. Carefully constructed double entendres would be wasted on some audiences.

Knives and How to Use Them

Sir Eric Phipps served as the British Ambassador to Germany in the early years of the Hitler regime, during which time he came to hate the Nazis passionately. He had a quick tongue and a dry sense of humour, both of which he was prepared to use against the Nazi leaders.

One evening Hermann Goering, Hitler's deputy, arrived late for a dinner at the embassy, not long after the massacre of the "Night of the Long Knives". He excused himself, explaining that he had only just returned from shooting. "Animals, I hope," replied Sir Eric.

Source: Ivone Kirkpatrick, *The Inner Circle*, p. 90.

Tribal Rituals

The diplomatic life is a life of rituals. One of the first of the many ceremonial occasions that an ambassador will face is that of presenting credentials to the head of state in the country to which he has been appointed. This is a highly formalized event: the ambassador presents a Letter of Credence, a formal greeting signed by his own head of state, in which his sterling qualities are attested to; the envoy then steps forward to recite an address expressing his immense pleasure at finding himself in this position, and assuring all concerned that he will earnestly endeavour to maintain and improve the cordial relations that exist between his country and that to which he has been accredited. The sovereign or head of state then replies in a similar vein, extends his hand to the emissary and brings the ceremony to an end.

"Let's Shake on it, King"

During the Second World War, John Cudahy was appointed Ambassador of the United States to Belgium with such haste, however, that he had no Letter of Credence. He did not even have the proper dress in which to appear; an outfit was quickly ordered for him, but when it arrived it was missing a few essential ingredients: one stiff shirt, one collar, one pair of white gloves, one white tie, and one top hat. A quick trip out to the shops of Brussels succeeded in replacing the missing items at the last moment, however, and the new ambassador was able to present himself at the palace as planned. But he still had no letter, nor did he have any written address to present.

Cudahy was ushered into the high-ceilinged rococo reception room, where he desperately looked for a lead from the Grand Marshal of the Court, Count Louis Cornet de Ways Ruart; he found none. "He was grave and immobile as a graven image, and as responsive. He bowed gravely to His Majesty; I bowed gravely. No American can bow gravely or otherwise without feeling and looking an ass, and certainly the situation required more than a grave bow."

Cudahy looked around the room at the dignified, uniformed attendants, his own grim staff who had accompanied him to the ceremony, and at last to the King; none of those assembled gave him a sign of what he ought to do. Deciding that he would have to take the initiative himself, "since there was nothing else to do, at last I crossed the room and inquiringly approached the King. He extended his hand cordially with a smile of genuine friendliness, and that was my official introduction to Leopold III, King of the Belgians."

Source: John Cudahy, *The Armies March: A Personal Report*, pp. 49-50.

*   *   *

As Ambassador Cudahy discovered, the diplomatic niceties that are expected of one can be particularly difficult to adhere to in times of crisis and upheaval, when it is not always possible to transact business in the manner to which the bureaucracy has become accustomed, and without which it hardly knows what to do.

The Old Ways

When the Churchill government was formed in Britain in May 1940, one of their first initiatives was to improve relations with the Soviet Union. For two months previously, the two countries had been discussing the possibility of re-establishing trade relations, but the Chamberlain government insisted that the Soviets should give them some reassurance that goods exported to it from Britain would not end up in Germany. The Soviets had refused to give such assurances, and there the matter stood until Churchill replaced Chamberlain.

On the evening of 20 May, Halifax, the Foreign Secretary, called in the Soviet Ambassador, Ivan Maisky, to inform him that the new Cabinet had just finished meeting and that they had agreed that the discussion of the trading relationship between the two countries should no longer be carried on by means of memoranda and counter-memoranda. Given the urgency of the situation, they had decided to send Stafford Cripps to Moscow in the capacity of "Ambassador on a Special Mission," in the hope of settling the question by means of direct negotiations. He asked Maisky to make the necessary arrangements for Cripps' journey as quickly as possible.

Meanwhile, events were unfolding dramatically in western Europe. On 14 May, the Germans broke through the French front at Sedan; their tanks and armoured vehicles began racing to the Atlantic coast; the Reynaud government appeared to be on the verge of disintegration; confusion reigned in Paris, and it seemed as if French resistance to Hitler might collapse shortly. Even before Maisky had received a reply from Moscow concerning the Cripps Mission, therefore, the Foreign Office contacted him on the evening of 24 May to inform him that they had decided to send Cripps to Athens the next day. Although the air link between London, Paris and Rome was still open, it might break down at any time, and they did not wish to see any days lost in travelling. So off went Cripps to Athens, to await word from his government that he was to continue his journey to Moscow.

On 26 May, Moscow replied positively to Halifax's suggestion of the 20th—but not to the idea of Cripps being "Ambassador on a Special Mission" to discuss trade. They insisted that he come as a regular "Ambassador of His Majesty," thereby replacing Sir William Seeds, who had demonstratively left Moscow "on leave" as a diplomatic slap on the wrist at the beginning of the year. The British reluctantly consented to this condition.

But now an awkward problem arose: how was Cripps to have delivered to him the necessary "credentials" that he would have to present to the head of state, in order to be a properly accredited emissary of His Majesty, the King? By this time the Germans were advancing on Paris, and the airline that Cripps had used to fly to Athens had ceased to operate. The alternative route to Athens was via North America, the USSR and the Balkans—not a very satisfactory alternative given the wish of both parties that he should appear in Moscow immediately.

The Soviet Ambassador thought that the solution was simple: "Send the credentials by cable."

"But will your Government accept cabled credentials?" asked Rab Butler, the Parliamentary Under-Secretary for Foreign Affairs.

Maisky burst out laughing: "Of course it will! You need have no worry about that."

Butler hesitated and continued to look worried. "I must consult with my experts," he cautiously replied.

A grey-haired sage of the most respectable appearance was called in to the meeting to provide his expert advice. Butler explained the problem to him and outlined Maisky's solution.

"No, that is impossible!" declared the expert.

"But why?" the dismayed and uncomprehending Soviet asked.

"During all the nearly 200 years of history of the Foreign Office there has never been a precedent for the King's signature being sent by cable." The credentials of ambassadors had to be signed personally by the King, he explained, in a tone that did not invite question.

"There you are," said Butler profoundly.

"Your argument does not convince me one little bit," Maisky told the Foreign Office man. "It may be that there has never been such a case in the history of the Foreign Office, but then in the history of mankind there has never been a war like the present one. One must keep pace with the times..." Look at the Houses of Parliament, he suggested: they had once been lit by candles, but had adapted to modern ways by having electric lights installed; surely the same principle held good for the transmission of credentials via telegraph?

The Foreign Office expert, Maisky later recalled, proved to be very obstinate and resisted his argument; Butler, the politician-parliamentarian, in the meantime, remained silent and gazed reverentially at the official.

Maisky, who was laughing inside at the nonsense imposed by these encrusted traditions, tried another suggestion: "Prepare Cripps's credentials, send them officially to me at the Soviet embassy, I will just as officially inform you that I have received them, and then I will myself transmit the contents of the credentials to Moscow by cable." Later on, when a suitable opportunity presented itself, he would forward the original documents to the People's Commissariat for

Foreign Affairs. The faces of the two bourgeois Englishmen suddenly brightened.

"That's splendid! That's what we'll do!"

One of the greatest, if unforeseen, obstacles standing in the path of an Anglo-Soviet alliance had been removed: a few days later, Cripps became British Ambassador to the Soviet Union, and on 1 July 1940 was received by Stalin.

Source: Ivan Maisky, *Memoirs of a Soviet Ambassador, 1939-1943*, pp. 136-39.

*   *   *

Ceremonies are both inevitable and persistent features in the lives of diplomats. They are much in demand for the opening of hospitals, bridges and roads and are expected, naturally, to perform their duties with dignity and to lend decoration to the occasion. Things, however, do not always go according to plan.

A Dignified Retreat

John Kenneth Galbraith, during his time as Ambassador in India, participated in numerous ceremonial occasions, but one in particular etched an indelible memory. He was to give an address on coal washeries and power plants at the inauguration of work on the Bandal power plant outside Calcutta, the cost of which was being borne entirely by the United States. The ceremony, he notes, "was one of the most disastrous events in diplomatic history."

After the motorcade slowly made its way twenty-five or twenty-six of the thirty badly-congested miles between the centre of Calcutta and the site at Bandal, a terrific storm hit them. Hail, several inches of rain, and winds of near-hurricane force struck so hard that drivers could not see the front end of their cars.

After waiting for twenty minutes, the motorcade attempted to continue, but most of the cars quickly bogged down in the mud that had been created. Galbraith, who was transferred to a jeep, did manage to reach the site, where the wind had succeeded in removing the *shamiana*, the tea tables, microphones, and decorations. A few people waded through the mud to stand on the porch of the only available building, where the Ambassador decided that it would be silly to read the speech under such conditions, and instead handed out copies of the text to reporters.

Galbraith then proceeded to plant a tree in order to commemorate the occasion, whereupon "I broke into two pieces the silver spade that was given to me for the digging. Then, feeling exceedingly silly, I symbolically watered the tree with a small silver sprinkling can amid the continuing torrential downpour."

The party agreed at that point to make a prompt return to Calcutta.

Source: John Kenneth Galbraith, *Ambassador's Journal: A Personal Account of the Kennedy Years*, pp. 354-55.

*   *   *

*E*ven *the smallest and simplest of things can go wrong.*

Diplomat in the Sail Set

Alexander Dumba, the Ambassador of Austria-Hungary to the United States before the First World War, rented a summer villa on the North Shore near Boston. His summer retreat happened to be located not far from that of President Wilson's closest adviser, Colonel Edward M. House, who invited him to attend a great international regatta on board one of the big government cutters. Following an excellent luncheon on board the ship, House and Dumba agreed that for non-sailing men, the time between the start and the finish of a race passed very slowly, and they agreed to go to shore ahead of time.

House pointed out that the cutter would fire the customary salutes as they departed, and asked the Ambassador to stand up in the small steam launch and acknowledge them. The unsuspecting Dumba, willing to perform this simple duty, had hardly risen "when the shots whizzed immediately above my head and the pressure of the air knocked me full length on to the deck."

Source: Constantin Dumba, *Memoirs of a Diplomat*, p. 217.

*   *   *

*I*nsofar as a ceremony is a highly formalized and ritualistic occasion, it is often devoid of political content: an ambassador present at a naval regatta is honoured with a salute, and returns the honour, regardless of the political relations that exist between his state and the one to which he is accredited; an ambassador from a friendly ally presents his credentials to the head of state in the same manner as would one from an adversary. But ceremonial occasions may also be used to make a political statement; and, if one party to the ceremony wishes to use it in this way while the other does not, it can give rise to some interesting innovations.

A Diplomatic Illness

The Rumanian Minister of Foreign Affairs, Grigore Gafencu, undertook in 1939 a journey through the capitals of Europe in an effort to attempt to avert the catastrophe that he saw coming. His official visit to Berlin finished on the evening of 19 April, and he thought that he had completed his sojourn there without any difficult incidents arising; but he discovered the next day that he had one trial left, for 20 April was Hitler's fiftieth birthday, and a huge military parade had been arranged in honour of the occasion in Berlin.

Before departing from Bucharest on his journey to Berlin, Gafencu had received from Ribbentrop, the German Minister of Foreign Affairs, an invitation to be his official guest on this occasion. The Rumanian had declined the invitation "since I wished my visit to be strictly diplomatic." And besides, "only the German people in the year 1939 had cause to fête Hitler." When he arrived in Berlin however, the Germans began to exert pressure on him to attend the festivities, and Gafencu agreed to meet them halfway, by attending as a private individual, as his formal diplomatic duties would have ended on the 19th. It was agreed that he would go to the diplomatic stand, accompanied only by the Rumanian Minister in Berlin. Gafencu was insistent that his appearance at the festivities should not be taken to indicate any degree of political approval for, or diplomatic affinity with, the Reich.

On the morning of 20 April, as Gafencu was preparing to go to the Rumanian Legation, he heard the voice of his chief of protocol arguing with Fabricius, the German Minister to Rumania, and a representative from the German Foreign Office. The Germans had arrived at the hotel with two open cars, and they were waiting for Gafencu to join them; he was to appear with the other two guests of honour in the procession that was making its way to the Führer's special stand. He protested that this was not what he had agreed to when he had consented to appear at the parade, but the Germans refused to give way: they had received a formal order that they were to fetch him and to see that he took part in the ceremonies along with the other guests of honour.

"I asked who were these guests with whom I was to share the honour of being received in the Chancellor's box. The reluctant reply was given that they were M. Hacha (the 'President' of what remained of Czechoslovakia) and Monseigneur Tiso (chief of the 'independent' republic of Slovakia)." The political message that would be conveyed by the Rumanian Minister of Foreign Affairs appearing as a guest of honour at festivities celebrating Hitler's birthday while standing in a special box next to two of his recently-installed puppets would be quite clear to all observers.

"I saw red and said that I set no store whatever on being paid so extravagant an honour. It was of no avail. The courteous but implacable pressure tightened around me; time was getting short and it was necessary to go."

At that moment Gafencu was inspired by a bright idea. He had already been suffering somewhat from the aftereffects of a liver complaint, which compelled him to adhere to a strict diet—as his hosts knew; perhaps he could draw on this to avoid a political scandal. "I played it up with appropriate moans; then, before the staring eyes of the two German diplomats, I flung off morning coat, collar, shoes, and the rest, and in an instant I was in bed, carefully tended by my secretaries, who had instantly grasped the significance of the 'crisis'."

Fabricius went to the telephone and, after a series of calls, returned smiling: if the Rumanian Foreign Minister's liver crisis should happen to pass, he could come to watch the parade as he wished. With this, Gafencu got dressed immediately and went to the diplomatic box along with his chief of protocol and the Rumanian Minister to Germany. "From that point I saw the celebrated march past which was intended to demonstrate to the world the surpassing power of the mighty German war machine..." For six hours he watched as the motorized troops of Germany marched past in what seemed to be an unending procession: "a grandiose display which began gaily with a joyful fanfare of trumpets under the cloudless spring sky, dragged on for hours with a besetting clangor of metal, finally to seem like the unending vision of Hell or a ghastly nightmare to the nerve-shattered spectators."

Gafencu watched Hitler, who remained erect and motionless throughout the parade, never taking his eyes off the immense army. "It was as though he was letting the army speak—supreme and irrefutable argument—so that by it he might win the full comprehension of the world." And there, at the foot of Hitler's podium, "in a special little box like a gilded cage, one saw MM. Hacha and Tiso, who had resigned themselves to participation in the Führer's triumph. Not without some disquiet, I saw the stall originally intended for me at their side—still vacant."

Source: Grigore Gafencu, *The Last Days of Europe: A Diplomatic Journey in 1939*, pp. 81-84.

*   *   *

And then there was the time that the Russian Court was paid the honour of a visit by the Shah of Persia—the first time that a Persian autocrat had visited a European city. At the Court reception held at the palace, the Shah was escorted into the *cercle* by the Tsar; the august visitor cast a wondering eye over an assembly which, in the great days of the Winter Palace, presented one of the most brilliant spectacles in Europe. The *Grande Maîtresse* was a lady, no longer young, of massive proportions, with an ample bust and shoulders. The Shah advanced towards her, with forefinger extended, pointing

to the *décolletage*, and, turning to his host, smilingly observed: *"Vielle, laide. Pourquoi nue?"*
["Old and ugly. Why is she naked?"]

*   *   *

Diplomacy is full of symbolic acts of various kinds. Participants and observers alike read the signs as carefully as any medieval astrologer studied his astrological charts. The manner in which things are done is sometimes more significant than what is done; it is not always what is said but how it is said, or who is saying it, or in what setting that really matters. The very chairs that diplomats sit on, and the table around which they sit, can, as a result of the significance attributed to symbols, become important elements of diplomacy. The symbolism is made vastly more complicated when parties whose existence is not altogether clear or universally recognized are introduced into the picture, as was the case in dealing with the Vietnams, the Koreas and the Germanies from the 1950s to the 1990s.

If I Had a Hammer

When the Foreign Ministers of the United States, Britain, France and the Soviet Union were to convene in Geneva for talks in 1959, they had great difficulty getting started. The cause of the difficulty was the nature of the representation and participation to be accorded to the two Germanies. Would the representatives of East and West be allowed to intervene in the discussion? The question provoked considerable debate, the conclusion of which was a rather elaborate, if ingenious, procedure: if one of the German groups wished to speak, they should give the chairman a sign of their intention to do so; the chairman would then ask if there were any objections among the Foreign Ministers to hearing from one of the Germanies (it being an unwritten rule to begin with that no one would object as long as the German representatives refrained from making provocative interventions); if any Foreign Minister did object, he could demand an immediate private session of the four principal participants alone.

More challenging than the procedure, however, was the question of the shape of the table and the configuration of representatives at or near it. The first meeting had to be cancelled because the carpenters had not yet been given instructions concerning what sort of table they were to build. The Americans wished the table to be square; the Russians demanded that it should be round; the British proposed that it should be oval.

A complete deadlock seemed possible until another elaborate compromise was worked out: the table would be round; two inches from it there would be two tables where each of the German delegations would sit; at a distance of two metres there would be an additional table for the secretariat.

The conference was saved by these imaginative constructions, and it was able to labour on for a full two weeks' worth of discussions.

Source: Harold Macmillan, *Pointing the Way, 1959-1961*, p. 63.

*　　　　　*　　　　　*

*S*ymbols are used, almost invariably, to make a statement of some kind, whether the expression comes from the weak or the strong.

With All Flags Flying

When Dino Alfieri arrived in Germany as the new Italian Ambassador in May 1940, he at once determined that it was going to be necessary to take a firm, resolute attitude. Especially with the Germans, he believed, such a policy was necessary to avoid being kept in a state of inferiority and subjection. He had almost immediately found their attitude offensive, when they kept throwing their military successes in the faces of foreigners, as if to say: "Our days of poverty and obscurity are over. Soon we shall be the masters of Europe—to some extent we already are—and everyone, including you Italians, will have to reckon with us." This posture reminded Alfieri of the *nouveau riche* who shows off his cars, his luxurious apartment, brags about the costly jewels he gives his wife and flaunts the vast wealth that he has accumulated. He was determined to respond in some way, but how?

When he arrived at the embassy on the morning of 24 May, Alfieri noticed that the Italian flag had not been hoisted. When he questioned the porter about this, he was regarded with open-mouthed astonishment. He tried an official instead, who immediately became embarrassed by the question, and pointed out that the flag had not been flown on this date in previous years, and that, in view of the existence of the Pact of Steel, to fly it now would certainly not please the Germans, and would be open to various interpretations.

The new Ambassador issued instructions for the flag to be hoisted, an act that caused an immediate stir in diplomatic circles, where the gesture was received with satisfaction. When the German Foreign Office expressed its amazement, Alfieri clarified the meaning of the gesture: that the friendship and the alliance between the two countries need not prohibit the commemoration of a date in history particularly dear to the hearts of Italians. And thus it was that on 24 May 1940, the anniversary of Italy's entry into the First World War on the side of the Allies, the Italian tricolour was flown from all Italian Government buildings in Germany.

Source: Dino Alfieri, *Dictators Face to Face*, pp. 28-30.

*　　　　*　　　　*

Ceremonial displays form part of the everyday existence of diplomats: some of them are splendid affairs, although most of them are humdrum and perfunctory. But even visits without fanfare or important personages can cause little miseries.

The Visit that Never Was

One evening during the height of the Cold War, an ebullient Czech official who was filled with the spirit of friendship (and a few glasses of wine) asked a member of the British embassy if he would not care to visit his paper factory, where the machinery was British. The

British diplomat, Cecil Parrott, replied that he would be delighted to undertake such a visit, and asked for directions to the factory; the Czech graciously insisted that he himself would call for his guest and drive him to the site.

A few days later the official called to say that the boilers had unfortunately broken down, so the visit would have to be delayed for the present; but they should soon be working again, and they would make the visit when they were. About three weeks later he called again to say that the boilers had now been repaired and the visit could proceed—but would Parrott mind making an application to the Protocol Department of the Ministry of Foreign Affairs, in order to obtain the necessary clearance?

Parrott minded very much indeed, and drew the line here. "It was insufferable that a high official, after having asked me to be his guest, should then ask me to beg permission to come. It would put an entirely wrong complexion on the episode and make it appear that it was we who were pressing to see the factory." The diplomat might very well find himself being accused of attempting to pry into things that were not of his concern—and all because he had accepted an enthusiastic offer of being shown a paper factory by a proud manager!

Parrott realized full well what had probably happened: the Party organization, on learning of the invitation, would have rapped the hapless official over the knuckles for not clearing the invitation with them beforehand. Communist Czechoslovakia's version of a Protocol Department was the Party apparatus, whose representatives would decide where and when foreign diplomats might travel within the country. "I took no further action and our would-be host never spoke about it again."

Source: Cecil Parrott, *The Serpent and the Nightingale*, p. 146.

*　　　*　　　*

Surely the most frustrating of diplomatic rituals is sitting through long and tedious speeches and presentations. But this is doubly the case when not a word of what is said can be understood. Although every foreign service is filled with diplomats who are multilingual,

*and although every service maintains its own corps of linguistic
experts to serve as translators and interpreters in case this facility
should prove insufficient, this is still no guarantee that meaningful
communication will be possible.*

Ålandese, Anyone?

After the First World War, a dispute arose between Sweden and
Finland concerning the ownership of the Åland Islands. Two diplomats, one British and one French, were called in to mediate the
dispute. In the early stages of consultation, a deputation of Åland
Islanders arrived in London to put their case before the British
diplomat. They immediately impressed John Gregory "by the cor-
rectness of their tail coats, the rotundity of their figures and the
weight of their gold watch-chains." But this was the only impression
he was able to derive because "Not one of them could speak a word
of any other language than Ålandese, whatever that may be, and so,
in order to make themselves intelligible, they brought with them a
Swedish interpreter whose function was to translate for my benefit
from Ålandese into Swedish. For all the good he was to me, they
might equally have brought a Swahili or a Chinaman..."

The hapless Gregory attempted to convey, by means of sign
language, the fact that he was unable to follow their remarks, but they
paid no attention to his gestures. "On the contrary, the spokesman of
the deputation without a moment's hesitation plunged into a long, loud
and impassioned harangue in his own tongue without pausing a second
for the Swedish interpreter to translate. It lasted the best part of an
hour, during which I did my best not to appear half-witted." When
the tirade finally stopped, the interpreter launched into a verbatim
translation; Gregory could do little but resign himself to listening for
another hour.

But quite suddenly the flow of completely unintelligible eloquence
stopped. "There was a loud detonation through the room. The chair
on which the Swedish interpreter was sitting had collapsed; and that
unfortunate and unnecessary gentleman had crashed on to the hard
floor. The accident caused so much consternation, chiefly because the

Swede (or pseudo-Swede) had been genuinely damaged, that the interview came to an abrupt end and the deputation bowed itself out."

In spite of these tragic circumstances, a treaty was signed in Geneva shortly afterwards that miraculously appeared to satisfy all the parties concerned.

Source: John Gregory, *On the Edge of Diplomacy: Rambles and Reflections, 1902-1928*, pp. 190-92.

Dining with the Diplomats

Diplomatic dining is conducted according to a rather rigid system of protocol. Like much of diplomacy, however, the rules are mainly unwritten and have to be learned through experience. This may be particularly difficult for those "amateurs" who find themselves occupying diplomatic posts without having been slowly trained in the niceties of such behaviour.

The Guest of Honour

Such was evidently the case when Clare Boothe Luce was appointed Ambassador of the United States to Italy and attended her first state dinner in Rome at the Spanish embassy. In Italy, unlike the United States, dining takes place later in the evening; and the Spaniards dine even later than the Italians. Dinner would normally begin at ten, and was expected to end at eleven-thirty. Mrs. Luce had been briefed beforehand that protocol dictated that no one was to leave the table before the guest of honour, so, although it was already late for her and she was tired, she nevertheless waited patiently towards the end of the meal, keeping a careful eye on the British Ambassador, the *doyen* of the diplomatic corps, to see when it might be possible for her to take her leave.

The food was finished. No one left. The British Ambassador continued to chat with those around him. Midnight came and went. Time passed. More conversation. Another hour elapsed. By one-thirty Ambassador Luce, who was by this time becoming very sleepy, turned in desperation to the wife of the Spanish Ambassador and, in a whisper, asked at what time they might expect the British Ambassador to rise from the table.

"When the guest of honor leaves" was the answer.

"But who is the guest of honor?" the new Ambassador asked.

"You are!" the Señora frigidly replied.

The Ambassador and her husband were gone from the embassy within minutes.

Afterwards, Mrs. Luce learned that as the only female ambassador in Rome she was often placed on the immediate right of her host, and that when this happened she was considered to be the guest of honour.

Source: Alden Hatch, *Ambassador Extraordinary*, p. 213.

*   *   *

*P*rotocol *certainly insists on a rather rigid system of placement at the table. As one might expect, the more formal the occasion and the setting, the more rigidly enforced is the protocol. Sometimes, however, practical necessities intrude in such a way as to mitigate the rigidity of the system.*

Protocol and Physique

Harold Eeman, when serving as Counsellor in the Belgian Legation in Moscow, did a good deal of diplomatic entertaining at his "official" Moscow apartment, which came to him fully furnished. The rooms were remarkably spacious by local standards, but for someone accustomed to the niceties of protocol, the furnishings presented some unique challenges. The drawing-room contained a huge sofa "obviously reserved for important guests, social V.I.P's who, once installed there, were virtually imprisoned behind a large circular table of dull glass. This voluminous piece of furniture was referred to as 'the Lubianka'."

The dining room presented an even more interesting challenge. The table, consisting of some rare tropical wood, polished to perfection, was neither round, nor oval, nor square nor rectangular: it was constructed in the shape of a double lyre. Although pleasing to the eye, its lovely shape presented some challenging situations, as the guests had to be accommodated to its curves, both convex and concave. Protocol had thus to be tempered by the requirements of anatomy: "It was clear that only thin, flat people could reasonably be asked to sit face-to-face with a bulge of the table, whereas fat people would not be comfortable unless their excess of flesh could dovetail into a corresponding convex curve."

Thus it was that the diplomat came to conceive of his own elaborate double system of protocol, based on both figure and rank.

Source: Harold Eeman, *Clouds over the Sun: Memories of a Diplomat, 1942-1948*, p. 76.

*   *   *

The issue of protocol arose in another context in Washington in 1946, shortly after Harry Truman had succeeded Franklin Roosevelt in the presidency. This time, however, the situation threatened to transcend issues of mere decorum, and to have political ramifications.

Protocol and Love

President Truman decided that the annual diplomatic dinner, which used to be given at the White House in the prewar years but had been suspended during the war, ought now to be reinstated. This created an unexpected problem for Stanley Woodward, the Chief of Protocol in the State Department, who pointed out that because of the tremendous expansion in the number of nation-states now represented at Washington, there was no longer sufficient room at the White House to include all of the chiefs of mission, their deputies, and the wives of both—not to mention the number of Americans who ought to be there in the official capacity of hosts. The dinner would have to be divided, but in such a way as to avoid the impression of first- and second-class affairs; the solution he proposed was to number the missions alphabetically, and to then invite the odd-numbered missions on one date, the even-numbered on another. This plan appeared to be a clever solution to a thorny little problem, and was immediately approved. Regrettably, no one thought to scrutinize the invitation lists that resulted from it.

On the afternoon of the first dinner, the Chief of Protocol received a telephone call from the Soviet embassy informing him that neither the Soviet Ambassador nor his Counsellor would be able to attend that evening, as both had been taken ill. The State Department immediately called Ambassador Novikov ("Old Novocaine") who seemed, when they reached him, to be both well and cheerful; when inquiries were made about his plans for the evening, however, he confirmed the poor health of the Soviet embassy in general. The dinner proceeded as planned, but in the absence of the Russians.

It was soon discovered what had caused this mysterious, and selective, bout of ill-health. The odd-and-even method of sorting out the delegations had resulted in the envoy of Lithuania being invited to the same dinner as the Soviet representatives, who regarded Lithuania as being an intrinsic part of the USSR, while the United States continued to recognize it as an independent state. Ambassador Novikov had probably received instructions from Moscow at the last moment. When President Truman the next day sent for Woodward and Assistant Under-Secretary of State Dean Acheson, they expected that they were in for a thorough scolding for their regrettable lack of attention to detail.

Instead, the President instructed them to inform the Soviet Ambassador that he was no longer welcome at the White House, since he had been inexcusably rude to Mrs. Truman. The two officials attempted to take the responsibility upon themselves, explained the political dilemma that their oversight had created for Novikov, and warned of the serious consequences that might follow from such a step as that which the President was now proposing to take. Truman remained adamant. But just as the die seemed about to be cast, an assistant entered the room carrying a telephone; Mrs. Truman was on the line.

The President listened for a while, and then said, "I'm talking with him now. He agrees with you." He handed the receiver to Acheson, who was told by Mrs. Truman that he must prevent her husband from going through with his foolish plan. Acheson agreed, but asked for her advice on how to proceed; she suggested that they try to delay action until Harry's temper cooled down, and added that if he went ahead as he was planning to do, his critics would have a field day in attacking him.

This gave Acheson a bright idea. While Mrs. Truman talked he began to murmur in horror, pretending to repeat phrases she had not actually uttered, such as "...above himself...delusions of grandeur...too big for his britches..."

The President took the receiver back. "All right, all right," he told his wife. "When you gang up on me I know I'm licked. Let's forget all about it."

He hung up the receiver and, smiling, handed Acheson a framed photograph of a young woman in an old-fashioned costume. "I guess you think I'm an old fool," he said, "and I probably am. Look on the back," he added. On the back was written: *"Dear Harry, May this photograph bring you safely home again from France—Bess."* It was dated 1917.

The President did not take lightly actions that might wound Mrs. Truman's dignity, whether they were intended or not. As Acheson and Woodward were leaving his office he shouted out to them, "Tell Old Novocaine we didn't miss him!"

Source: Dean Acheson, *Present at the Creation: My Years in the State Department*, pp. 149-50.

*   *   *

*U*nsuspected challenges always lie in wait for the organizers of diplomatic dinners. Protocol is not the only worry; dining can be particularly challenging when it comes at the end of a long day of heated debate and strong arguments. To then sit down at table with one's adversaries for a pleasant meal and engage in civilized conversation can be a challenge worthy of even the most experienced and sophisticated of diplomats.

Singing for Supper

This was certainly the case when the Council of Allied Foreign Ministers met in London during the Second World War. The arguments at this meeting were particularly intense, with real bitterness arising between the British Foreign Secretary, Ernest Bevin, and the Soviet Commissar for Foreign Affairs, Vyacheslav Molotov. The US Secretary of State, James Byrnes, recalled afterwards the particularly awkward situation that arose when Prime Minister Attlee gave a state dinner in honour of the assembled ministers.

The tensions of the day continued on into the evening, in spite of the splendid setting in which the dinner was held, and in spite of the best efforts of their genial host to lift their spirits. The dinner speeches were unusually abrupt—so abrupt, in fact, that they ended long before the diners were scheduled to depart. During one of the long lulls in the proceedings, Byrnes could hear the British Foreign Minister quietly singing to himself. The American complained that Bevin was no singer, but claimed that a member of his staff, present at the dinner, was a *real* singer.

Byrnes was immediately challenged to produce this man, but he warned the Englishman that he would not like what he heard "because all he knows is Irish songs. It's too bad, though, that this is St. James Palace, because he is the best singer of Irish songs you ever heard." Bevin challenged him to go ahead anyway, so Byrnes called upon Colonel Hugh Kelly, the security officer of the American delegation, to sing an Irish song for the British Foreign Secretary.

Colonel Kelly rose splendidly to the occasion. He was soon standing in the middle of the room, directing nearly a hundred people (including Comrade Molotov) in a community sing. Molotov was so impressed that he enthusiastically called out for a repeat performance of *"Johnny Doughboy Found a Rose in Ireland"*.

Conclusive evidence that the evening had been saved by this unexpected twist to the festivities came as the Americans were departing. The butler who had served the dinner, and performed his duties as stiffly, correctly and impassively as one would expect, was helping Colonel Kelly into his coat, when he suddenly bowed and said: "Begging your pardon, sir, I wish to say that precedent was set here tonight. But all of us had a ripping good time."

Could the Cold War have been prevented if community singing had been made an integral part of post-war diplomacy?

Source: James F. Byrnes, *Speaking Frankly*, pp. 106-7.

*   *   *

It is not only at the table itself where the nuances of diplomacy come into play, but wining and dining can, under certain circumstances, be incorporated as part of the public relations efforts undertaken by an astute ambassador.

Honouring Local Customs

Witness, for instance, the extraordinary sensitivity to American opinion demonstrated by a British ambassador to Washington, Sir Esmé Howard during the era of prohibition in the United States. With only a few months remaining in his ambassadorial tenure, Howard announced that the British embassy would, while he was Ambassador, honour the spirit of the American laws governing the prohibition of alcoholic beverages. Although American citizens were prevented by these laws from selling, purchasing, transporting or consuming spirits, diplomatic missions were, naturally, exempt from these limitations. As a consequence, receptions and dinners given by diplomats during this time were met with the most extraordinary enthusiasm on the part of those Americans who were fortunate enough to be invited to attend.

Nevertheless, the British Ambassador admitted that, while diplomatic immunity and other privileges did exist, it was the duty of diplomats to respect and observe the laws of the society in which they found themselves. He announced, therefore, that in the months that remained to him in Washington, he would no longer ask permission to import any further liquor supplies; he could not, however, commit his successor to such a policy; the next ambassador would have to make his own decision concerning this difficult problem.

The announcement was a public relations success, especially among those elements of the American public who were jealous of the special privileges enjoyed by the diplomatic community. What they did not realize was that the embassy had been sufficiently well stocked in liquor supplies that there was no need to ask for further import permits. Howard had, moreover, been quite careful to refrain from announcing that he intended to discontinue serving wines and liquors at his parties—which, not surprisingly, remained as popular as they had been prior to this tactfully astute announcement.

Source: Kenneth P. Kirkwood, *The Diplomat at Table: A Social and Anecdotal History Through the Looking-Glass*, pp. 162-63.

*   *   *

A certain amount of liquid lubrication is one of the ingredients that organizers of diplomatic entertainments rely on in attempting to make the social machine run smoothly. But this too can give rise to some unanticipated situations. Entertaining in the style of the diplomats may be challenging, but occasionally the "challenge" involved might be more literally interpreted.

A Challenging Reception

Such would appear to have been the case in a story told by Dean Acheson, the US Secretary of State, who described a reception in Berlin given by General Maxwell Taylor. General Taylor, who was serving a tour as commandant of the US sector in Berlin, had invited the other commandants to attend, but had been informed that his Soviet counterpart, General Chuikov, was not likely to come, as he had not attended a Western social function for months.

The reception had been going on for about an hour when the Soviet general, along with his staff, arrived quite unexpectedly. A waiter immediately approached them, carrying a very large tray full of cocktails. General Chuikov studied the drinks carefully, then began to drink them, one by one: he knew a diplomatic challenge when he saw one!

When Acheson realized what Chuikov was doing, he assured him that no challenge was intended, and that the General did not have to rise to the occasion. He remarked to the General that, in order to even think of attempting such a feat, "You must have a tin stomach!"

The remark was translated for the General. "No," he said, shaking his head, "steel."

Source: Kenneth P. Kirkwood, *The Diplomat at Table: A Social and Anecdotal History Through the Looking-Glass*, pp. 250-51.

*　　　　*　　　　*

Some rise to the challenge—whether real or imagined—others do not.

Falling to the Challenge

And then there is the story of the Turkish diplomat, Sermet Effendi, who at one time served as a Secretary at Stockholm. Being totally unaccustomed to the consumption of alcohol he had, unfortunately, allowed himself to be persuaded into imbibing rather too much Swedish punch at a reception, with the result that he had made rather a fool of himself. He later recounted his unfortunate experience to Arthur Hardinge, a British diplomat, when they were later posted to Madrid at the same time.

"What," Hardinge asked him, "did your Minister say to this mishap: did you not have an awkward interview with him?"

"No," Sermet replied, "most fortunately for me, a few minutes before my own mishap, he was borne downstairs to his carriage by the servants of the Palace, for the effect of the Swedish punch on him had been even more disastrous than on myself. He was in fact utterly helpless and swayed about, unable to keep his balance, or even to stand!"

Source: Arthur Hardinge, *A Diplomatist in Europe*, pp. 49-50.

*　　　　*　　　　*

Tastes differ. So do manners. Representatives of the United States posted to missions in the Old World frequently found themselves criticized for their lack of refinement at the table; but sometimes they found that the performance of the Europeans themselves left something to be desired.

A Diplomatic Mouthful

One American Consul in Greece, George Horton, recalled how a particularly overwhelming and pompous European diplomat finished each meal by taking a mouthful of water from the finger-bowl, rinsing his teeth, and then spitting the water back into the bowl. But this curious procedure seemed quite restrained when compared with the Secretary of a Legation who later dined with Horton. The American Consul happened to mention, during the course of the meal, that he needed to have some dental work done, and that he was encountering some difficulty in finding a reputable dentist. His dinner companion immediately snapped a dental plate, which contained three or four teeth, out of his mouth, rinsed it in his finger-bowl, dried it on his napkin and placed it in front of the startled Horton.

"I had that done here," he explained. "It would be hard to find better work than that." Seeing that Horton was more than slightly taken aback, he exclaimed: "Pick it up, it won't bite you!"

Source: George Horton, *Recollections Grave and Gay: The Story of a Mediterranean Consul*, p. 83.

*　　　　*　　　　*

While we might imagine that diplomatic dining is conducted with style, in splendid surroundings, such is not always the case. Diplomats are not always afforded the luxuries that we might imagine to be due to them according to their station.

Dining in Style

The Council of Foreign Ministers met in Moscow in November 1948, and the meeting proved to be yet another disastrous affair in the early days of the Cold War. The British Foreign Secretary, Ernest Bevin, returned to London in a gloomy mood; he had hoped to create a workable Four-Power system or, at the very least—as a Labour Minister—to act as some sort of a bridge between East and West. Not long after the conference ended, a couple of his friends spotted him coming in to lunch in the dining room at the House of Commons and, seeing his apparent despair, joined him to see if they could cheer him up a bit.

One of them remarked that, although the conference might have been a failure, they must have had some nice things to eat and drink, especially in comparison with the limitations that diners still faced in London, where rationing was still in full force.

"No," Bevin bitterly told them, "You see, I was at the embassy."

Of course, with rationing still in effect in the British Isles itself, the British embassy could hardly be seen to be providing a flow of champagne and caviar to its own people. The Foreign Secretary concurred with the principle of the policy, so he was in no position to complain. With a twinkle in his eye, Bevin surprisingly asked his companions, "Do you know Brindle?"

Brindle, it turned out, was the elderly Scottie dog that was the pet of the British Ambassador and his wife. How did Brindle come into the story of rationing at the British embassy?

"Well," said Bevin, "it was like this. Towards the end of our little meal, they gave me, with the cheese, what I took to be dog biscuits..." By way of a joke, and quite unsuspecting, the Foreign Secretary said, he had turned to his hostess and asked, "Lady Peterson, these look to me like dog biscuits?"

"As a matter of fact they are, Secretary of State, but we like them."

After a brief pause, Bevin responded. "Lady Peterson, I 'ope I'm not depriving Brindle of his dinner?"

"That's quite all right, Secretary of State, Brindle won't eat 'em."

Source: Hubert M.G.B. Gladwyn, *The Memoirs of Lord Gladwyn*, pp. 206-7.

Dressed to Deal

Diplomats are most frequently portrayed in popular works of fiction and film as grey, dispassionate and humourless; they are invariably attired in impeccable fashion, rarely give a glimpse of their own emotions and hardly seem human at all. Above all, their manners are restrained, their dress fastidiously conservative. There are, however, some occasions on which the humanity and the personality has broken through the surface of appearances.

Pale Rider

When the Algeçiras Conference met on the Moroccan coast opposite Gibraltar in 1906, an American diplomat, Lewis Einstein, became acquainted with the Secretary of the Italian delegation, Count Sforza (who would become the Italian Minister for Foreign Affairs after the First World War). Einstein was soon impressed with Sforza's brilliance in speech, and perhaps even more with his humour.

One day during a temporary lull in the conference, some of the delegates and their ladies decided to go walking along the beach. Lying down on the sand, they were deeply moved by the scenery. The waves lapped at their feet, an amphitheatre of cliffs rose behind them to frame a picture of wild beauty, with no sign of human habitation to be seen. For a moment they felt near to the ancient gods of the Mediterranean, when Count Sforza suddenly appeared on horseback. One of the ladies in the party remarked that, given the setting, it would seem more appropriate if, rather than a modern man astride his horse, an ancient centaur were to be seen dashing through the waves. Sforza soon disappeared.

"Moments later he reappeared as a fleeting silhouette against the setting sun, galloping madly along the water's edge but without a stitch of clothing on his back."

Source: Lewis Einstein, *A Diplomat Looks Back*, p. 14.

*　　　　*　　　　*

The American diplomat who recorded this scene, Lewis Einstein, has also given us an engaging portrait of another diplomat who he came to know during his time at Constantinople.

How Do I Look?

Einstein found that the Spanish Minister at Constantinople, the Marquis of Campo Sagrado, had a distinctive old-world charm that seemed the product of a more leisurely age. The Marquis never allowed official duties to interfere with his life, and rarely communicated with Madrid. When he did find it necessary to send some report he would simply borrow the despatches of his colleagues—which would later be returned to them with most of the text struck out, having been marked by him as "superfluous".

The Spanish envoy once explained to his young American friend that his dream of happiness would be to live as a rich king in exile in Paris. Einstein thought that this short, fat and ungainly man would have performed this role brilliantly if he had been given the opportunity: "he possessed a grand manner and an incomparable charm which made him loved by everyone and left him with no enemy other than himself. Not even Franklin Roosevelt could smile more winningly, and I have never known any man who gave the impression of being so great a gentleman."

Much like an exiled king, the Marquis took little interest in such mundane affairs as his personal finances. In spite of having ruined his family by indulging his extravagant tastes, he nevertheless upon his arrival in St. Petersburg immediately purchased a magnificent sable coat. He had himself photographed in it and sent a copy to his brother in Madrid, inscribing on it "Behold how I am." His brother responded by sending to his spendthrift brother a picture of himself stark naked, inscribing on it, "This is how you have left us."

Source: Lewis Einstein, *A Diplomat Looks Back*, p. 62.

*   *   *

Diplomats are, quite naturally, accustomed to seeing one another not only properly, but fully, attired. They are about as far removed from the rough-and-tumble as can be imagined; theirs is not the world of manual labour or locker-rooms. To maintain the proper bearing and to display the necessary level of seriousness and solemnity requires the dignity of fastidious dress. There are many stories of how hard diplomats have struggled to maintain the proper decorum under trying conditions; but one episode proved more than merely trying—it was positively humiliating.

The Last Judgement

When, in the course of the First World War, the British government found it necessary to give up voluntary service as the method of recruiting for the armed forces and introduced conscription in its place, it was decided that the staff of the Foreign Office would have to be subjected to the same treatment as those who found themselves in other organizations. This meant that members of the staff would have to undergo a physical examination. It was agreed, however, that those conducting the examination would be able to do so within the sacred precincts of the Foreign Office itself, and a set of large rooms on the top floor were given over for this purpose.

Whereas individuals undergoing examination throughout the rest of the country might have found it humiliating to be stripped naked and handed over to the tender mercies of military doctors, at least it was done in an impersonal way, amid strangers in strange premises.

Such was not the case in the Foreign Office examination, when more than a hundred gentlemen, well-known to one another, accustomed to maintaining the highest standards of dress and decorum,

123

"were herded, completely nude, into familiar surroundings, looking for all the world like a Signorelli *'Last Judgment'*." At least one of those examined on this occasion "felt that the dignity of the Office would never be the same again after this anatomical exhibition...and, as the whole proceeding was totally unnecessary, since not one of us was ever taken for military service," that they were all owed some *amende honorable* to compensate them "for this violation of our diplomatic modesty."

Source: John Gregory, *On the Edge of Diplomacy: Rambles and Reflections, 1902-1928*, pp. 74-75

*　　　*　　　*

Quite apart from the travails involved in adhering to proper diplomatic decorum in the matter of full dress to be worn while doing business, attending ceremonies or receiving visitors, there is also to be considered the matter of dress referred to in most military messes as "relaxed". Within one's own culture such a designation is quite easily understood, even without a guide-book of rules and regulations. But diplomats regularly find themselves in "relaxed" situations where both the expectations, and the dress itself, might be imperfectly understood.

Tennis, Anyone?

There was, for instance, the case of the English diplomat attending the San Francisco Conference, which met for the purpose of creating the new United Nations organization. The work was unusually intensive, particularly when it came down to the crucial drudgery of translating the Charter into Russian, which meant long hours for all the participants, who regularly worked sixteen and seventeen hours a day. The pressure was relieved somewhat on the weekends, when the diplomats frequently retired to a country estate for tennis, parties and swimming.

On one such weekend a British statesman who longed for a refreshing dip in the pool, but who had arrived without his own bathing costume, inquired of his hostess whether there might be an extra suit available. She replied that if he went into the bathhouse he would find plenty of extras there.

When he emerged from the bathhouse he asked the giggling guests, what was he supposed to do "with this"? "Does one put it over one's shoulder?".

Not quite. He had emerged wearing, over top of his bathing suit, a jockstrap!

Source: Charles E. Bohlen, *Witness to History, 1929-1969*, pp. 233-34.

*   *   *

*I*nformal occasions might take the unsuspecting diplomatic traveller by surprise, but it can sometimes be quite unnerving when, on formal occasions, one member of the diplomatic community fails to adhere to the rigid code established by precedent for such occasions. It might raise that most excruciating of questions: what should one wear?

Of Top-Hats and Tails

One such moment occurred during the embassy of Joseph Grew to Tokyo in the 1930s. A new Chinese Minister, General Tsiang Tso-ping, was appointed to Tokyo and, as was the custom, initiated a series of formal calls on other members of the *corps diplomatique*. But the dress that he wore on the occasion of his visit to Grew left the American Ambassador stumped. The Chinese Minister had arrived wearing a short black coat and a top hat, thus combining two distinct levels of dress and formality.

The question for Grew was, should he, in making the return visit that was dictated by custom, attire himself correctly in tail coat and top hat—and risk offending the Chinese Minister by exceeding the dress standard he had set; or should he attire himself in short coat and bowler hat—and risk jeopardizing relations between China and the

United States by failing to meet the Chinese Minister's dress standard? Monumental questions indeed.

In any case, Grew reflected, "I refuse to commit so heinous a breach of sartorial convention as that of which the Chinese Minister was guilty. This is a real problem with which I shall have to wrestle during the next few days, for of such stuff is diplomacy made."

Source: Joseph C. Grew, *Ten Years in Japan*, pp. 35-36.

*   *   *

Issues of dress are not necessarily limited merely to questions of decorum and appearance. Sometimes, when occurring in the midst of crucial negotiations, they seem to jeopardize even the most important political considerations.

Breeching Protocol

Early in the twentieth century, the protocol of Buckingham Palace still prescribed that gentlemen who were invited to ceremonial occasions there appear attired in knee-breeches. This practice caused some concern in 1903, during the early days of the *Entente Cordiale* between Britain and France. The President of France, M. Loubet, and his Minister of Foreign Affairs, M. Delcassé, were to come to London to return the visit paid by King Edward VII to Paris the previous year.

The knee-breeches, which were a time-honoured custom in the British court, also had an historical resonance in French history. Many of the founders of the first French republic had, after all, referred to themselves as the *sans culottes*—those who did not wear knee-breeches—in order to distinguish themselves from their aristocratic enemies in the *ançien régime*. Neither the head of the French Republic nor his chief minister could reasonably be expected to appear before a foreign monarch attired in the dress of the traditional enemies of the Republic without risking the ridicule of the French press and the song-writers of Montmartre.

This earth-shaking issue came to be discussed at the highest levels. One evening shortly before the visit was to take place, at a party given by Lord Rothschild, King Edward took the opportunity of speaking to the French Ambassador on the subject, expressing his hope that the President would appear before him properly attired in knee-breeches. M. Paul Cambon replied that the President intended to dress as he did in Paris. The King, expressing his disappointment, said that the Americans, whose republic was older than that of the French, had no difficulty appearing before him in the prescribed fashion.

Cambon refused to give way and thought that he had succeeded in convincing the King, but Lord Lansdowne, the British Foreign Secretary, was soon sent over by the King to return to the charge. But Cambon stuck to his guns, insisting that it was simply impossible for President Loubet to comply with the royal wishes.

Reluctantly, the King finally gave in and the matter appeared to be settled. A few days before the visit was to take place, however, the British Ambassador in Paris received a communication from the King telling him that, while the President was free to come to Buckingham Palace dressed as he pleased, his Minister for Foreign Affairs was expected to appear in knee-breeches.

Delcassé, who was the chief architect of the *Entente*, flatly refused. Cambon told Lansdowne "that it was up to him to choose between a Minister without breeches or breeches without a Minister" and, as the visit had already been announced, if it were to be cancelled now "people would ask themselves what could be the reason of his absence and when these became known in Paris and London everyone would laugh at the King."

In the end, the French dignitaries made their visit to Buckingham Palace—attired as one would expect representatives of the republic to be—the *Entente Cordiale* was saved, and history unfolded as it should have. Paul Cambon always suspected that King Edward had been enjoying himself greatly at the expense of the French.

Source: Jules-François Blondel, *Entente Cordiale: Fifty True Stories, Mostly from Diplomatic Experience*, pp. 91-93.

*   *   *

*A*ware *of overly punctilious attention to dress, observers of the diplomatic process conclude that the professionals are overly concerned with matters of decorum.*

Suede Shoes and the Coming of the Second World War

The British Air Attaché in Finland, "Freddie" West, travelled through Germany by car in order to meet with his counterpart in the Berlin embassy shortly before the outbreak of the Second World War. When he arrived there, he met with Air Commodore John Vachell and the Naval Attaché, who agreed with his sombre views of the situation, and who believed that they were very close to war. They warned him, however, that the Ambassador, Nevile Henderson, did not share their views. West had an appointment to meet with the Ambassador later in the evening.

Henderson, receiving him cordially, politely enquired as to the state of his wife's health and the success of their journey down from Finland. Coming to the point, he finally said: "I understand, West, that you're pessimistic about the German situation, and, like your Service colleagues on my staff, expect Germany to start a war very soon. Why are you so pessimistic?" West proceeded to describe the conversations that he had had with the attachés of all the countries bordering on Germany, and the discussions that he had recently had with the Finnish general staff. All the information that he had been given, he concluded, pointed to war.

Henderson, who listened politely to West's assessment of the military situation, but remained silent throughout, suddenly spoke up when West had finished. "Do R.A.F. officers, when in dinner jackets, wear black suède shoes?"

West began to laugh. "Are you serious, sir?" he asked the Ambassador.

"Yes, I am."

It was plain to West that this subject was of greater interest to the Ambassador than his assessment of the strategic situation in eastern Europe. "Well, we don't normally wear black suède shoes with dinner jackets in the R.A.F.," he told him.

"That being so," the Ambassador commented, "I can't understand why Vachell does. It irritates me."

This concluded their conversation. War broke out the next month.

Source: P.R. Reid, *Winged Diplomat: The Life Story of Air Commodore "Freddie" West*, p. 142.

*   *   *

To outsiders, fussiness in matters of dress may appear bizarre indeed. Insiders soon learn that these trivial issues can have unexpected consequences. Nor are the professionals alone when it comes to matters of the dress code: their families are inextricably drawn into the same, or similar, difficulties.

This Dress is Killing Me

The wife of the British Minister in Bucharest, Rumania was not entirely pleased to receive an invitation to a ball given by the municipality of the city in honour of the recent marriage of the Crown Prince. Some of the events held to mark the occasion of the Royal Wedding had already proved to be somewhat unusual, including the simultaneous marriage of thirty couples of Rumanian peasants in the Cathedral, where each was presented with a dowry from the State.

What was unusual about the ball, and the cause of Winifred Hardinge's displeasure, was the requirement that the ladies of the *Corps diplomatique* should appear in Rumanian dress. Their husbands, on the other hand, were to appear in their diplomatic uniforms. She objected strenuously to this, and had the temerity to tell the King himself that she would decline to wear such a costume. The King said nothing, but on the morning of the ball he sent to her at the Legation a magnificent Rumanian costume, along with a note asking her to do him the pleasure of wearing it at the ball. She really had no choice but to comply with this wish and to wear it as requested.

As fate would have it, by that evening poor Winifred felt very ill and would certainly have declined to attend the ball had this awkward question of Rumanian dress not arisen. She had a high temperature and a splitting headache, but not to attend now would appear to be a determination to persist in refusing to wear the dress that had been requested, even though the King had gone to special efforts to provide her with one.

Fortified by champagne, the Ambassador's wife dutifully put on the dress and went off to the ball. But she and her husband stayed only a short while, "and when the doctor came to see her next morning he pronounced her to be suffering from an acute attack of scarlet fever." She was fortunate indeed that she did not catch a chill while doing her duty, as the fever might otherwise have proved fatal.

Source: Hardinge of Penshurst, *The Old Diplomacy*, pp. 52-53.

*　　　　*　　　　*

The expectations underlying the dress code of diplomats have frequently led to a variety of difficulties. American diplomats were quite regularly embarrassed by the absence of a diplomatic uniform that might be worn on formal occasions. Their colleagues, on the other hand, often appeared in a stunning array of splendid outfits.

The Crow among the Parrots

The embarrassment that the absence of a uniform caused to American diplomats was not relieved by the contention of foreigners that the wearing of common evening dress was a mere pose to call attention to their pseudo-democracy. One representative of the United States recalls that, save for his white shirt, in a group of his diplomatic colleagues he resembled "a crow in a flock of parrots."

This embarrassment led to a certain touchiness amongst members of the Foreign Service. One particularly sensitive "Envoy Extraordinary" was once approached at a crowded reception by a lady who was obviously in some distress. "I beg your pardon," she asked him, "are you the butler?"

To which inquiry the Envoy snapped back: "No! Are you the chambermaid?"

Source: George Horton, *Recollections Grave and Gay: The Story of a Mediterranean Consul*, p. 74.

Sex, and Other Diversions

Diplomats, particulary those of the young and single variety, are placed in rather difficult circumstances when it comes to relations with the opposite sex. Situated in a different cultural environment, with different codes and patterns of behaviour, young diplomats frequently find themselves placed in embarrassing situations; but, like the young everywhere, they often find the challenges more stimulating than restraining.

Boys will be Boys

Two young members of the British Legation in Osaka, Japan in the later nineteenth century found themselves cloistered within a compound for Europeans, or, when they chose to venture beyond the compound, escorted by an armed guard. This made the fulfilment of certain desires rather difficult. But they gave it their best effort, as one of them, Ernest Satow, tells us:

> The street in which the foreign representatives lodged was shut in at each end by solid wooden gates, at which a number of the *betté-gumi* were stationed on guard day and night, and it was impossible to get out into the city without an escort, as the guard had instructions to follow us wherever we went. This was very irksome to Mitford and myself, until we found out a gap in the wall which surrounded one of the temples, and from that time we used to make nocturnal excursions to all parts of the town, accompanied by my retainer Noguchi. The sense of a certain peril to be encountered, combined with a sort of truant schoolboy feeling, rendered these explorations into the night life of Japan very enjoyable. On one occasion young Matsuné joined us on an expedition to the quarter occupied by singing and dancing girls; it

was a moonlight night, and the chance of detection by the guard was so much the greater. After getting through our gap, we doubled back, and passing behind the legations, got into a lower street running parallel to that in which we lived, where we ran along for some distance keeping close in the shadow of the houses, then darted into another street at right angles, turned to the right again until we felt sure of having baffled any possible pursuers, after which we walked on quietly, and crossing one of the long bridges over the river, found ourselves at our destination. A room had been taken in Matsuné's name, and some of the bepowdered and berouged girls were awaiting the arrival of the Japanese party they had expected to meet, when to their surprise and horror three Europeans were ushered into their midst. We were at that time objects of more alarm than interest to the women of Ozaka [sic]. The fair damsels starting up with a scream fairly ran away, and no assurances from our friend would induce them to return. The keeper of the house besought us to leave, as a crowd might collect, and if there was any disturbance he would get into trouble, and so we had to submit to our disappointment. But even the slight glimpse we had of the native beauties seemed to compensate for the risk run, for here in Ozaka [sic] no foreigner had ever been admitted to the quarter.

The adventurousness did not go unrewarded. A short time later they succeeded in "enjoying the society of some *gei-shas* for several hours"—and in this they were apparently secretly abetted by some of the local Japanese authorities.

Source: Ernest Satow, *A Diplomat in Japan*, pp. 200-1.

*   *   *

The risks that it may be necessary for the young diplomat to run in order to accommodate the stirrings of youth is not necessarily limited to the last century. Even in the modern age there are dangers to overcome, with numerous variations being played on the old theme of boy wishing to meet girl and, in foreign parts, finding this a difficult wish to fulfil.

A Near Miss

The young Hubert Gladwyn, a junior official in the British Legation at Teheran in the 1920s, quickly discovered that the needs of bachelors were not provided for at all. Persian women were *tabu* and those that were not proved to be either unavailable or not tempting. Soon after arriving, he was told the cautionary tale of an earlier member of the staff who had gotten himself dressed up as a *Mullah* and taken to a house of ill-repute; this little episode had resulted in the young man's prompt dismissal from the Diplomatic Service. "So, not unnaturally perhaps, I led a monastic life the entire two and a half years that I was there though towards the end I very nearly broke this dismal record."

One evening at a costume party at the club frequented by western diplomats Gladwyn met a ravishing creature: "Snow-white skin, jet-black hair, blue eyes, red cheeks, perfect figure..." Unluckily, she turned out to be the young Georgian wife of a Soviet official by the name of Golubiatnikoff. Although the two young people could converse only in Persian and inadequate French, they got on well together. Following the party, Gladwyn dropped her off at her home, which was not far from the Soviet embassy. In spite of the obvious risks, he made a date with her for the following week, when her husband was to be out of town.

When he arrived at her home, however, she would do no more than talk to him while they sat on hard chairs in her bleak sitting room. Her children were asleep next door. "So I felt I could not take risks for nothing and abandoned the siege. What the Minister would have put on my file had I in fact been caught *in flagrante delicto* with the wife of a Soviet official I can hardly imagine." Most likely, Gladwyn's adventure would have been regarded even more seriously than being discovered disguised as a priest in a Teheran brothel.

Still, "I did try later to get her to come to a hotel but she failed to turn up. I can only think that I was specially protected by Providence."

Source: Hubert M.G.B. Gladwyn, *The Memoirs of Lord Gladwyn*, pp. 28-29.

*   *   *

*These sexual-cultural misunderstandings are shared by diplomats
moving in both directions: east to west, as well as west to east.
Although the sinfulness of western cities may obviate the necessity
for disguise and subterfuge, and although ideological tensions might
be minimized or nonexistent, misunderstandings can still occur.*

Sex and the Single Diplomat

One such disconcerting episode concerns the career of a young
Persian diplomat, newly-arrived as the Third Secretary of the Legation in London. He was lonely and overcome with a longing for
female companionship, if only for a few moments. Seeking a
companion, he set out on the streets of London, where it took him
but a short time to find that which he sought.

When he returned to the street one-half hour later, however, he
discovered that his wallet, which contained a considerable sum of the
Legation's money, was missing. He immediately sought out a policeman and, finding one, took him to the scene of the crime. Unfortunately, as a stranger in a strange land, he took the policeman to the
wrong apartment and the wrong girl was arrested. Protesting that she
was no thief, she immediately instituted proceedings for defamation
of character.

What was the hapless young man to do? He might claim diplomatic
immunity, but if he were to do so the case would certainly be reported
in the British press, the Persian Minister would be forced to send an
account to Teheran, to which the young man would almost certainly
be recalled to suffer some horrible punishment. If, on the other hand,
the Persian Minister pointed out to an official in the British Foreign
Office, the case were to go to court, the headlines would likely be
most regrettable as they might include references to the Shah himself.

John Colville, a young clerk in the British Foreign Office, was told
by his Head of Department to deal with the situation. He at once set
out for the Home Office where he met with an ancient and dignified
official, to whom he outlined the subtleties of the diplomatic difficulties involved in this case and to whom he unwisely suggested that it

would be best settled out of court or perhaps quashed altogether. The reply ought to have been foreseen: did the Foreign Office really propose that the Home Secretary should interfere with the administration of justice? But the ancient official took pity on young Colville and sent him away with a promise that he would consider whether there was anything that he might be able to do in order to get everyone involved out of a sticky situation.

On the following day, Colville was informed that the case would be heard in one of two adjacent courts—and, by some lucky chance, the case being heard next door concerned a particularly horrifying and sensational rape that had already captured the imagination of the British press.

Not surprisingly, the reporters flocked to the rape trial and ignored the young Persian, who apologised to the young woman and agreed to pay her substantial damages. The case was ignored by the newspapers, and the only punishment suffered by the unfortunate young diplomat was the monthly deduction from his salary, which continued until the Legation's money was paid back.

Source: John Colville, *Footprints in Time*, pp. 60-61.

*   *   *

Not all senior officials are as generous as the Persian Minister was when it comes to recognizing the needs of younger members of their staff.

At Your Service

When the Spanish diplomat, Quiñones de León, was serving as a young Secretary in the embassy in Paris, he one day turned up an hour late for work in the morning. When the Ambassador confronted him about his tardiness and lack of conscientious attention to his duty, the young Spaniard excused himself on the ground that he had been involved in an amorous adventure the night before.

The Ambassador proved to be entirely unsympathetic, though for a reason that must have surprised the younger man: "That is no excuse, my young friend. I am an older man than you are; and I serve the Ambassadress every night, yet I am at my desk at nine o'clock every morning."

Source: Salvador de Madariaga, *Morning without Noon: Memoirs*, pp. 28-29.

*   *   *

Perhaps there is a pattern here, a pattern of age suspecting youth, or of failing to perform according to the standards prescribed by a previous age. A young Secretary of the American embassy at Rome shortly before the First World War made the surprising discovery that it would not be possible to study the Italian language within the confines of the embassy building.

The Scent of Promiscuity

The American Ambassador in Rome at the time was firmly convinced that all secretaries were in the diplomatic service simply in order to get whatever fun out if it that they could. He insisted that they attend church every Sunday. He maintained that it was bad enough for young men to be in Rome with something to do, but to be there and to be idle was going to lead them straight to the devil.

It seems that the young Secretary had neglected to inform the Ambassador that he had engaged a lady to instruct him in the Italian language: "a most respectable old soul who had the one fault of covering herself with the strongest perfume I have ever encountered." Shortly after his first lesson, the Ambassador came into his room, sniffed the air, and immediately threw the window wide open.

"Who've you had in here?" he asked severely.

The unlucky young Secretary replied, respectfully, that it was his Italian teacher.

"You may call her that. Where I come from there is another name for them. I can't keep up with you when you leave this office; but I can while you are here; so you had better write that lady not to come back."

As long as this particular ambassador was in charge, the American embassy in Rome was guaranteed to be a respectable institution.

Source: Norval Richardson, *My Diplomatic Education*, pp. 100-1.

*   *   *

The pursuit of entertaining diversions flows in both directions; seniors have attempted to prevent the natural inclinations of youth from bringing their mission into disrepute, or covering things up when trouble is discovered. But sometimes the diplomats find themselves having to deal with the requests of those who they find it difficult to refuse. Entertaining, and being entertained, is one of the essential tasks contained within the job description of every diplomat. But the description of this task is always implied, never implicit; no one knows what the requirements are to be. While many of them will certainly be routine, consisting of the usual round of cocktail parties, dinners and receptions, there are also bound to be unusual requests that the diplomat will have to attend to, whatever his personal disinclinations might be.

A Bourgeois Education

A number of embarrassing requests were presented to a Soviet diplomat, Grigory Bessedovsky, the Chargé d'Affaires in Paris in the late 1920s. When the People's Commissar for Education arrived in Paris, for example, he had visited a night club with his wife, who wished to dance; but, as he himself did not dance, a professional was summoned. Unfortunately, the professional turned out to be a White Russian emigré officer, who refused to dance with the Commissar's wife for less than 200 francs; the visitor paid the fee demanded, then left as quickly as possible.

As a result of embarrassing episodes such as this, Bessedovsky issued a circular that members of the embassy staff were no longer to accompany Soviet visitors who wished to participate in the pleasures that Paris offered. He soon had to override his own rule, however, when the People's Commissar for Transport, who was also a member of the Politbureau, turned up with his two secretaries, immediately announced that he wished to "study bourgeois debauchery", and invited the Chargé to accompany him as his guide. Bessedovsky refused, but felt he had little choice but to place two of the embassy's secretaries at the disposal of the Commissar.

The Commissar's tour lasted all night, and the secretaries reported that the debauchery of the bourgeois had been studied in some detail, that they had visited several houses of dubious reputation, and that the Commissar had been honoured at one such house in the Rue Chabanais by being given a room frequented by some of the crowned heads of Europe.

The evening of educational enlightenment had cost the Soviets 10,000 francs, but it must certainly have been money well spent.

Source: Grigory Z. Bessedovsky, *Revelations of a Soviet Diplomat*, pp. 209-10.

*　　　*　　　*

Sex is not the only leisure activity pursued by diplomats abroad. There are other diversions offered by foreign cultures: music and theatre; folk-festivals and villages; art and architecture. At one time or another, almost every diplomat who has spent time serving outside his own country has developed in interest in one of these, or other, cultural opportunities. One might assume that pursuit of these interests would be easier and less complicated than some of those described above—an assumption that is not necessarily correct.

Culture in the Cold War

One member serving in the British Legation in Moscow in the 1950s, Cecil Parrott, had developed a genuine fascination with Russian baroque architecture. There were, apparently, four examples of this style in churches located in and around Moscow, and Parrot succeeded in finding and studying three of them. The fourth, the Church of the Trinity in the village of Troitsky-Lykov, proved to be more elusive, as it appeared to sit on forbidden ground. Parrott proceeded to the limits of what he knew to be safe territory—and then rashly ventured into the unknown.

He found himself in a beautiful part of the countryside, walking down a road in the forest, when he saw a curious procession advancing in his direction. At first it looked like a funeral, but there appeared to be no hearse, so this seemed unlikely. As the procession came closer, he could see that two people, engaging in earnest conversation, were at the head, followed by a group of about ten others in civilian clothes; on the wings of the group were two more people, who appeared to be guards of some kind. He wondered who these men could possibly be, "when all of a sudden I recognized the leading two as Kaganovich, a member of the Presidium, who was shortly to be expelled as a member of the Anti-Party group, and Shepilov, the Soviet Foreign Minister, who was to share the same fate."

It looked as though Kaganovich was wearing a dressing gown and pyjamas, but as he drew nearer it became apparent that the outfit was, in fact, hospital garb. Parrott immediately concluded that the Soviet was recuperating in a nearby sanatorium, "and that I must be treading on very dangerous ground, having, in fact, stumbled on to the spot where the great ones received their medical attention."

By this time Parrott had gone too far to retreat; nor could he casually walk past the procession pretending not to have noticed them or to have failed to recognize the two important figures, both of whom he had previously met. He greeted the two men, who left the procession and walked to the side of the road to speak with him while their followers maintained a respectful distance. The situation was made still more awkward by the fact that the British diplomat had a camera hanging around his neck.

After some of the customary formalities, Parrott thought it wise to explain what he was doing there. He was looking, he said, for the Church of the Trinity in Troitsky-Lykov, and felt that it must be nearby. Could his Soviet friends tell him if he was headed in the right direction?

"Yes, indeed," Kaganovich said, staring at the camera, "it's a few hundred yards down the road."

Parrott thought that some further explanation was called for, and explained that he was hesitant about proceeding, "because I am not quite sure whether this is a protected area where diplomats are not supposed to come. Is it all right for me to be here, because, if it is not, I will naturally withdraw to permitted territory." Kaganovich continued to stare at the camera.

Parrott added, "Yes, I've brought this camera with me because I wanted to take a photograph of the church which is of a rare type. I suppose it will be in order for me to do this?"

Kaganovich paused thoughtfully, and, with a twinkle in his eye, turned to Shepilov and said, "Well, that church is no longer a church and is now being used as the headquarters for all the army bands in Russia. All the same I don't think it is a military objective, is it, Shepilov?" The Soviet Foreign Minister agreed that it was not.

Kaganovich asked Shepilov how to say *Do svidaniya* in English, "and after he had made a rather comical attempt to say 'goodbye' the cavalcade moved off and I felt secure and was able to carry out my 'non-military objective' and photograph the church."

Source: Cecil Parrott, *The Serpent and the Nightingale*, pp. 117-19

*   *   *

*P*arrott had gone off on what he assumed to be a straightforward pursuit of aesthetic appreciation and almost landed himself in an awkward adventure instead. An American diplomat, on the other hand, had earlier prepared himself for a sporting adventure, only to discover that his Japanese hosts had a somewhat different idea of sport.

The Duck Hunters

When Hugh Wilson, an American Counselor in Japan in the 1920s, found himself, in the absence of the Ambassador, temporarily in charge of the embassy, he was honoured to receive an invitation to an "Imperial Duck Hunt"—a diversion that he knew was usually limited to chiefs of mission. Uncertain as to the type of sporting dress required on such an occasion, he consulted the Japanese Secretary, who told him that since the invitation came in the name of the Emperor, and since the Emperor would be represented by one of his Imperial relatives, the proper costume for Mrs. Wilson would be an afternoon gown, while for the Counselor, a cutaway coat would be appropriate. Wilson began to suspect that this hunt might be rather different than those to which he was accustomed at home.

On the morning of the hunt, the invited guests met on a private train that was to carry them into the country. They were received by an uncle of the Emperor, an extremely exalted gentleman who let it be known, during their journey, that he desired to speak with Wilson. The American was pleased to have such an opportunity, particularly as he was aware that, since Marquis Ito's famous trip to Europe, French had been made the foreign language of the Imperial family; he should, he thought, be able to engage in an interesting conversation with his host.

His Highness, after the introductions, asked Wilson a question in French about his previous posts. Delighted to have the opportunity to speak freely, without the aid of an interpreter, he answered at some length. His Highness would, occasionally, bow and smile while the American rambled on contentedly. Eventually, the elderly Japanese man called over the embassy's Japanese Secretary and said something to him in Japanese. The Secretary's face turned crimson with suppressed emotion, but he gravely turned to Wilson and said, "His Imperial Highness says if you will talk French to him he can understand it."

The day's festivities were not off to the best possible start. But, as the Japanese Secretary later explained to Wilson, tradition did not tolerate the presence of foreign tutors in the Imperial Family; French therefore had to be taught by a Japanese tutor, and thus the imperial students never became accustomed to the sound of the French tongue in voices other than Japanese.

They did eventually arrive at the scene of the hunt: a circular lake about a quarter of a mile in diameter, entirely surrounded by a tall bamboo fence. The lake was a sanctuary; no gun had been fired there for years. When guests peered through holes in the fence, they saw the water almost covered by gaily-feathered Japanese duck, looking,

Wilson thought, like bright toys in a child's bathtub. Out of the lake radiated a dozen trenches, each of them about a yard wide; a zigzag entrance to the lake screened these trenches from the sight of the duck on the lake, as well as hiding the lake from the hunters. Decoys were tethered in the trenches, and food was abundantly provided there, so the ducks would get into the habit of swimming into these trenches whenever they wanted a meal.

Each of the trenches was marked with a number on a large plaque; a Head Huntsman formed a party of ten by passing out numbered buttons which were pinned on to the hunters; the five odd numbers would line up on one side of the bank, the five even on the other. The gentlemen, in their cutaway coats, the ladies, in their high-heeled shoes, lace gowns and fancy hats, were then presented with their weapons: a butterfly-net on the end of a long pole. The hunting party then marched off to their trench in two columns, maintaining a respectful silence, as they followed their Huntsman, who carried hooded falcons on his arm. The hunters took up their positions along the banks of the trench, the Huntsman waved his net over the trench, whereupon the duck rose with a squawk and the hunters plucked them down from the air with their butterfly-nets. When a duck escaped, a falcon would be loosed, who would streak for it like gray lightning and bring it back to earth—the Huntsman explaining that no duck could be permitted to escape from the trench because he might return to the lake and tell his fellow duck about the hunt, which would spoil everything.

After these sporting exertions, a magnificent meal of—what else?—pressed duck was served in a shady pavilion by another lake. After the respite, the hunt was renewed. This time, Wilson was assigned the number three position, while placed alongside him in the number five spot was a gentleman unknown to him, dressed in a black cutaway, gray derby, check trousers and white spats. "I addressed him in every tongue I knew but got only mutters for reply. I decided he was a bad linguist or that he had done more than justice to the admirable Burgundy they had just served with the pressed duck."

When they had finished hunting their first trench, and moved to another to take up their places along the bank, they discovered that number five was missing. Wilson conferred with the Huntsman;

together they ran back to the previous trench, fearing the worst. But when they got there, number five was alive and well. "He was kneeling on the embankment, fishing the decoys out of the water with his butterfly-net, and wringing their necks one by one. I learned subsequently that he represented one of our sister Republics in the Americas, and that he was, in fact, a competent linguist."

Each of the hunters was given a present of duck on the way back to the city: seven for ambassadors, five for ministers and three for chargés.

Source: Hugh Wilson, *Diplomat between Wars*, pp. 135-38.

*   *   *

A more traditional diplomatic entertainment, at least in the West, is that of the ball. Diplomats respond variously to the pleasures offered by such an occasion: some regard it as a delight that ought not to be tempered by contemplation of official business; others regard it as a bore that prevents them from getting on with their work; a few regard it as the quintessential scene of diplomacy, in which a lavish setting, elegant style and polished manners are combined with the intrigue of high politics.

The Dance of Diplomacy

The Rumanian Minister of Foreign Affairs, Grigore Gafencu, had occasion to observe these various behaviours and to participate in such an event himself at a reception given in his honour at the Ankara Palace when he visited Turkey in July, 1939. The German Ambassador, von Papen, made his entrance into the ballroom surrounded by his political and military staff "and with most ostentatious grandeur performed his evolutions among the first couples who took the floor to the strains of the jazz orchestra. He excelled in the art of playing at peace."

Approaching Gafencu, von Papen congratulated him on his efforts to maintain peace, which was what he himself aimed at in his mission: "For my part, that is what I am trying to do here and, above all, in my own country. We don't want war. War is a misfortune I should like to spare the regime which governs Germany at the moment." With a knowing smile, he shared with Gafencu his sense of responsibility for the creation of the Third Reich: "You doubtless understand my solicitude for the regime. I have more reason than anyone to wish that the little experiment now being tried by my country will not cause too many disappointments."

Gafencu found the French Ambassador, Massigli, less inclined to mingle the cares of office with the amusements of the dance. "On the other hand, His Britannic Majesty's Ambassador could profit by the happy relaxation afforded by an evening's dancing. After a good dinner and eloquent speeches, over coffee and liqueurs, when the first tango is played—is not that often the propitious moment for great decisions?"

Knatchbull-Hugessen, the British Ambassador, was seeking to create a *bloc* of countries opposed to German expansionism in the south-east of Europe. He was convinced that Bulgaria could be brought into the Balkan Entente if only the perplexing question of the Southern Dobruja could be overcome; he attempted to persuade Gafencu that a gesture of conciliation and concession on the part of Rumania would win Bulgaria for the common cause. Knatchbull-Hugessen was joined by the Turkish Minster of Foreign Affairs, Sarajoglu, in persuading the Rumanian: "I was invited to come away from the place where attentive young secretaries were inviting the wives of ambassadors to dance, so that I might meet, in a less noticeable corner of the room, a pale, sad man with a feverish look, M. Christoff, the Bulgarian Minister."

It quickly appeared that Christoff had come prepared to negotiate, notwithstanding the jazz band and the crush of dancers. He expounded warmly and eloquently the benefits that would accrue to all the states of the Balkans if Bulgaria and Rumania could reach an agreement. The cession of Southern Dobruja by Rumania to Bulgaria could establish a lasting peace in the region. Gafencu responded by assuring the Bulgarian that he had always desired an entente between their two countries, and that no act would seem to him to be excessive if it would really guarantee peace in the Balkans. But was Southern Dobruja enough to accomplish this aim?

Christoff, delighted at his unexpected success with the Rumanian Foreign Minister, confirmed that Bulgaria could not be satisfied with so little, but that it was unfair to expect Rumania alone to pay the price of a Balkan reconciliation: Yugoslavia should cede Tzaribrod and part of Macedonia; Greece must give up western Thrace. Gafencu, now enlightened, felt that nothing remained to prevent him from rejoining the dancers.

"Well," asked the British Ambassador, who had been keeping an eye on the conversation from a distance, "did you come to an understanding?"

"Beyond all your expectations," the Rumanian gaily replied.

"You have allowed him to hope for the return of Southern Dobruja?"

"If only that were all! I have given up everything: Tzaribrod, Macedonia, western Thrace...."

"What?" an incensed Ambassador exclaimed. "He has again asked for everything?"

"Everything."

Disappointed, the Ambassador and the two Foreign Ministers made their way to the buffet table, where they consoled themselves by feasting on the delicacies that had been provided for their pleasure.

Source: Grigore Gafencu, *The Last Days of Europe: A Diplomatic Journey in 1939*, pp. 192-94.

*   *   *

*T*he dance of diplomacy is an endless one, and the ball, like the show, must go on, whatever the circumstances.

The Icy Ambassadress

There is the story of the Russian Ambassador in London who was responsible for acting as the official host to Tsar Alexander II when he came to London for the marriage of his daughter to the Duke of Edinburgh. Unfortunately, during his stay in London, the

Ambassador's wife fell ill and died. This unexpected calamity caused great distress to the poor Ambassador, because he was to give a ball at the embassy the next day, in honour of the Tsar.

The Ambassador called together his staff and announced that protocol required that an ambassador's wife could not die when he was entertaining his sovereign. Nobody was to be told that his wife had died; her body was to be taken down to the cellar and put on ice until the entertainment had ended.

The ball went ahead as scheduled although, during the royal quadrille, the Tsar did ask his Ambassador how his wife was feeling. He replied that she was much better.

Did he have to resist the temptation to say that she was still feeling a little chilly?

*   *   *

It is doubtful that a certain French Ambassador in South America could have restrained himself from making such a flippant remark.

A Debauched Nuncio?

The Papal Nuncio at Rio, who, as an Italian, tended to be somewhat jealous of France, one day remarked to the French Ambassador there that it was a pity "that almost all the women of your nationality should be known abroad because of their low morals."

M. Conty replied that this was surprising news to him, that apart from the ladies in the French diplomatic colony, the French women in Brazil consisted of the Daughters of Charity, who directed thirty schools and orphanages, thirty-five hospitals and a school for nurses; the nuns of the Sacred Heart, of our Lady of Sion, of the Assumption and the Blessed Sacrament, and the Franciscan sisters of Marie. They seemed, to the Ambassador, to be doing a fine job in contributing to the upbringing up the female youth of Brazil.

Then, moving nearer to the Nuncio, the Ambassador delicately whispered in his ear: "Monseigneur, as you seem to know only flighty Frenchwomen, be a sport and introduce me."

Source: Jules-François Blondel, *Au fil de la carrière: Récit d'un diplomate, 1911-1938*, p. 104.

My Mistake

Although it may seem difficult to believe, many of the most embarrassing mistakes in diplomacy, as in ordinary social life, arise from cases of mistaken identity. And these mistakes can occur at the highest levels.

The Two Berlins

One such instance occurred in Britain during the Second World War when Winston Churchill, after reading a heap of papers that contained the latest summary of the views contained in American newspapers, asked for the name of the author who had written the "brilliant" summaries. His Private Secretary made the customary enquiries, to discover that they were written by a Fellow of All Souls College, Oxford, the well-known philosopher and historian, Isaiah Berlin.

Some weeks after this, the Churchills gave a luncheon party at 10 Downing Street, which included the Chief of the Imperial General Staff, Sir Alan Brooke, and his wife; the Chief Whip of the Conservative Party; the Duchess of Buccleuch, and a few others. Mrs. Churchill reported that the Prime Minister had, at short notice, insisted that she should also invite Mr. Irving Berlin, who was currently in London to entertain the American troops, and whose arrival had been widely reported in the newspapers. She was delighted to include him in the party, but was not certain why it was that her husband wished to meet him.

Irving Berlin duly arrived and was introduced to the other guests but, as they were really unknown to him, he sat quietly throughout the meal that followed while Churchill discoursed on the war situation. The trouble began near the end of the luncheon, when Churchill,

148

turning to Berlin, asked him to tell the party gathered around the table, "what in your opinion is the likelihood of my dear friend, the President, being re-elected for a fourth term?"

Berlin was deeply flattered that the Prime Minister would ask of him "a question of that importance on which I am so little qualified to speak."

Churchill continued to prod him, insisting that his impressions would be of great interest. Berlin obliged by providing a rambling disquisition in which he explained that Roosevelt would win the election because the American people "were so dynastically minded". Churchill was unimpressed, and was saved from an embarrassing interruption only by the timely intervention of one of his assistants, who had recognized that an error had been made.

When Churchill was informed of the mistaken identity afterwards, he claimed never to have heard of Irving Berlin, although he knew and liked many of his songs. John Colville, who recorded this story, could not resist adding that, "it got back to Isaiah Berlin who received it with ecstasy. I hope it did not get back to Irving Berlin."

Source: John Colville, *Footprints in Time*, pp. 168-70.

*   *   *

At least Churchill had managed to avoid saying anything that would embarrass his luncheon guest, even though he did not really know who he was. Cases of mistaken identity certainly increase the likelihood that the unwary diplomatist might put his foot in his mouth.

Short-Sighted Diplomacy

On a cold, gray afternoon in late March 1918, the American Chargé d'Affaires in Switzerland, Hugh Wilson, received a telephone call from a friend at the Swiss Telegraph Agency, who read to him a German communiqué that had just come in. "Our troops have broken the British line and penetrated thirty kilometers. We have taken fifteen thousand prisoners, two hundred guns. Our long range guns are shelling the fortified city of Paris." This sounded like devastating news indeed; not having heard of "Big Bertha" yet, he thought the Germans must have reached the outskirts of Paris itself.

Wilson, who was shaken and depressed by the news, returned to his room at the Hotel Bellevue around eight o'clock that night. As he neared the elevator, he spotted an acquaintance, a Swiss officer, already inside. The Swiss General Staff was also quartered in the hotel at that moment, where they messed together in a private dining room, in the company of Switzerland's one officer of general rank, General Wille. It was the General—short, rotund, absent-minded and sleepy-eyed—that Wilson recognized in the elevator; even though the Swiss military found it easier to maintain their aloof neutrality by keeping strictly to themselves, the American had met the General and had spoken with him in the past. So when he stepped into the elevator, he nodded politely and said, *"Guten abend, Herr General."*

Wilson was amazed when General Wille turned to him with a delighted smile, clapped him on the shoulder and exclaimed in German: "Have you heard the latest news? We have taken twenty thousand prisoners and two hundred guns. We are bombarding Paris. *Kolossal!*"

A stunned Chargé stepped off the elevator and onto his floor. Wilson knew that the General had married a Bismarck, and assumed that he supported the Germans in his heart, but he had never before given any sign of partiality. For him now to have spoken in this manner to an official of the United States of America was shocking behaviour indeed. Wille had identified himself with the Germans by his use of "we": *"Wir haben,"* he had said. Wilson returned to his room in a fury, pacing back and forth, trying to cool himself down, and composing a protest note when he heard footsteps racing down the hall; the door suddenly flew open, and in burst the General's aide.

"Mr. Wilson, what a terrible thing!" the aide exclaimed. "You know that the General does not see very well…[and] it's a fact that you are not unlike Alfred von Hohenlohe in appearance. So when you entered the lift and greeted the General in German, he took you for Prince von Hohenlohe of the Austrian Legation and was being diplomatic."

The General's idea of what correct diplomatic behaviour consisted of was too funny for Wilson to bear: "I fell into a chair convulsed with laughter, the Aide gave me a startled look, began to grin and was soon in the same helpless state as myself. Needless to say, after this exhibition I could never make a protest."

Source: Hugh Wilson, *Diplomat between Wars*, pp. 50-52.

*　　　*　　　*

Churchill had not said anything to humiliate his guest; General Wille had placed the American Chargé in an embarrassing situation, but was quickly able to prevent any damage. Sometimes, however, the consequences of such errors are more difficult to overcome.

An Honoured Guest

Another case of mistaken identity occurred before the First World War began, at the court of the Emperor Wilhelm I in Berlin. A recently-appointed Portuguese diplomat, serving as Secretary to the Portuguese Minister there, was surprised to receive one day an invitation to dine with the Emperor as one of a small and intimate party. His first reaction was to assume that he had been invited in order to accompany his Minister—who betrayed some annoyance when the Secretary, Soveral, approached him to ask if he had received a similar invitation. Soveral began to worry that some mistake had been made, but his fears proved groundless: when he arrived at the Imperial Palace on the evening of the dinner, he received a warm welcome and most flattering and complimentary attentions from the German sovereign.

"I am so sorry," His Majesty said, "to learn that you are leaving us: but it would not be fair or right for me to stand in your way, or object to your well-merited promotion in your Royal Master's service. I desire, however, to bestow on you a personal mark of my regard at your departure, and I should like you to accept this decoration." At which point the Emperor handed to the astonished Soveral the insignia of a high German Order; the Portuguese Minister was even more astonished when he beheld the decoration.

It seems that what had happened was that the German government, which was at that time anxious to draw Spain into the Triple Alliance, had been persuaded by their representative at Madrid that a young relative of the Spanish Prime Minister, Don Antonio Canovas del Castillo, might usefully receive a decoration in order to secure the goodwill of a powerful member of the government. Don Antonio, however, was a retiring diplomat, barely known in Berlin society; somehow the German Foreign Office confused him with Soveral and suggested the wrong man for the dinner and the bestowal of the Order.

Apparently, when Bismarck heard of the mistake he was furious; he saw to it that Soveral was informed of what had actually occurred and let it be known that he expected the decoration to be returned. This the Portuguese diplomat flatly refused to do. "The Emperor," he replied, "had assured him that it was his own personal gift. For him to doubt the truth of this Imperial assurance would be a mark of ingratitude and disrespect to the venerable monarch, and should he have no descendant deserving of such an heirloom, he would wish it to be buried in his own tomb." After this reply, it would seem that the German government thought better of pressing for the return of the decoration.

Source: Arthur Hardinge, *A Diplomatist in Europe*, pp. 52-53.

*   *   *

Errors of identity are not the only ones made by diplomats. An excessive consumption of alcoholic beverages at the inevitable cocktail parties and receptions certainly increases the likelihood of mistakes being made. Some diplomats regard the social side of diplomacy as an opportunity to consume vast quantities of food and drink; others restrain themselves, departing from the scene at the first opportunity that protocol allows.

A Party Animal

Both policies were demonstrated during an international conference at "The Homestead" in Hot Springs, Virginia. The first reception was given by the Russians, who made an abundance of vodka and caviar available. The head of the British delegation, Richard Law, did his duty by appearing at the reception, but took his leave for a night's rest at the first possible opportunity.

Law went to his room, which was one of the grand suites reserved for VIP's, where, exhausted from his travels, he quickly fell into a deep sleep. Some considerable time afterwards he was awakened by what appeared to be a hairy gorilla moving towards his bed. Terror-stricken, he sat up and shouted, whereupon the gorilla scooped up some clothes from the floor and fled down the hallway, naked.

The next day the British delegate received a shipment of vodka and caviar, along with an apology from his Russian colleague who, it seems, had an identical suite to his, but on a different floor.

Source: Dean Acheson, *Present at the Creation: My Years in the State Department*, p. 75.

*   *   *

Another variety of mistake in diplomacy involves that of wounded vanity, of which there are many examples. But one story illustrates the problem particularly well.

Wounded Vanity

On 22 May 1940, the recently-appointed Italian Ambassador to Germany, accompanied by his military attachés, found himself visiting Hermann Goering at his General Headquarters, in order to present the Deputy Führer with a decoration on behalf of the King of Italy. Goering, with his pink, chubby face, large light-blue eyes and infantile expression, was almost overcome with emotion. He had been waiting for some time to receive this visit. Exactly one year before, on the occasion of the signing of the Pact of Steel in Berlin on 22 May 1939, a great banquet had been given by the Italian Ambassador, Attolico, at the Italian. All of the most important figures in the German Government and in the Nazi Party were in attendance. Hermann Goering, widely recognized as second in importance only to Hitler in the Reich, was there in all his splendour. As always, he was extremely anxious that he should be given the respect that he believed to be due to him; and, as frequently happens with those who are overly sensitive to such matters, he behaved in a ridiculous and childish way.

Goering took care to see to it that the chief place at the banquet had been reserved for himself. Seeing that Ciano, the Italian Minister of Foreign Affairs, had gone off into a corner of the drawing-room with Ribbentrop, his German counterpart, Goering walked casually into the great dining-hall, went over to the top table and found that the seat he had been assigned was to the left of Ciano, while the place of honour on his host's right had been given to Ribbentrop. Without the slightest hesitation, he quickly changed the place-cards.

But poor Goering must have suffered a shock to the system when he re-entered the drawing room and discovered what had been going on in the corner between Ciano and Ribbentrop. While he had been busying himself with the seating arrangements, Ribbentrop had been presented with the Collar of the Annunziata, the highest honour that Italy could confer. The decoration, which dated back six centuries, was rare: there were only twenty copies in existence, each of which bore its own serial number. The Collar consisted of a series of flat, rectangular gold links, together with the three knots of Savoy, known as "love-knots", the legend *Fert*, and a reproduction of the scene of the Annunciation. The collar was to be returned to the King of Italy at the death of the holder; in the meantime, the holder became a Cousin of the King.

When Goering saw Ribbentrop with the open case containing the Collar and receiving the congratulations of the other guests, he was outraged; his colleagues had considerable difficulty in restraining him from leaving the embassy. He had no difficulty in making his displeasure known, and in the year that followed, Ciano repeatedly pestered the King about conferring the next vacant Collar on Goering. The King, with great reluctance, finally gave way to the pressure, and it was arranged that the new Italian Ambassador in Berlin, Dino Alfieri, would present the Collar to Goering on the first anniversary of the signing of the Pact of Steel.

And thus it was that Alfieri found himself presenting this ancient honour in a special railway coach, which was concealed by camouflage netting of the type used to disguise artillery batteries and surrounded by anti-aircraft guns, to a man wearing yellow boots, slate-blue Air Force trousers and a white jacket: a uniform of his own design. The Ambassador made a short speech, to which Goering uttered a few words of gratitude in a voice quivering with emotion. When Alfieri indicated that the time had come for him to take his leave, Goering asked him to wait a moment and departed through a doorway, a difficult feat, given his bulk; he finally had to negotiate it sideways. He soon returned looking pleased and self-satisfied, having slipped the Collar around his neck. He gazed lovingly at his reflection in the mirror and called for one of his photographers to capture the moment forever.

Source: Dino Alfieri, *Dictators Face to Face*, pp. 24-26.

*   *   *

Much of the distrust and resentment that arises in the course of diplomacy comes simply from the inevitable, and unintentional, human errors involved in keeping records, transcribing and reporting. These errors are compounded, of course, when suspicions of bad faith are already present—and, in diplomacy, such suspicions are almost always present.

Drafts as a Cause of the Cold War

In the spring of 1944, an American official, John R. Deane, was in Moscow attempting to arrive at an agreement with the Soviets for the installation of a radio system as part of the Allied war effort. He tells the story of how one small incident almost wrecked the project.

The negotiating procedure that was being followed consisted of Deane making a draft, taking this with him into the meeting-room, and making notations in pencil of changes that were agreed upon in the course of the discussion. This meant that from time to time a clean copy had to be produced in order for the participants to see where the proposals stood.

One day, following a meeting, Deane agreed to have clean copies typed in both English and Russian and to send these to his Russian colleague, Fortushenko. He rushed back to his office, and in his haste to get to another appointment, mistakenly handed his stenographer not the latest revision arrived at that day, but one that had been discussed weeks earlier. This version was sent to Fortushenko before Deane had an opportunity to look it over.

The Russian was infuriated. He accused Deane of attempting an underhanded strategem for reinstating clauses they had long since agreed to delete, and for leaving out a clause that they had since agreed to include. "My explanations were finally accepted, but only reluctantly, and thereafter I was not trusted at all."

Source: John R. Deane, *The Strange Alliance: The Story of Our Efforts at Wartime Co-operation with Russia*, pp. 70-71.

*   *   *

Another recurring feature of diplomatic negotiation is the necessity of translation, the difficulties of which have given rise to a variety of curious situations.

Gaining something in Translation

When an Assembly of the International Labor Organization was meeting in Spain, at that time governed by the dictatorial Primo de Rivera, the government was deeply embarrassed by an attack on it by the working class leader, Largo Caballero, who accused it of a multitude of crimes. To face these attacks while an international audience was gathered there was very difficult for the Rivera government to accept. The representative of the Spanish Government to the I.L.O. was so agitated by the attack and the gravity of the issue involved that his French, which was rather fragile to begin with, went completely to pieces. He made a vehement speech in a language that, unfortunately, was known only to him. So there sat the baffled reporters, précis writers and the translators with a speech, but no text.

The English translator, fortunately, was a certain Russell—a man known to be more than fond of a good glass of whiskey; or even several glasses. He understood very little of what the Spaniard said, but he knew Spain, he was acquainted with the facts of the situation, and he was able to make a fairly good guess at what the Spanish Government's attitude was to the attack that had been made on it. Sitting there, staring at his blank notebook, he asked himself, "What would I say in his place?" And he said it. The reporters and writers immediately began transcribing the English version of the Spaniard's speech, which was now preserved for posterity.

All seemed well until the Spanish representative telephoned the Secretariat during the lunch hour to explain that the speech was crucial both for Spain and for his own political career, "so please let me have a text at once so that I can correct it before it is cabled to Madrid."

Telephones began ringing throughout the offices of the Secretariat, where much cursing was heard in many languages; a group of translators set about transforming Russell's English improvisation back into the "original" French in which the speech had been given. About an hour later they sent the new rendition to the Spaniard and waited for the inevitable catastrophe to strike. At last, the Spaniard called the office: "Perfect. No corrections."

Russell's next whiskey was paid for by the head of the Secretariat.

Source: Salvador de Madariaga, *Morning without Noon: Memoirs*, p. 59.

*   *   *

The experience of the fortunate Russell is less common than the reverse, for the history of diplomacy is littered with the broken careers of diplomats and would-be diplomats. The mistakes that men have made in pursuing careers in the craft are as varied as the personalities of those who have made them. But one story illustrates how a career can be unmade even before it has begun.

Following Instructions

At the beginning of the Taft administration in the United States, the President decided to offer the Legation at Peking to one of his political supporters, Mr. Charles R. Crane, a plumbing magnate from Chicago. He unfortunately chose to make the offer without first consulting his newly-appointed Secretary of State, the feisty Philander C. Knox. Taft had persuaded Knox to give up a safe seat in the Senate, partly by promising him that he would have the freedom to run his own department as he saw fit. Knox was not pleased that he had not been consulted on such an important appointment, particularly as one of his objectives was the expansion of US business in China. But he said nothing to the President, choosing instead to bide his time and wait for an opportunity.

Crane duly proceeded to Washington in order to receive the customary instructions from the State Department before setting sail for his new post. Curiously, he found that the Secretary was not available to see him; poor Crane had to make do with an interview with the permanent Assistant Secretary, the near-deaf Alvey Adee, who seemed unable to hear any of Crane's questions about China. The only advice offered by Adee was that he should take up photography while in China, and perhaps take along a microscope: Crane's interest in marine biology might help him to pass the time.

As a number of banquets were planned in Crane's honour before he departed for China, and as he would be expected to give speeches on these occasions, he sought out the advice of the President himself. Taft was rather vague, but suggested that his new Minister should give it to his audiences "red hot"—advice that Crane regrettably took to heart. In speaking to various groups of American businessmen before his departure, he predicted the coming of a war between the United States and Japan. It also became public knowledge that he planned to take with him to Peking a secretary known for his outspoken anti-Japanese opinions.

Not surprisingly, the Japanese government strenuously protested the appointment of such a Minister to a potentially volatile position. Crane already had his baggage placed on board the ship on which he was to sail from San Francisco when he was handed a telegram recalling him to Washington. His resignation promptly followed.

Secretary of State Knox, who had wisely bided his time, insisted to the President that Crane be recalled because of his "undiplomatic" speeches. Taft realized that unless he yielded to Knox's demand he would lose the leading figure in his Cabinet at the very beginning of his administration. Sadly, he had to ask for the resignation of his own appointee before he had even arrived at his post.

The unlucky Mr. Crane apparently learned his lesson, however. He became a supporter of Woodrow Wilson, who eventually appointed him as Minister to China in 1920.

Source: Lewis Einstein, *A Diplomat Looks Back*, pp. 83-84.

*   *   *

Crane's mistake was in "going public" with his opinions, which he believed to have the support of the President; perhaps he could have avoided disaster if he had taken the indirect approach of "leaking" his views to journalists. Or perhaps not.

Off the Record

An American Ambassador in Athens, known to be a tremendous snob, requested that he be given the posting in Madrid when it became available. He achieved his dream and was posted to the great historical monarchy, with its gold, its lace and its ebony coaches. But not long after he had arrived his dreams of splendour came crashing down, as the monarchy was soon replaced by a vulgar Republic.

The disappointed Ambassador could not refrain from making his views known, but he chose to do so carefully, off-the-record, by holding a press conference for American journalists only. Unfortunately for the ambassador, there was one journalist present who, although meeting the technical requirements to be there, was actually a Frenchman and a bit of a troublemaker. This journalist let out the story that, when the American Ambassador had been asked what he thought of the new Spanish government, he had answered: "I never saw such a pack of jailbirds in my life."

The ambassador was recalled to the United States shortly thereafter.

Source: Salvador de Madariaga, *Morning without Noon: Memoirs*, pp. 231-32.

*   *   *

As unsuccessful as this particular effort was, those diplomatists who disagree with the policy being pursued by their masters have frequently resorted to underhanded methods in order to make their disagreement known. In the twentieth century, press leaks have become a recurring, and particularly troublesome phenomenon for those in positions of power.

Stopping Leaks

Henry Kissinger tells the story of the advice he got from the outgoing President, Lyndon Johnson, on how to deal with leaks. Kissinger, when he met with the President, noted how the walls of Johnson's Oval Office were lined with television sets and news tickers; in spite of having access to all the information provided by various intelligence agencies, the President appeared to be most concerned with what was being said in the press.

The advice that Johnson gave to Kissinger helped to explain his fascination with the media: his government, as he saw it, had been destroyed by systematic leaking from within, and he advised Kissinger to take steps to ensure that the bureaucracy of the new administration would be loyal.

"I have one piece of advice to give you, Professor," the President said—and here Kissinger leaned forward to profit from the advice of a man who had been engaged in the public service for decades—"read the columnists...and if they call a member of your staff thoughtful, dedicated, or any other friendly adjective, fire him immediately. He is your leaker."

Source: Henry Kissinger, *White House Years*, pp. 18-19.

*   *   *

Everyone pursuing a career is aware that certain things are expected of them: some things must be said, others must be avoided; some things must be done, others must be done without being seen to be done. Sometimes these expectations are clearly inscribed in black and white; at other times they are implicit—inexplicable and yet understood. But doing the right thing, saying the right thing, can still land the unfortunate diplomat in hot water—or Siberia.

The Good Comrade Kouzmin

A Soviet Consul-General in Paris, Nicholas Kouzmin, had been appointed to that post as a reward for services rendered during the revolution. He had commanded the Red Army in the White Sea district, where he succeeded in driving the White counter-revolutionaries and the British out of Archangel. In 1921, as a member of the Revolutionary Council in Petrograd, he had been imprisoned by the Kronstadt rebels. Kouzmin, who had lived as an exile in Paris before the revolution, longed to return there to revisit his old haunts, Montparnasse and Montmarte. Merely to breathe the air of Paris was for him an unending pleasure—and thus it seemed only right that the Party appoint him to the post on which he had set his heart.

On one of his occasional visits from Paris to Moscow, however, poor Kouzmin made a rather unfortunate error in judgement. He complained of having to live as an exile in a bourgeois country—one of those remarks that were thought to be proper in Bolshevik circles. The Consul-General, who undoubtedly thought that he was simply adhering to one of the expectations implicit in a revolutionary regime, discovered, when he returned to Paris, that he had gone too far in attempting to say the right thing: opening a telegram, he learned that he had been appointed to a military post in eastern Sibera. Kouzmin's senior comrades, taking pity on the unfortunate revolutionary who was suffering semi-exile in Paris, had attempted to see that his wish to participate more directly in the creation of a socialist state would be fulfilled.

Like a good comrade, Kouzmin took up his post, but the contrast between the glories of the *Rotonde* and Irkutsk or Krasnoyarsk appears to have been too much for him: he got mixed up in an awkward affair over a woman; when he took over the Arctic shipping line, he was blamed for the smashing-up of an ice-breaker. Finally, during the purges of 1936-37, it was remembered that he had been one of Zinoviev's collaborators during the Civil War, and this poor old Bolshevik was declared to be "an enemy of the people". And all because of a few phrases that he uttered because he thought they would ring nicely in the ears of his comrades!

Source: Alexandre Barmine, *Memoirs of a Soviet Diplomat: Twenty Years in the Service of the USSR*, pp. 250-51.

*   *   *

A simple expression, an unfortunate word uttered in the wrong place at the wrong time, can easily result in unforeseen complications. Occasionally even the simplest of acts can also cause unexpected difficulties, such as that which occurred in Berlin in 1938.

Frayed Nerves

During the May crisis of 1938, when stories of German troop concentrations along the Czechoslovakian border abounded, and when the Czechs mobilized 170,000 troops, some fairly stiff words were exchanged between Britain and Germany concerning the upholding of Czech sovereignty. Europe seemed to be moving close to war, and everyone in a position of official responsibility was becoming very nervous.

The Naval Attaché to the British embassy in Berlin, Troubridge, was proceeding with his family on 21 May to take his annual leave. Another member of the embassy's staff regarded this as a good opportunity to send his own small children away for a vacation under the thoughtful care of the good Mrs. Troubridge. Unfortunately, when this staff member went to purchase tickets for his children, he was informed by the railway company that the train was full; they would, however, consider putting on an additional coach, if they could be assured that it would be filled. He managed to persuade two other members of the embassy staff to send off their families as well, thereby filling the coach, which the railway company now agreed to put on.

The British Ambassador, Sir Nevile Henderson, who had been having some harsh words with the German Minister for Foreign Affairs concerning the French commitment to uphold their guarantee of Czechoslovakia's frontiers, returned to the embassy later in the day, where he found the French Ambassador waiting for him: was it true that the British Ambassador was evacuating the whole of the British colony? The news had even reached London; a phone call was received from the Foreign Office asking the Ambassador to cancel the evacuation arrangements. When he put the receiver down, the telephone rang again. This time it was the German Foreign Ministry, telling him that they had received a number of embassy passports for visas and begging him not to be an alarmist.

The Ambassador assured the Germans that he had only just learned of the situation on returning to the embassy, and that the Naval Attaché was simply taking his normal leave with his family. Furthermore, he promised to see to it that the extra railway carriage was cancelled and that he would forbid the departure of any other members of the embassy staff.

Henderson recognized that everyone's nerves were wearing thin, and he recalled afterwards how such little things could be misconstrued. Later that night he dined with Frau von Dirksen, the stepmother of the German Ambassador in London and a friend of Hitler's. The French Ambassador, François-Poncet, was also there. During the course of the dinner the municipal authorities began demolishing a small hotel down the street by dynamiting it, part of Hitler's design for rebuilding Berlin. Henderson leaned across his hostess and remarked that "the war seems to have begun."

Months afterward he discovered that this "humorous" remark had been conveyed to Goering, who took it as evidence of how frightened Henderson was at that moment.

Source: Nevile Henderson, *Failure of a Mission: Berlin, 1937-1939*, pp. 139-41.

*   *   *

It may be impossible to anticipate where trouble is going to come from, but overzealousness, especially on the part of the young, is, as the experienced know, one of the leading causes of mistakes in any profession.

The Energetic Consul

An energetic young British Consul was appointed to a post in South America. As was frequently the case, he appears not to have been given very explicit instructions outlining his various duties and the requirements involved in performing them. Early on in his posting he had performed the Consular marriage ceremony for six or seven British subjects residing in his district. He filled up the Registers (which he should not have had) and sent home to London certified copies of the entries (for which he should not have had the forms) at the end of the year.

He soon received a rather frantic telegram from the Foreign Office instructing him that, as he had not obtained a Marriage Warrant, he was not entitled to perform the marriage ceremony. He must therefore inform all the couples involved that their "marriage" was not a legal one, and that if any offspring were on the way, they would have to take the necessary steps to legitimize them. The poor young man wrote remorsefully—and fearfully—to each of the couples involved. He then prepared to escape from the wrath of those he had misled: he made his way down to the pier to await the arrival of the monthly steamer, which was due in shortly; escape seemed to him to be his only possible salvation.

"But the steamer was late and the couples reached him first, not with guns, stones and staves, but with presents of fruit and cigars in grateful acknowledgement of the news that they were not married after all."

Source: Gerald Campbell, *Of True Experience*, p. 12.

*　　　　*　　　　*

The young are not the only ones to be carried away by energetic ambitions. Even those who ought to know better have occasionally attempted to stimulate better relations between their people and those of their hosts by promoting "culture" of one kind or another, the assumption being that a better understanding of one another's customs may lead to a more favourable impression; such efforts may have unforeseen results.

Playing the Game

When William Bullitt was appointed to Moscow in the 1930s—the first Ambassador to be appointed by the United States to the Soviet Union since relations had been broken during the Revolution—he began his term with an enthusiastic belief in the possibility of improved understanding, which included some interesting cultural initiatives. What, for instance, could be more American than baseball? Bullitt encouraged his staff to teach the Russians to play, and sent home to the United States for bats, balls, and gloves.

About once a week the embassy staff would meet in a park to instruct the Russians on how to play the game. Their students did not appear to be particularly keen, having apparently been commanded from above to participate. One of the American players, Charles Bohlen, remembered that, "Their interest declined even further when a Russian who was learning to catch missed a fast ball. The ball hit him in the head and knocked him out."

165

An intriguing experiment in cultural diplomacy was quickly abandoned.

Source: Charles E. Bohlen, *Witness to History, 1929-1969*, p. 23.

*   *   *

*A*stute *diplomats are, in spite of the examples given above, adept at getting themselves out of sticky situations. Of all the qualities required of the diplomat, an ability to think on one's feet, to be quick-witted, is certainly chief among them, a characteristic nicely illustrated by the following story.*

Telling Tales

There is, for example, the story of the great Georges Clemenceau, reputed to have been the wily old diplomatist who outfoxed the hapless Woodrow Wilson at Versailles, and whose mind and tongue were legendary for their sharpness. Following an assassination attempt, Clemenceau was laid up in the hospital at the Rue Georges Bizet. During the crisis of his illness, when death seemed a likely prospect, and grateful for the kindness and attention given to him by the staff of the hospital, he called for the Mother Superior and asked her what he might be able to do in return for the care he was receiving. She replied that the nuns were deeply concerned for his spiritual welfare and would like him to confess. The old sinner was not at all pleased by the prospect but promised to sleep on it.

The next day, when he had begun to feel better, and it was becoming obvious that he would recover after all, he sent again for the Mother Superior. He wished, he said, to tell her about the dream that he had had following their conversation yesterday. He had dreamt that he had died, been transported to the gates of heaven, and met by St. Peter, who had denied him admittance until he went back and confessed his sins. The Mother Superior, deeply moved and thankful, wished to know what happened next.

Clemenceau told her that at this point in the dream he had complained to St. Peter that he was a very old, and a very tired man who could not possibly go back all that long way: "Bring me out a priest and I will confess here." St. Peter agreed and disappeared. After many hours he returned and said, "I am very sorry, M. Clemenceau, there isn't one."

Source: Tom Bridges, *Alarms and Excursions*, pp. 301-2.

The Rewards of Service

Diplomacy is a profession that offers many rewards: a staff of servants in residence; the power of a bureaucratic machine to smooth one's path; the pomp and splendour of official duties and entertainment; travel to interesting and exotic places at the taxpayer's expense. Some of these apparent benefits can be more illusory than real, and diplomacy can be a more dangerous profession than outsiders sometimes imagine it to be.

The Bewitched Diplomat

Take the case, for instance, of the British Minister to Panama, Eric Cleugh, who, when he arrived in Panama City discovered that the staff who maintained his official residence were not up to the standards that he expected. One day he returned unexpectedly from the office to discover a naked baby playing on his bed while the maid was doing his room—a scene that he found to be deeply offensive. He quickly made up his mind to dismiss the entire staff and to replace them with his own group of carefully selected West Indians.

After bidding a formal farewell to the former members of his household staff and seeing them off the premises, Cleugh went upstairs to be surprised by what appeared to be a sprinkling of water around the tiled veranda and on the walls of the bedrooms. He called in his new, but rather elderly, West Indian butler, who immediately became uncomfortable and who seemed rather frightened. Cleugh noticed that the butler was careful to avoid stepping across the water marks. After some careful prodding, the butler reluctantly explained to the Minister that the marks were signs of witchcraft, and that a spell had been placed on the room that would lead to Cleugh's death.

Alas, the Minister did survive—although it took weeks of scrubbing to remove the marks left by the witches' brew.

Source: Eric Cleugh, *Without Let or Hindrance*, pp. 195-96.

* * *

Dealing with embassy staffs that are frequently composed of foreign nationals can be one of the minor challenges confronting a diplomat abroad. Cooking, in particular, may be a troublesome matter if one is not prepared to "go native".

Cooking the Books

Diplomats living in China found the Chinese rendition of European food less than appealing: it normally consisted of a poor imitation of English cooking, comprised of chops, stews and overcooked vegetables. Not surprisingly, it was a French diplomat who, around the turn of the century, solved this problem by bringing with him to Peking his own chef, who was also to instruct a few promising Chinese cooks in the noble traditions of his native art. The experiment proved a great success, and the disciples who were so trained were greatly in demand by other diplomats, who were prepared to pay a high price and put up with a good deal in order to secure and to retain their services.

The American Secretary of Legation at Peking in 1909 managed to secure the services of one of these practitioners of the culinary arts, a man who was always addressed as the "Great Master," and who appeared at the Legation each morning attired in spotless black silk. The Secretary's wife, wishing to demonstrate her knowledge of local market conditions, once mentioned to the "Great Master" the price of eggs, one hundred of which cost twenty-five cents. He concurred that this was indeed the price; but at the end of the month, when he rendered his accounts, she discovered that they had been charged for two thousand eggs! When she pointed out to him that their diet had not consisted entirely of eggs, he assented that this was so. The result was that the next month they were charged for a mere fifteen hundred.

When the poor Americans compared notes with colleagues in the *Corps diplomatique*, they discovered that they were not alone: a French friend who had accused his cook of being the greatest robber in Peking was assured that this was not the case, that the honour of being the greatest thief of all had to go to the Russian Minister's chef. The Italian envoy suffered a more humiliating defeat. When he attempted to cut down on his cook's brigandage, the latter responded by waiting until the next official dinner to make his feelings known: every dish was a triumph—until they arrived at the dessert course, when none appeared. The cook, summoned to explain, simply declared, to the everlasting embarrassment of his host, "No money, no sweet."

Source: Lewis Einstein, *A Diplomat Looks Back*, p. 93.

*   *   *

But the staff problems faced by diplomats are not necessarily limited to those created by dealing with foreign servants and cooks. Those serving abroad frequently have difficulties in their relationships with the permanent members of their own department—especially when those permanent members have never left the comfortable confines of Washington, London, Paris or Berlin.

Helping Hands

John Kenneth Galbraith, serving as Ambassador to India, was glad to return there following a visit back to the United States. He was particularly glad to get away from Washington and the State Department. "It suffocates me with its endless, undirected meetings, its prideful commitment to the clichés of foreign policy and its pomposity," he noted in his diary. He wished he could find a way of filing an inefficiency report on the desk officer who had been assigned to him, an annoying bureaucrat who combined, "a great verbal felicity with a remarkable inability to accomplish the most minute task, a considerable reluctance to try and a total unawareness of any inadequacy."

When Galbraith became ill and was forced to rearrange his travel plans for returning to India, he called on the officer to ask him to make the arrangements. "He advised me that there should be a travel office in my hotel. I assume he had once been in the Biltmore."

On future trips from India to Washington, the State Department managed to keep the unfortunate officer out of the Ambassador's sight.

Source: John Kenneth Galbraith, *Ambassador's Journal: A Personal Account of the Kennedy Years*, p. 301.

*   *   *

Those who ascend to the uppermost levels of the diplomatic profession soon become accustomed to the pomp of ceremonial travel whether they like it or not. Consider, for instance, the experience of President Carter's National Security Adviser when making his first diplomatic procession through the streets of Paris.

A Stately Escort

Zbigniew Brzezinski visited Europe in October of 1978, where he was impressed by the security arrangements that had been made for him. In Germany he was accompanied by several police cars and a massive armoured car. But the French exceeded this standard by a wide margin. "Three extremely tough-looking detectives followed me wherever I went, on foot or by car, and in addition there were two motorcyclists in elegant dark leather coats and white helmets who would race ahead of my motorcade at enormous speed, weaving in and out of traffic..." And they brought a flair to their task that made a lasting impression on the visiting American, as they roared through the streets "acrobatically waving cars off the road to the right and left, occasionally even standing up on the motorcycle with both hands pointing in opposite directions in order to make the traffic yield..."

Brzezinski's escorts demonstrated much greater concern for his safety than for themselves or for that of their fellow citizens. "They would occasionally pull up to cars which would not yield the way and kick their fenders or pound their windows with their fists..." Again, they accomplished this while continuing to drive full blast. "At one stage, we drove literally on a sidewalk for a brief period of time; at another time we went around a rotary in a direction which met the onrushing traffic head on, forcing it rapidly to pull off to the side."

Source: Zbigniew Brzezinski, *Power and Principle: Memoirs of the National Security Adviser*, p. 294.

*   *   *

It hardly need be added, however, that there are risks and dangers involved in travel undertaken in the line of duty. Not all travel is done through the streets of Paris—and even there a gunman or bomb-thrower might be waiting. Nor is all travel simply ceremonial.

Getting There is Half the Fun

In February 1941, the British were hard-pressed to decide whether to treat Greece or Turkey as their principal line of defence against the Germans in the Middle East. Most strategists argued that Turkey was the more important of the two since, if Greece fell, they would still have Turkey to fall back on. If the British failed to divert whatever resources in arms and men that they could spare for Turkey, the Turks might give way to German demands, or perhaps fall victim to a German attack. On the other hand, the Turkish government had recently refused to accept a British offer of armaments and aircraft, while the new Greek Prime Minister had informed them of General Metaxas' determination to resist the Germans, even single-handed. Because of the importance of the decision, and the need for speed in arriving at it, the British Foreign Secretary, Anthony Eden, and the Chief of the Imperial General Staff, Sir John Dill, were dispatched on a special mission to Ankara. Getting there turned out to be as difficult as making the strategic choice.

The five members of the mission made their way from Paddington station to the Royal Air Force station at Plymouth on the afternoon of

February 12 with the intention of taking off that night, but the weather was too bad for them to leave. They remained in Plymouth throughout the next day, waiting for the weather to clear. The Prime Minister called in the middle of the night, urging them to take no risks, and expressing fears that they might be shot down off the coast of France. Finally, two days later, at 11:30 p.m. they took off from Plymouth in a Sunderland, manned by an Australian crew.

Within an hour things began to get rough. Piers Dixon, a Foreign Office man who kept a diary of the trip, recorded that "I was sick for the first time about 4 a.m., and from then onwards spent most of my time near a sink in the galley. Never having been in a flying-boat before, I imagined that these weather conditions were not abnormal." Before long everyone on the airplane was sick, including the crew. About 6.30 a.m., the 22-year old Australian pilot approached Dixon to announce that: "We've run into a b——— hurricane. I don't think we've enough petrol to make f——— Gibraltar. We can go into b——— Cadiz, but you don't want to be interned, do you? But, if we don't, we shall probably flop into the f——— ocean."

They were, at that time, about 100 miles north of Cape St. Vincent. The pilot thought that if they cut the corner and he used his reserve tanks, he might just possibly make it to Gibraltar; but this would mean infringing Portuguese neutrality. Or they could head for the North African coast, where the water should be calmer, and on which they could land if they ran out of petrol; but this would mean using the reserve tanks, which involved stopping the engines—which might or might not start again.

The Foreign Secretary was awakened and asked for his opinion. Eden thought that they would have to push on: they certainly could not run the risk of landing in Spain and being interned. He asked the Chief of Staff to decide, and Dill (who had been sick on and off throughout the night) after discussing things with the pilot, decided to make a bid for it. The reserve tanks were duly employed, the Sunderland dropping almost to the sea while the engines were stopped, and by 12.45 that afternoon they were off Tangier and landing in Algeçiras Bay. They had ten minutes' worth of fuel remaining. Dixon recorded that he spent the last four hours of the flight in a lifejacket, but that he felt less frightened than "very sick and angry with fate at the trick we were being played."

Three Sunderlands had started out on the trip, but only two made it; the third had been forced to make a landing in Portugal. What had hit them was a southerly gale that had gone unrecognized at Plymouth; it had wrecked sixteen ships in Lisbon harbour and had blown shipping and a Sunderland ashore at Gibraltar. The storm was so intense that it knocked out the instruments in the plane carrying the diplomatic mission, so the pilot was not certain of his direction or altitude, or even whether the plane was rising or falling. Just before dawn they had in fact been pointed in the wrong direction, flying north instead of south, heading out into the open Atlantic. Fortunately, the second Sunderland had met them at this moment and signalled to them to change direction. Otherwise, they almost certainly would have disappeared. Whether the course of the Second World War would have changed direction as well is more difficult to say.

Source: Pierson John Dixon, *Double Diploma*, pp. 56-59.

*   *   *

It might easily be supposed that the advantages to be gained in the process of travelling are entirely one-sided, in favour of the rich and famous. It is true that such people can pay for service and luxury, and that because they are well-connected they may be able to gain privileges and opportunities denied to lesser mortals. Although the ledger may be unbalanced, however, there are some entries in the other column that testify to some occasions on which the poor and downtrodden may enjoy advantages denied to others.

The Proletarian Diplomat

Listen, for instance, to the story told by Angelica Balabanoff, a Russian refugee living in Italy before the First World War. She had fled her native country around the turn of the century, having become a communist and a committed revolutionary. Articulate and energetic, she had established a sufficient reputation to be chosen to serve as the representative of Italian Socialism on the Executive Committee of the Second International. After the assassination of the Archduke Ferdinand at Sarajevo, the international crisis that followed, and the declarations of war by the Great Powers, the Executive Committee decided that it must hold an emergency meeting in order to determine how the workers of Europe should be guided. Comrade Balabanoff, receiving the message that her presence was required immediately in Brussels, dashed to the railway station and boarded the train headed to Milan, where she would then catch the express for Brussels.

Unfortunately, in her haste, she boarded the wrong train. Although she had been living in Italy for more than a decade, and although her political activities had taken her all over the country, although she had never missed a meeting or an appointment, she had now managed to get on a train headed for Rome, rather than Milan—and she would miss the most important meeting of her life as a result. The train, which was an express, would make no stops before it arrived in Rome. By the time she got to Brussels from Rome, the emergency meeting would likely have ended.

She explained her mistake to the conductor who had come to check her ticket and who, fortuitously, recognized her. "I have seen you so often at the station," he told her, "and I know who you are. Is it important for the Party that you get to Milan tonight?"

Balabanoff realized that, having found a friend, she could speak freely: "Listen, comrade, the war has begun. We must stop it if we can or keep it from spreading over all Europe. The International Congress in August will be too late. The Executive Committee must act now. We meet in Brussels tomorrow." The conductor knew what to do: "Don't worry, comrade. You will be in Brussels in time."

Half an hour later, as they approached a station, the train slowed down. The conductor entered Balabanoff's compartment, opened a window, lifted her in his arms, thrust her through the opening and lowered her into the outstretched arms of a startled station employee who had come running along the platform in response to his shouts. The train quickly regained its momentum and disappeared into the night.

"What are you doing here at this time of night, Comrade Balabanoff?" the station master asked. When she told him, he explained that there was no train to Milan that night, "but I will see that you get there." He was as good as his word, and proletarian diplomacy was able to continue: she arrived at Milan in a baggage-train just in time to catch the express to Brussels.

Source: Angelica Balabanoff, *My Life as a Rebel*, pp. 2-3.

*　　　*　　　*

Unlike the young proletarian above, diplomats soon recognize that they are also bureaucrats; they are both caught up in, and responsible for, operating a large organization. And, as in all bureaucracies, this has its advantages and disadvantages, its ironies and its paradoxes.

The Rewards of Bureaucracy

One of the more delightful ironies occurred in conjunction with Dean Acheson, at that time Under Secretary of State for Foreign Affairs in the United States, who was asked to give the commencement address at Bryn Mawr in 1946, partly because his daughter was one of the graduating class. He chose to speak on the theme of the development of an independent critical spirit as one aim of education. But in doing so he chose an example that infuriated at least one member of his audience.

Acheson explained that to characterize a proceeding today as a "star chamber" was to apply a highly pejorative epithet; the original Star Chamber, a room in Westminster Palace so-called because its ceiling was decorated with stars, was vilified by the Puritans because it was in that room where the king's counsellors sat, sometimes in secret, to try offenders who were deemed to be too powerful to be judged in the ordinary courts of law. And yet this chamber was, Acheson suggested, one of the principal instruments by which the Wars of the Roses had been brought to an end and which permitted England to emerge as a modern centralized state.

Fulton Oursler, senior editor of the *Reader's Digest* immediately protested the use of this illustration by writing to the President and to the Secretary of State that, "such views are treasonable to the philosophy of American government," and that, "no man holding such views deserves public office."

Alas, Oursler's protest was soon caught up in the workings of the bureaucratic machine, which provided Acheson with an unexpected reward. The letter to the President was referred to the State Department for a reply and, in the temporary absence of the Secretary of State, the task of responding was left to the Under Secretary—Dean Acheson, who took great pleasure in being excessively patient and polite and in regretting that the Under Secretary had failed to make himself clear, and that this had caused Mr. Oursler to be disturbed.

Source: Dean Acheson, *Present at the Creation: My Years in the State Department*, pp. 183-84.

*   *   *

The bureaucratic tides move in both directions. Acheson was the unsuspecting beneficiary of one of its many ironic movements; George Kennan was the unlucky victim of one of its operating procedures.

What Gets Read

Kennan was living in Berlin in 1940, after serving at the American Legation in Prague while it was under Nazi occupation. If only for intellectual diversion, he took to studying their policies of occupation, as the months he had spent in Prague gave him both an interest in the subject and a basis for comparison; he was particularly interested in the efforts the Nazis were undertaking to have the Germans play the role of a *Herrenvolk* throughout the whole of Europe. He began, on his own, to write reports on various regions of Europe and, in the spring of 1941, produced a long report that analyzed the German occupational policies and experiences in general.

After the war, when he returned to Washington, Kennan approached the official who sat at the German desk in the State

Department to ask whether they had received his report, and whether it had been of any interest. "The answer was: yes, they had received it, but it had been of no use because the discussion was not broken down by individual countries and therefore it could not be cut up and distributed to the 'country desks' in the various Washington agencies."

"Know thyself" might be a dictum worth attending to, but for diplomats serving abroad, "Knowing thy bureaucracy" might be of more practical utility.

Source: George F. Kennan, *Memoirs, 1925-1950, pp. 127-28.*

*   *   *

At least Kennan did not have to pay a price much beyond that of wounded vanity. He may have felt himself to have been unduly ignored by a system that was incapable of monitoring itself and its own procedures—but careful scrutiny can sometimes involve costs that are more directly felt by unfortunate diplomats.

The Gratitude of the Crown

The British Diplomatic Service, in the early part of the century, placed a variety of demands on those who received appointments to the high rank of ambassador. Although the government, through its Board of Works, partially furnished its embassies, much of the cost of the establishment was borne by the ambassador himself. He was expected to supply uniforms for a butler, a groom, three or four footmen, coachmen and chauffeurs, as well as the carriages and cars. An ambassador was expected to possess sufficient silver, china and glass to entertain anywhere from ten to one hundred guests at dinner. And most ambassadors, wishing the embassy to look something like home, usually supplied their own furniture, pictures and ornaments.

George Buchanan, who served as Ambassador to Russia before and during the First World War, lost everything when the revolution broke out in 1917. He desperately sold what furniture he could in the autumn of that year, and managed to collect £3,000 from the sale. As a sum of this size was too large to transfer to England, he invested it in the Lena Goldfields, which were then taken over by the Bolsheviks, making it impossible to recover the investment. He estimated that he had lost, in addition, £5,000 in various personal effects. After fleeing Russia, he entered into a protracted diplomatic negotiation of his own with the British Treasury, in an attempt to recover his losses.

These negotiations were still proceeding when Buchanan was appointed Ambassador to Italy in 1922, and found himself without those possessions that one would normally have accumulated by that point in a career. He therefore found it most distressing when the Treasury offered him only £3,000 as complete compensation for his losses, which amounted to approximately one-third of his estimated losses. Furthermore, the Treasury insisted that, in the event of the recovery of any of his personal effects, he would have to refund the appropriate amounts to Exchequer. He found it especially frustrating that the Treasury refused to give him any compensation for those articles considered to have a purely artistic value, which they classed as *"articles de luxe"*, and yet they insisted that if any such articles were eventually recovered he would have to pay back a percentage of their value. He did his best to argue against the Treasury's case, but they remained obdurate and he was eventually forced to accept their offer, which he found humiliating and which filled him with resentment. He would undoubtedly have been even more humiliated and resentful had he lived to see the dénoument of the case.

About three years after his death, a few items that had been salvaged from the embassy eventually found their way back to England, whereupon his daughter was presented with a bill from the Treasury for £1,000. The returned items consisted of two white and gold Empire chairs (from a set of twelve), one or two small tables, a high-backed chair, a few silver spoons and forks, some china snuffboxes and three trunks—two of which were packed with odd small pieces of fabric, while the other contained letters and photographs. The trunk of memorabilia was the only item that Meriel Buchanan was able to keep, because her Trustee advised her that the remaining items were not worth the £1,000 demanded; "I had to let them go, although I confess that those white and gold chairs brought a lump to my throat, recalling memories it was wiser to forget."

Such was the generosity of a grateful government for faithful service abroad through years of crisis, war and revolution, and which had cost the family most of their personal treasures.

Source: Meriel Buchanan, *Ambassador's Daughter*, pp. 209-10.

*   *   *

Even those who are themselves bureaucrats are not immune from the machinations of the bureaucratic machine; if diplomats, consuls and members of foreign office staffs become hardened cynics, it is not simply as a result of becoming familiar with the realpolitik that governs international life. Cynicism also arises from living their daily lives according to the rules and procedures that govern large organizations. Sometimes, as we see in the following story, these rules can pursue the hapless official even to the grave.

Poor Puffkins!

In the early days of the First World War, John Gregory, an official in the British Foreign Office, was in charge of a department responsible for consular administration and with the protection of British subjects who were resident or travelling abroad. One day his clerk announced, for about the hundredth time that day, that there was a gentleman to see him. Gregory asked who it was, to be told that it was "Vice-Consul Puffkins" who was outside in a taxi.

"Show him up," Gregory instructed.

The clerk, hesitating, said, "I can't, Sir."

"Why not?" Gregory asked.

"He's dead, Sir."

"Dead!" Gregory exclaimed, "But you said he was below in a taxi."

"So he is, Sir," was the reply.

Gregory sent another member of the department outside to investigate, and to explain that, as there was no mortuary chapel at the Foreign Office, he could not be of much assistance. But no taxi was to be seen.

The next day, however, another clerk announced that there was a gentleman to see him.

"Who?"

"Vice-Consul Puffkins, Sir."

This time Gregory succeeded in seeing the young lady who had escorted the defunct gentleman all the way from the South Sea Islands with the expectation that a grateful government would provide the means with which to give His Majesty's loyal servant a proper funeral in a decent burial ground. She had not realized that the red tape of the bureaucracy would prevent her from achieving this laudable objective.

The archives of the Foreign Office were searched for precedents, but none being found, the verdict was inexorable: only Mrs. Vice-Consul Puffkins was entitled to receive burial fees, and this lady, if she existed at all, was nowhere to be found. The deserving young woman who had brought the extinct official several thousands of miles across the ocean and conveyed him by taxi to the centre of Imperial Generosity was refused the simple request that she asked for. By the time that Gregory reached the end of his service and sat down to write his memoirs, he still had no idea what had finally become of poor Vice-Consul Puffkins, "whether he is still circulating round Whitehall in a ghostly taxi: or whether his one-time admirer successfully mislaid him in a railway cloakroom: or whether he was taken back by her to the South Sea Islands: or whether he is reposing securely in a corner of Kensal Green."

Source: John Gregory, *On the Edge of Diplomacy: Rambles and Reflections, 1902-1928*, pp. 21-22.

*   *   *

*D*ying in office is, of course, one way to bring a career in diplomacy to a close. Fortunately, poor Puffkins was not himself able to witness just how grateful the government was to him for the services that he had rendered. Such was not the case with an American diplomat, who had apparently outlived his usefulness.

The Right Stuff

Lewis Einstein had served abroad for thirty years, the last eight of which were spent as Minister to Czechoslovakia, and was coming to be rather tired of the monotony of diplomatic life in Prague: "Such glamour as it ever possessed for me had long ago worn off, and though I liked the work, when work there was, I was bored by diplomatic entertainment and the continuous obligation of attending tedious banquets and talking to tedious people." He decided to retire unless he was offered a more important and interesting post.

President Hoover saved his Minister the difficulty of making a decision by accepting a resignation that had not actually been tendered: not a particularly courteous way of dismissing a public servant who had devoted his working life to the representation of his country abroad, but not a particularly unusual one. "Mr. Hoover liked to be known as the great Engineer, but his zeal in advocating the preservation of natural resources did not extend to the human ones that were at his disposal." Einstein was not alone; Hoover dropped a good number of career men from the service. "The presidential purpose was only one of utilising diplomatic posts as a hidden subsidy for administration politics. My successor at Prague obtained his training for world affairs by operating a taxi company."

Source: Lewis Einstein, *A Diplomat Looks Back*, p. 207.

*   *   *

*D*iplomats make their exit from diplomatic lives in a variety of ways. Most, of course, retire with honours and a pension, after a long career. Some departures, however, are less dignified.

A Hasty Departure

One Soviet Chargé d'Affaires in Paris, Grigory Bessedovsky, had, in the later years of his diplomatic career, developed what were seen by his masters in Moscow to be dangerous political tendencies. He was counselled to admit that he suffered from hereditary neurasthenia and to return home voluntarily, but he refused, denouncing Stalin as the embodiment of Oriental despotism and members of the communist party as caring only for their income, political careers and promotions: "You are the gravediggers of the Revolution. You are criminals, and from this day forward I shall fight relentlessly against you."

The officer who interviewed him reminded Bessedovsky that he was, by virtue of being in the compound of the Paris embassy, on Soviet territory, and ordered that neither he nor his family was to leave it. Bessedovsky rose from his chair and walked out, slamming the door as he left. He went to his wife's room and told her to get ready to leave immediately, grabbed two revolvers and extra ammunition, went down to the courtyard and into the waiting-room of the embassy—where he was confronted by one of the concierges of the Trade Delegation.

The concierge, white and trembling, ordered him to return to his apartments. Bessedovsky replied that, as the Chargé, he had no intention of obeying such orders. The concierge pointed a revolver at him nevertheless, declared himself to be a Party member and announced that he had orders to stop him. If Bessedovsky took another step he would be a dead man. The Soviet diplomat thought of shooting him, but through the doorway he could see another armed man. Turning his back on them, he returned to the courtyard to look for another means of escape.

Bessedovsky realized that, if he did not escape at this moment he and his family would probably be overpowered sometime during the night, and he recalled that two diplomatic couriers had arrived that very day with an enormous trunk—sufficient for packing three corpses. Knowing that he would not be able to contact friends on the outside by telephone, there seemed only one route left: the wall. Taking off his overcoat and throwing it over the wall, he pulled himself up and climbed over. There remained another wall, three and a half metres high. He found a chair and managed to get over this one as well. A powerful voice called out from the nearest building, asking who was there, but the inquirer turned out to be friendly and assisted him in getting to the police station. An hour and a half later

Bessedovsky returned to the embassy with a policeman, where he succeeded in retrieving his wife and his son. His diplomatic career was over.

Source: Grigory Z. Bessedovsky, *Revelations of a Soviet Diplomat*, pp. 269-73.

*   *   *

*S*talin's reputation for dealing harshly with recalcitrant officials was well known to the diplomats who worked with him.

Stalinist Humour?

When coffee and brandy were served following a diplomatic dinner of the "Big Four" in Moscow, Averell Harriman, then the American Ambassador to the Soviet Union, found himself seated next to Charles de Gaulle—who soon proved to be in a mood to provoke the Russians. Pointing to Nikolai Bulganin, a member of the Soviet Military Council, de Gaulle asked Harriman in a loud voice: "Isn't that the man who killed so many Russian generals?" a remark that was certainly overheard by the Russian interpreter.

At the same time, the Russian and the French foreign ministers, Vyacheslav Molotov and Georges Bidault, had moved to a separate table where they continued to engage in a heated argument arising from that day's negotiations. They showed no signs of stopping now that the day's work was done. At this point Stalin called out to Bulganin, in a voice that could be heard by everyone: "Bring the machine guns. Let's liquidate the diplomats."

Source: W. Averell Harriman and Elie Abel, *Special Envoy to Churchill and Stalin, 1941-1946*, p. 377.

Amateur Adventures

The circumstances in which diplomats work are often fortuitous: they find themselves placed in situations that are not of their own making; they are required to deal with people who appear on the scene with attitudes and prejudices already formed and with which they must deal. Sometimes this means overcoming hostile opinions, sometimes it means dealing with indifference, and occasionally it means receiving unexpected gifts.

Queen Elizabeth and the Anglo-American Alliance

One such story involves Franklin D. Roosevelt's friend, adviser and unofficial diplomatist, Harry Hopkins, who was reputed to be anti-British, a reputation he quickly dispelled when he began to work with the British during the course of the Second World War. He explained to one of Winston Churchill's assistants that although he had once been anti-British, his attitude had been altered by a single dramatic incident that had led him to reconsider his prejudice.

Following the death of his wife, Hopkins had been invited by the Roosevelts to move into the White House, along his small daughter. They were in residence when, in 1939, the first British reigning monarch to visit the United States, King George VI, arrived in Washington. This meant little to Hopkins, who considered the monarchy to be among those British institutions that he disliked; but it meant a great deal to his daughter, who had a fairy-tale image of queens and was thrilled at the prospect of actually seeing one.

On the night of the State Banquet at the White House, the little girl was, unfortunately, taken ill with fever and under strict instructions to stay in bed: she was not even to be allowed a glimpse of her fairy-tale queen from the staircase. Many tears were shed.

Some thoughtful soul mentioned the child's disappearance to Queen Elizabeth who, when she was fully dressed for the banquet (complete with crinoline, Order of the Garter, jewels and tiara) made her way to the child's room. She must have appeared just as a little girl would imagine a queen to be; and with her gift for charm, she must have made a splendid impression on young Miss Hopkins, who then transmitted this impression to her father.

"And that", reported Hopkins in later years, "is how I first came to think you people must have some good in you after all."

Source: John Colville, *Footprints in Time*, pp. 146-47.

*   *   *

Many of the most curious diplomatic situations have arisen from the interventions of "unofficial" diplomatists, who believe that the professionals are unwilling or unable to do the job properly.

The Hess Mission

Perhaps the most famous example of this type of diplomatic activity came from the strange mission undertaken in 1941 by Rudolf Hess, the Deputy Führer of Nazi Germany. He had decided that an accommodation could be reached between Britain and Germany to bring about an end to the war—if only he were able to meet with the Duke of Hamilton, reputed to be sympathetic to Germany's case, on a face-to-face basis. To this end, he undertook to fly to Scotland and parachute into the ducal estate.

Hess arranged with his friend, Willy Messerschmitt, to have a two-seater fighter plane with an auxiliary detachable gasoline tank placed at his disposal at the airport in Augsburg, where it apparently sat for some months while he waited for the most opportune moment for undertaking his mission. On 10 May he had an aide drive him to Augsburg, where he climbed into the aircraft and, without a word of explanation to either his aide or to Messerschmitt, took off for an unknown destination.

Arriving off the coast of Scotland rather sooner than expected, while there was still daylight, Hess circled over the North Sea until nightfall; around midnight he reckoned that he had arrived at his destination, and attempted to bail out, only to discover that the wind would blow him back into the cockpit. He then attempted to turn the aircraft upside-down in order to drop out, and eventually he succeeded. In doing so, however, the tail smashed into his back, and when he pulled the ripcord the jolt knocked him unconscious. He was still unconscious when he hit the ground, miraculously suffering no more than a broken ankle in the process. The next thing he knew a kindly cottager was at his side, offering to take him in and give him a cup of tea.

Ironically, Hess's quarry, the Duke of Hamilton, who was serving in the Auxiliary Air Force, happened at this moment to be in command of the station at Turnhouse, about fifty miles away from the estate, and it was Hamilton who received a report from observers that a Messerschmitt had been spotted in his sector—a report that he discounted, knowing that these fighter aircraft had insufficient fuel to make the return flight home. Nevertheless, the report was confirmed, some aircraft were sent up to pursue the intruder, and they duly reported that he had crashed somewhere in the vicinity of Glasgow. Reassured, Hamilton went to bed.

When he awoke the next morning, he was given a message that the German pilot, a man named "Horn", had been taken to hospital, placed in the custody of the Glasgow police, and was now asking to see him. When Hamilton arrived at the hospital the pilot announced that he was, in fact, "Reichminister Hess" but, as Hess had not had the foresight to bring documentation with him in order to prove his identity, and as Hamilton had never met Hess, the great diplomatic meeting never got off the ground.

Hamilton flew down to London, where he was put in contact with the Prime Minister, who was greatly annoyed to be disturbed by such a ludicrous story. The next day, however, the Foreign Secretary asked the Permanent Under-Secretary whether someone might not be found who knew Hess and could thus attest to the validity of the pilot's claim. Alexander Cadogan called up Ivone Kirkpatrick to ask if he would be able to recognize Hess if he saw him; Kirkpatrick, then working for the B.B.C., assured him that he would. He and Hamilton were immediately flown to Scotland for another meeting with the German pilot; delays with the aircraft meant that Hess had been in the country for 48 hours by the time that they arrived in Scotland, where another report from the Foreign Secretary awaited them: a German radio report, announcing that Hess had gone missing, had been intercepted. They were ordered to see the pilot without a moment's delay.

By this time Hess had been moved from Glasgow to Buchanan Castle, which was serving as a military hospital. Kirkpatrick and Hamilton, driving to the castle, became lost and arrived after midnight. They had left London shortly before 5 p.m., and were tired and dinnerless by the time that they were finally shown in to the pilot, who by that time was sound asleep. Hess awoke, dazed and confused, eventually recognized Kirkpatrick, and began to read from a series of notes he had prepared in order to provide the British with a grand summary of Germany's grievances against England. By 3 a.m. he had yet to finish his oration.

Exhausted and impatient, Kirkpatrick demanded that Hess briefly define the object of his visit. Hess replied that it was to convince the British of the inevitability of a German victory and to bring about a negotiated peace. The British were now alone, and if they continued with their ineffective resistance the German air force would begin a program of systematic destruction; the British Isles would be reduced to rubble and millions would be killed. On the other hand Hess, who enjoyed the confidence of the Führer, could give his assurance that Hitler had always had the highest regard for the British and their Empire and that he would be prepared to conclude a magnanimous peace. The foundation of this peace was to be German hegemony on the continent and the return of the colonies taken from her at Versailles in 1919; in return, the British Empire would remain intact. The German army and the British fleet together would rule the world. Hitler could not, of course, be expected to negotiate with Churchill, so negotiations should be initiated immediately with Hess. Hess's speech finally ended around 4 a.m. Kirkpatrick and Hamiliton finally managed to get to bed for a short sleep by 6 a.m.

A full day elapsed before the government decided how to respond. Kirkpatrick was ordered to pursue the discussion with Hess, although it remained unclear what purpose the government had in mind. When they arrived at Hess's room some 36 hours after the initial interview, he was visibly disappointed that negotiations had not yet begun, insisting that they must move quickly or risk missing the bus, as Hitler was not a man to be toyed with. Moreover, the treatment that he was receiving was unworthy of a *Reichminister*: the room was too brightly lit; he was humiliated by the constant surveillance; when he had undergone a medical examination the physician had failed to lay a clean sheet on the couch beforehand, which might have resulted in him picking up some distasteful skin disease; and it was much too noisy in his room—the sentries wore heavy boots and deliberately stamped around to annoy him.

When Kirkpatrick was ordered to interview Hess again the next day, he decided to ask for Hitler's views on Ireland. Hess replied that Hitler took no interest in Ireland and that the British were free to do as they liked there. As for the Soviet Union, Hess gave his assurance that Hitler was a man of his word and that there would be no attack in the east. Kirkpatrick was convinced that Hess really was unaware of the preparations for such an attack that were already underway. In the meantime, Hess had decided that there was a plot to poison him, and he insisted that the officer of the guard should taste his food. The British government, almost equally fearful, had decided to deploy an infantry battalion around the castle in case Hitler should attempt to rescue his deputy.

The next day Hess was shipped down to London, where he remained locked up in the Tower for the duration of the war. The "negotiations" initiated by the would-be diplomat got nowhere.

> Source: Ivone J. Kirkpatrick, *The Inner Circle: Memoirs*, pp. 170-181.

News of the Hess Mission soon spread through Germany, which led to the circulation of "Hess jokes":

> BBC Report: "On Sunday night no further German cabinet ministers flew in."
>
> German High Command Communiqué: "Goering and Goebbels are still firmly in German hands."

"The 1,000-year Reich has now become a hundred-year Reich. One zero is gone."

Churchill asks Hess: "So you are the madman?"—"No, only his deputy."

*   *   *

People who enter the world of diplomacy as amateurs may unwittingly put themselves at risk. Even with the best of intentions, their activities may not be well received and, unlike the professionals, they have no code of custom to protect them when things fail to work out as planned.

Get Thee to a Nunnery!

During the First World War, Kaiser Wilhelm II of Germany made a number of attempts to negotiate a separate peace with Russia. He seemed to believe that, if he could regain the friendly ear of Tsar Nicholas II, they would be able to find grounds for an agreement. One channel that he selected for such an overture was a Mlle. Wassiltchikoff, who belonged to an old Russian family, but was living in Germany when war broke out. Late in 1915 she was invited to Darmstadt by the Grand Duke of Hesse, who then sent her off to Petrograd charged with the mission of concluding peace with the Tsar.

Mlle. Wassiltchikoff was empowered to say that the Kaiser was prepared to grant Russia very attractive terms; that England had already made overtures to Germany for a separate peace—and therefore the Tsar should have no qualms about negotiating directly with Germany; and that a reconciliation between Russia and Germany was desirable from the point of view of the two ruling dynasties. She arrived in Petrograd armed with a letter for the Russian Foreign Minister, Sazanov, as well as two open letters from the Grand Duke for the Tsar and Tsarina. She went immediately to the Foreign Ministry, where she presented the documents to Sazonov, who told her that she had acted disgracefully in undertaking such a mission.

Tsar Nicholas, when he received Sazonov's report on the episode, was so angry that he issued orders to have the unlucky Mlle. Wassiltchikoff interned in a convent.

Source: George Buchanan, *My Mission to Russia*, p. 252.

*   *   *

Poor Rudolf Hess imprisoned, and poor Mlle. Wassiltchikoff sent into a convent, do not establish encouraging precedents for the forays of unofficial diplomatists.

The Counterfeit Diplomat

At the beginning of 1923, Prince Lajos Windischgraetz, one of the leaders of the official opposition in the new state of Hungary, undertook a daring diplomatic mission on behalf of the Government, which he was patriotically willing to support on matters of national interest. One point on which he agreed with the government was the need to help those organizations dedicated to recovering the "Lost Lands" that had been taken from Hungary by the Treaty of Trianon. Unfortunately for the Hungarian nationalists, such support was illegal under the treaty and, as Hungary's expenditures remained under Allied control, it was most difficult to supply these organizations with arms and other resources.

Windischgraetz went to Berlin, to talk to Gustav Stresemann (who would soon become German Chancellor) because, in Windischgraetz's words, "Under immediate post-war conditions Hungary lacked a diplomatic service equipped to handle delicate major issues." So the government would use, instead, members of the opposition to conduct such business for them. Windischgraetz had been asked to approach Germany in order to outline the possible advantages that might be gained from presenting a united front in international affairs. Stresemann smiled and shook his head.

"No, no, my dear Prince, there would be little point in such a manifestation of solidarity. An alliance between the lame and the halt suffers from notorious handicaps."

On the other hand, he hastened to add, this did not mean that they should not help each other as much as they could, but that they should refrain from making a public exhibition of their cooperation. Stresemann obviously had something in mind. As their discussion continued, he mentioned the difficulties involved in paying the Allied reparations in the present difficult circumstances. He did not, however, suggest any remedy for the situation. Only after the meeting did Windischgraetz discover what it was that Stresemann had in mind: there was a plot being hatched to forge French franc and British pound notes in order to purchase gold and thus strengthen the German currency. Apparently, two senior civil servants in Germany had been instructed to look into the technical aspects involved in such an undertaking.

When Windischgraetz discussed the idea with an old friend, Colonel Bauer, one of Ludendorff's closest collaborators and former head of the Artillery and Munitions Department during the war, a plan began to take shape: the notes could be produced in Hungary using German technicians and machines; in return Hungary would get a third of the forgeries.

"Supposing Hungary were ready to consider your proposal, what would be the next step?" Windischgraetz asked.

"Somebody nominated by your Government would have to come to the Rhineland to see on the spot what factories there are doing."

Bauer proposed that they travel to the Rhineland together and look at the operations there before Windischgraetz approached his government. Forty-eight hours later they were in Cologne, which was still occupied by the British; cautiously, they stayed at different hotels while conducting their inspection of the factories. In Cologne they met up with a Balt named Arthur Schultze, a former employee of the Russian printing works who had fled from the Bolsheviks; he had come to Cologne to study bank-note production, where he had been recruited by the Germans to work on the forgery project.

Schultze confided that he had devised a new method of paper production that obviated the need for special machines; a factory in a small town nearby was testing the process. They travelled there in darkness, walking the last mile until they reached a huge iron gate, through which they passed after Schultze gave the password. Entering the factory, they were guided by a porter along dark corridors and down innumerable stairs through subterranean rooms until they reached a laboratory; all of those working there were former officers, sworn to secrecy. Schultze went to a cupboard and took out samples of genuine French francs, along with his paper substitute; they studied the graining of the fibres through a magnifying glass, and Windischgraetz was convinced that they appeared to be identical.

"Success is as good as guaranteed," Bauer exclaimed. "Everything else is easy! Wouldn't it be a shame to back down?"

"I'll tell my Government," Windischgraetz replied.

"And?"

" What happens thereafter is not up to me."

Windischgraetz quickly returned to Hungary, where he met with other leaders of the irredentist movement; they agreed that they ought to approach the government through Count Teleki, the Commissioner for the Lost Lands. Teleki was duly informed of the proposal, and he was prepared to support it, provided that the Minister-President approved as well, and that the Military Cartographic Institute was willing to produce the forgeries, as it alone possessed the appropriate technical resources. They estimated that the proceeds from the operation would amount to some fifty million gold francs, which would be allocated partly to the Lost Lands Commission and partly to propaganda to influence the elections to be held in Slovakia in 1925.

The Cartographic Institute received instructions to undertake the project, but Windischgraetz was reluctant to begin without the direct support of Count Bethlen, the Minister-President. A meeting was set up, but Bethlen put off a discussion, explaining that he must have no formal cognizance of what was being done.

That summer the Institute was extended by digging deeply into the ground and building concrete cellars lined with steel. The necessary machinery for the operation began to be circuitously imported from Britain and Germany, as the destination had to be kept secret. Schultze arrived from Cologne to instruct the technicians in the paper-making process. Months of experimentation had to be devoted before the counterfeit notes were sufficiently good to pass inspection. Plans were made to convert the forgeries once they were ready, which was no easy task for such a quantity of notes. A General Staff officer was appointed to study and test a selection of effectual methods of conversion; he travelled through Europe to study banking practices, clearing system techniques, and so on. A number of technical and mechanical problems had to be overcome in producing the notes, but Windischgraetz was more concerned that Bethlen continued to refuse to take official cognizance of the operation, and that Teleki had withdrawn from the chairmanship of the National League, the chief irredentist executive organization.

Finally, in the spring of 1925 (already too late to influence the elections in Slovakia) bundles of notes were ready to pass. The Director-General of the Post Office Savings Bank, Baross, who was chosen to initiate the disposal of the currency, described the series of thousand franc notes that were shown to him as a great success. He asked for six weeks to study the best means for dealing with them; meanwhile the whole production was sorted, packed, and moved under police escort to a really secure spot: the palace of Bishop Zadravesz.

Baross came up with the method to be used: renting a safe at a bank, and depositing a certain sum of money in it; the bank clerk would normally make a cursory scrutiny of the notes' authenticity, count them, and issue a receipt. The receipt constituted a bill for the value of the amount deposited, which could then be tendered in ordinary payment or used in stock exchange dealings. Baross planned for the forgeries to be placed in safe-deposits in a hundred different cities and for the receipts all to be negotiated on one and the same day. Official couriers were selected, passports were forged, and the couriers took an oath of secrecy administered by the Senior Army Chaplain. The notes had been conveyed by diplomatic bag to embassies and legations abroad, who were to hand them over to the couriers when the moment arrived. By late autumn of 1925 everything was ready to go. But no signal came from the Minister-President.

Windischgraetz was uneasy. He could not believe that all the details of the operation, particularly those involving the Foreign Affairs Ministry, could have gone ahead without Bethlen's approval. The delay was inexplicable. When he was out in the countryside in November, shooting and playing cards with friends at an estate, an urgent coded message arrived from Budapest, asking him to return immediately: Colonel Jankovich, the staff-officer assigned to disperse the notes in Holland had been arrested.

When Windischgraetz arrived in Budapest, he was told the story. Jankovich, who was to deliver his packages to the embassy, crossed the border without trouble, using his diplomatic courier papers. But, instead of continuing to The Hague as planned, he decided to stay the night at Rotterdam, meeting there with two of the disposal people. He took them up to his room, opened his bag, took out one of the packets, and showed some of the notes to them. After they had admired the quality of the forgeries, he had placed the packets back in his bag and closed it up. "Then he noticed that three of the bills had fallen under the table. To save reopening the bag, he stuffed them in his wallet. Among genuine ones of the same face-value." The next morning Jankovich travelled to The Hague, "arriving too early to find anyone at the embassy. So he strolled around the town until it occurred to him to change some money. When he passed a thousand franc note across the counter, the bank clerk declared it to be counterfeit."

To make matters worse, Jankovich's next move was to attempt to stuff the remainder of his notes into his sock. A policeman confronted him, but Jankovich identified himself as a diplomatic courier, "So the two of them went to the embassy, where the most incredible of all happened. In front of the policeman Jankovich burst into tears and confessed everything."

"That's not possible."

"I assure you that it is. We've got our ambassador's report."

A cable had been sent round immediately to all the embassies and legations that the forgeries, most of which had already been deposited in bank safe-deposits, were to be destroyed. Several of the conspirators had been arrested. Bethlen indicated that he intended to deny all official complicity, and to maintain appearances had instructed the police to find some culprits, and to do so quickly. The French sent their own agents into Hungary, armed with genuine franc notes to be used to obtain information from the poorly-paid Hungarians who had participated in the production of the forgeries. They soon learned of Windischgraetz's activities. Within days, the Minister-President let it be known that he expected Windischgraetz to make a "noble gesture" and assume full responsibility for everything that had been done. And in the end, this is more or less what Windischgraetz did.

While in prison awaiting trial he received secret messages from Stresemann, Bauer, and his German friends, thanking him for not implicating them in the proceedings. Eventually, Prince Windischgraetz was sentenced to four years in prison. It is difficult to imagine what the consequences of success would have been: the counterfeit notes would have more than filled a railway car, and the face-value of the notes at prevailing prices was fifteen hundred million francs.

Source: Lajos Windischgraetz, *My Adventures and Misadventures*, pp. 129-174.

*　　　　*　　　　*

The most frequent forays of amateur diplomats in the twentieth century are to be found not in secret missions or in the activities of unseen advisers, but in the insinuation of political figures into affairs for which they have no responsibility. Organizations of various kinds feel that they must take a position on the important issues of world politics: municipalities declare themselves to be "nuclear-free"; university senates insist on boycotts of multinational corporations that do business with sovereign states whose social policies do not meet with their approval; officials seeking election attempt to use the nationalistic or xenophobic inclinations of their constituents in order to gain popularity. Though often well-informed and frequently well-intentioned, these interventions of outsiders are not usually welcomed by the professionals who are frequently placed in the position of having to deal with the consequences of their declarations.

Making the World Safe for Democracy

When "Big Bill Thompson" was campaigning for Mayor of Chicago in 1928 his speech writers began to run out of good material towards the end of the contest. Thus it was that he promised one night that if he were elected he would "keep the British Navy out of Lake Michigan".

This idea went over so well with his audience that the night before the election he announced that he was prepared to go even further: "If King George ever comes to Chicago," he proclaimed, "I will personally throw him out."

Someone in the crowd called out to ask: was he referring to King George III or King George V? To which the would-be statesman is said to have replied, "My God, don't tell me that there are two of them."

Source: Chester Bowles, *Promises to Keep: My Years in Public Life,*
p. 465.

*   *   *

At least "Big Bill" was not actually in the presence of George V or his ambassador to the United States; what he might have said or done in such a situation must be left to the imagination. But such situations are not unknown.

Facing the Dictator

In 1946, for instance, a group of American congressmen were planning a trip to the Soviet Union, and they let it be known that they expected the State Department to arrange a meeting with Stalin for them. Surprisingly, the request was granted—with consequences that came perilously close to disaster.

The congressmen duly arrived in Moscow, and were being shown the sights prior to their meeting with Stalin, which was to take place late one afternoon. Immediately prior to the meeting the visitors were to tour the Moscow subway system. Their host, George Kennan, having seen the glorious subway more than once, declined to accompany them but arranged to pick them up at 5:30 p.m. at the Mossovyet station. When 5:30, came however, there was no sign of the congressmen. Inquiries revealed that they were being entertained at "tea" somewhere deep in the bowels of the system. When the visitors eventually emerged a bare ten minutes before they were scheduled to meet with Stalin, Kennan discovered that tea was not all that they had been served: "varying amounts of vodka, depending on the stoutness of character and presence of mind of the individual concerned, had been poured into my charges while they were on the verge of their interview with the great Soviet leader."

The two limousines placed at their disposal immediately tore off in the direction of the Kremlin. As they approached the gate, which was guarded by the world's most elaborate security system, Kennan heard a raucous voice shouting from the back seat, "Who the hell is this guy Stalin, anyway? I don't know that I want to go up and see him. I think I'll get out."

Kennan knew that if anyone were missing from the group the whole meeting would be thoroughly ruined; elaborate arrangements had been made, including the submission of every passport to the Foreign Office. So he turned to the tipsy congressman and told him that he would do nothing of the sort: "You will sit right there where you are and remain with the party."

The limousines passed the inspection at the gate. A car full of armed guards escorted them at the front, while another followed from behind. As they proceeded up the short incline that led into the heart of the Kremlin, the same voice was heard again: "What if I biff the old codger one in the nose?"

Kennan's heart froze. He spoke as earnestly as he could to the elected representative of the American people, and enlisted the support of some of the other, more sober, congressmen in containing the exuberance of the one. He came along meekly enough to Stalin's office, where he sat facing him at the end of the long table, doing "nothing more disturbing than to leer and wink once or twice at the bewildered dictator, thus making it possible for the invisible gun muzzles, with which the room was no doubt studded, to remain sullenly silent."

The interview passed without further incident, but it was an educational experience for Kennan nevertheless. When taken with other episodes of a similar kind, it gradually induced in him a deep scepticism about the value of "people-to-people" contacts for the improvement of international relations.

Source: George F. Kennan, *Memoirs, 1925-1950*, pp. 275-77.

Spies, Skullduggery, and other Sensations

Although much of diplomacy is conducted in a highly refined and formalized atmosphere, there are those moments when diplomats behave more like James Bond than characters in a Henry James novel.

A Difficult Meeting

On the morning of 17 October 1942 an urgent message was received by General Eisenhower at his office in London from General Marshall in Washington, relaying a surprising report from the Counsellor of the American Embassy in Algiers. The French General, Charles Mast, currently commander in Algiers and the best contact that the United States had in North Africa, wanted to hold a secret rendezvous to discuss plans for the proposed Allied operations in North Africa.

As part of Operation *Torch*, the Allied counterattack in North Africa, the American and British planners had thus far been counting on some resistance from the French. This message suggested, however, that there was some prospect of arranging for cooperation instead, and implied that General Henri Giraud, who had been captured by the Germans early in the war but had managed to escape, might be able to make his way to Algeria to take over the command of French forces in the region. The U.S. Counsellor reported that, shortly after he arrived in Algiers, he had a secret interview with the head of French Intelligence who told him that both German and Japanese sources reported that the Allies were planning an attack on Dakar, Casablanca, or both. The Germans were urging the French to take precautions against such an attack, and had implied that they might themselves occupy French North Africa if no action were taken. The Axis was reported to have about 100,000 troops massed along the Tunisian frontier. The Counsellor further suggested that Admiral Jean Darlan, perhaps the strongest figure in the French government at Vichy, might be prepared to come to Africa and to bring the French fleet with him. If he did, the French military and naval forces in North Africa would surely obey his command. Under these circumstances, the possibility of winning the cooperation of the French for the Allies was most attractive.

Eisenhower and Churchill immediately put together a team of five experts, led by General Mark Clark (Eisenhower's deputy commander), to undertake the secret mission.

Mast's message had stipulated a specific place for the rendezvous: a lonely house on the shore about sixty miles west of Algiers; a specific time: a mere four days away; and a specific mode of transportation for the American negotiators: submarine. It was decided to send the team to Gibraltar in two Flying Fortresses—a risky operation, as no B-17 had previously attempted to land at the field in Gibraltar, and it was uncertain whether a landing could be accomplished. Consequently, the team was divided between two planes, so that if one were lost, the remaining members could carry on with the mission. From Gibraltar they would be taken to the Algerian coast by a British submarine, which was given a specific latitude and longitude at which it was to surface on the night of 21 October. A single, steady white light would be shone from a window of the house if the coast were clear and the landing could proceed.

General Clark, disguised as a lieutenant-colonel, spent most of the night of 18 October awake, waiting for the bad weather to clear, keeping out of sight of the personnel at the Polbrook bomber base, and worrying that his team could not reach the rendezvous in time—not to mention that the whole thing might be an elaborate Nazi trap to capture him and thus jeopardize the whole of the *Torch* operation.

By 6 a.m. of the 19th the weather cleared sufficiently for the planes to take off, but without a fighter escort (for fear of attracting too much attention) and with the pilots under strict instructions to avoid landing in Spain or Portugal no matter what the circumstances. The planes did manage to make their way successfully to the landing in Gibraltar, but before the team could get out the British rushed up to tell them to remain seated, that German agents would be observing them from Spanish soil a mere 300 yards away. The officers on the team were advised to take off their hats and coats, while a big car with drawn curtains pulled up as close to the plane as possible. The team quickly jumped out and were taken to the governor's house, where they remained while Clark discussed the submarine plans with British navy officials—who were less than optimistic about the chances of success, given the heavy shore patrols and spotting planes along the Algerian coast. Nevertheless, the mission was bound to go ahead; the team was taken on board the submarine H.M.S. *Seraph*, where the six-foot-two Clark discovered that he could get to the "head" only by crawling along the passage on all fours.

The submarine, which was an old and slow one, eventually arrived at the appointed destination, but too late to permit safely the planned disembarkation of the team. Fortunately, a message had reached the French on shore that there might be some delay, and they were prepared to try again the next night. At midnight of the second night the light from the house on the shore was spotted, and the team made their way into four little "folbots"—collapsible, wood-framed canvas canoes—to paddle their way through the remaining two miles of surf.

Finally, the team arrived on the beach and scrambled to hide under the cover of the olive trees located at one end of the beach, where they were greeted by the same American Counsellor who had sent the initial message; "Welcome to North Africa." Clark, who had rehearsed a speech in French, could only respond with, "I'm damn glad we made it."

They were taken to the house, where the Arab servants had been sent away, to await the arrival of General Mast, who was driving out the sixty miles from Algiers. Clark managed to grab a little sleep while they waited. Shortly after 5 a.m. the American general was sharing a *petit déjeuner* of coffee, bread and jam, and sardines with the French general, while they discussed military strategy and the situation in North Africa. Mast proved willing to place the French forces under his command at the disposal of the Allies. They discussed a hypothetical Allied invasion, which the French general preferred to take place in the south of France; Clark could not tell him that *Torch* was much more than hypothetical, that General Patton had already set out from the United States with a contingent of the American invasion force. But Mast assured him that, if the Germans attacked French North Africa, the army there would fight them in any case, although he expected that the French navy might resist any orders given by him or Giraud.

They were continuing their discussion of strategy after a lunch of chicken with hot Arab sauce, red wine and oranges—cooked up by the owner of the house and one of Mast's junior officers—when the telephone rang: the police would be at the house in a few minutes. The French officers scrambled to change into civilian clothes; one of them grabbed a suitcase and ran for the car, which immediately took off in the direction of Algiers; others fled through the windows and disappeared into the brush along the beach. The British commandos who had aided the American team in getting ashore were sleeping upstairs; Clark dashed up to tell them to grab the canoes and hide in the brush. But there was no time. The owner of the house locked up the room containing the boats, while the remaining occupants rushed down through a trap door in the patio into a wine cellar, taking with them bags of incriminating French documents, which would make things pretty tough on them if they were discovered.

It was pitch black in the cellar, and those hiding there could hear every word spoken above; they had to keep absolutely still. The owner, the American Counsellor and two others remained above, drinking, singing and acting as jovially as they could. The police had been tipped off by the Arab servants who had been suspicious about being sent away and who had seen footprints on the beach. The police searched corners and behind furniture while Clark knelt at the foot of the stairs in the cellar, carbine in hand, ready to fight his way out. One of the British commandos was seized by a coughing fit: "General," he whispered to Clark, "I'm afraid I'll choke."

"I'm afraid you won't!" the general replied, slipping the unfortunate soldier the wad of gum that he had been chewing on. The soldier later commented that he had been surprised American chewing gum was so flavourless; Clark didn't tell him that he'd already chewed out all the flavour.

The French police continued their search for half an hour before leaving; but they obviously suspected something, and announced that they were returning to Algiers to ask for further instructions. Those hiding in the cellars made a dash for the beach; by this time, however, the wind had come up, making a canoe trip out to the submarine extremely hazardous. Clark and the leader of the commandos decided to experiment; they stripped down to shorts and undershirt, knowing that they would be soaked, and headed for the most promising spot, where they were immediately overturned by a wave. They returned to the woods to wait and hide. One Frenchman was sent to the nearest village to see if he could buy or rent a fishing boat to take them to the submarine, but he failed to find anyone willing to risk such a mysterious mission.

By midnight the police had failed to return; Clark was cold, wet, nearly naked, and very hungry; they had not eaten since lunch. He decided to risk going back to the house for some food and clothes; the owner was less than happy to see him again, but agreed to give him some things. Just as Clark was putting some bread and a couple of bottles of wine under a sweater, the police showed up. He dashed out of the house in his bare feet, jumped over the cement wall separating the house from the beach, and landed on the path some ten feet below. It was 1.30 a.m. by the time he rejoined the others.

After waiting for two more hours, the group decided that they had to make a try to get out to the submarine. They took one boat to the most promising looking spot along the beach, stripped, and waded out into the cold water, trying to push it through the breakers. They got through the first one all right, and Clark heaved a sigh of relief. "Just then the second loomed up ahead, gleaming just a little in the starlight and appearing about a hundred feet high. I knocked Wright's Navy hat off trying to call his attention to what was coming, and he grabbed it in mid-air." Miraculously, they made it through this breaker and found themselves in the clear. The other boats followed their route, but every one of them capsized. Their bags and the brief cases containing the secret papers were soaked. They paddled for what seemed like hours before they finally spotted the outline of the *Seraph* in the blackness.

Each of the boats eventually reached the submarine safely, but as the last one approached, an enormous wave knocked it against the side of the submarine and broke its frame; the boat filled with water and disappeared, along with the musette bag. This was a dangerous clue to leave behind: the folbots had air pockets at either end, which might keep the wreck afloat; if it washed up on shore it could cause real trouble, especially for their associates who had remained behind. As daybreak was now close, however, they had no choice but to submerge and leave the wrecked boat to its fate. It was never found.

As they went below, everyone was thoroughly soaked and completely exhausted. Clark asked the lieutenant in charge, "Haven't I heard somewhere about the British Navy having a rum ration, even on submarines?"

"Yes, sir," answered the lieutenant, "but on submarines only in emergencies."

"Well," Clark said, "I think this is an emergency. What about a double rum ration?"

The lieutenant agreed that this would be possible, if an officer of sufficient rank would sign the order.

"Will I do?" Clark asked.

The mission ended with Clark signing a formal written order for the dispensing of a double rum ration to the crew and passengers of the submarine.

Source: Mark W. Clark, *Calculated Risk*, pp. 67-87.

*   *   *

A somewhat less adventurous exercise in clandestine diplomacy, but equally illuminating, was that conducted by John Deane, on special assignment from the Joint Chiefs of Staff to Moscow during the Second World War.

Negotiating with the NKVD

Toward the end of 1943 Deane undertook to establish a working arrangement between the Office of Strategic Services, headed by Major General William Donovan, and Russian Secret Intelligence. The British had already established a Mission of their Secret Operations Executive in Moscow, and Donovan, in November of that year, had succeeded in getting the approval of the President to establish a similar Mission by the OSS Donovan himself came to Moscow shortly before Christmas to participate directly in the negotiations to establish the working arrangements with the NKVD

Two days after Christmas, Donovan and Deane, accompanied by Chip Bohlen as interpreter, arrived at the Commissariat of Internal Affairs for a meeting with Lieutenant General P.M. Fitin, head of the Soviet External Intelligence Service, and Major General A.P. Ossipov, head of the section conducting subversive activities in enemy countries. "We were met at the door by members of the police," Deane recalls, "and whisked to the office where our meeting was to be held with an eerie quietness that was a bit chilling."

They were introduced to the Soviet Generals. Fitin, who seemed about forty, was wearing an army uniform with blue piping to indicate his police status; he was smooth-shaven with long blond hair and blue eyes; he had a pleasing smile, "and did not impress us at all as a man who would be high in the circles of the secret police." Ossipov was shorter, with brown eyes, wavy brown hair and a sallow complexion; he wore civilian clothes, spoke English perfectly, and quickly impressed the Americans as being smooth and suave.

As Donovan entered the room, he spotted a seat that faced a light which would shine in the face of whoever sat there. He went out of his way to sit in this particular seat, which was obviously intended for those unlucky souls who were required to account for their activities to the police. He announced to the Soviet Generals that he was now ready for the third degree. Fitin and Ossipov took the joke in good humour, and a productive and agreeable meeting followed in which the two sides agreed to an exchange of representatives between Moscow and Washington.

Donovan, who had quickly accomplished his purpose in coming to Moscow, was now anxious to return to Washington—but it proved easier to negotiate with the Soviets than to get away from them. The Americans planned to have Donovan fly back to the United States via Cairo in the special four-engine plane that Ambassador Harriman and General Deane had brought with them to Russia as a transport aircraft, and which they had kept there for their use. The four-engine plane offered the advantage of being able to fly directly from Moscow to Teheran without refuelling, whereas the smaller two-engine planes of the Russian Civil Air Administration had to stop once, and frequently twice, for refuelling. Because of the short hours of daylight and the risk of delays due to bad winter weather at Moscow or any of the refuelling stops, at least one more day would be added to the journey if the smaller plane was used. When Harriman asked permission for Donovan to leave in the American plane, the request was flatly refused on the grounds that it was authorized solely for the use of the Ambassador.

Harriman protested vigorously that to unnecessarily delay Donovan's departure, whose duties required his immediate return to Washington, was unfriendly and detrimental to the war effort. But Molotov, the Soviet Foreign Minister, refused to budge. He did agree to set up one of their special two-engine planes for Donovan's use, however. For the next eleven days Donovan's party, the Harrimans and General Deane "would get up at six in the morning and go in sub-zero weather to the airport. Just as the plane was about to take off we would be told that the weather in Stalingrad, Astrakhan, or Baku was bad and there would be no flight that day." The group would return to the Embassy to hold a war council over breakfast, where they invariably agreed that Harriman should see Molotov again. The result was always the same until finally, on the eleventh day, the Foreign Minister agreed that Donovan could use the American plane with the proviso that it would not be returned to Russia until a formal agreement covering its use there had been reached. Donovan left the following day. After this experience the plane was kept at Cairo and was used only to shuttle Harriman or Deane in and out of the Soviet Union.

The OSS-NKVD agreement proved as difficult as the flight from Moscow. Arrangements for the exchange of Missions were going smoothly when, in March 1944, the Ambassador received a telegram from President Roosevelt indefinitely postponing the project. Harriman and Deane attempted to change his mind, but Roosevelt replied that domestic political considerations within the United States prevented him from altering the decision, and assured them that Stalin would understand the situation. Meanwhile, they were to emphasize that the exchange was to be delayed only because of timing. Quite clearly, the possible political ramifications of introducing members of the NKVD into the US during an election year could have been tremendous.

General Deane now faced the unpleasant task of telling the Russians of the President's decision. He telephoned Fitin, who set up a meeting and sent over one of his men to take Deane to the meeting place. "At about six-thirty a typical bomb tosser in a long black overcoat, thick glasses, and a disreputable black hat appeared at my office, saying that Fitin had sent him." Deane suggested that they take his car, which was sitting near the entrance, but his escort declined, taking him instead to a long black limousine with dark curtains on all the windows.

Deane told his chauffeur to follow them, which apparently did not go down very well with his escort, who fired some instructions in Russian to his own driver as they got in, and who then settled back into his seat in silence. The streets that day were a mass of slush as a result of a thaw that followed a heavy snowfall. "We careened away from my office, up one street and down another, following a zigzag course at a tremendous rate of speed for perhaps twenty minutes." Deane realized that the driver was trying to lose his chauffeur so that he would not know where he was being taken. "The slushy snow was thrown in a fan-shaped stream far onto the crowded sidewalks, and people attempting to get on streetcars were drenched as we passed them."

The Russian driver could have saved himself the trouble: Deane's Buick was much faster than any Russian car, and his chauffeur enjoyed putting his foot to the floor. "Sure enough, when we emerged from behind the curtains in front of a dilapidated apartment house in a neighbourhood that was strange to me, there was Naum parked in back of us with his motor turned off and looking very bored."

Deane never met Generals Fitin and Ossipov in the same place twice. They apparently kept hide-outs all over town. "On this occasion we climbed a few flights of stairs, a door was opened cautiously while I was identified and then was thrown open by Ossipov, who invited me in. I found a table set with vodka, cognac, fruit, and chocolates, and they insisted that I indulge." Dean hesitated to join them in any serious drinking, but found that the vodka stiffened his courage in giving them the bad news. And perhaps it mellowed his hosts, who took the news as well as the President had suggested they would. They agreed that the co-ordination between the two agencies could be carried on in Moscow, with Deane acting on behalf of Donovan. This arrangement lasted throughout the remainder of the war.

Shortly after the clandestine meeting in the dilapidated apartment block, Deane received an invitation from Fitin and Ossipov to dine at the *Aragvi*, Moscow's only restaurant-night club. Dinner there cost $45 US per plate, so Deane, who had never entered the place, was delighted to accept. "We found a beautifully appointed restaurant with deep rugs, soft lights, and enough room for twenty or thirty tables, most of which were empty." At each end of the high-ceilinged room was a balcony, one of which held a string orchestra, while the other contained the private dining room in which Deane was entertained. "We left the door to our balcony open and could thus look down on the diners below and at the orchestra in the balcony opposite us. It was a setting such as...I would not have believed existed in Moscow."

While they had pre-dinner cocktails, Deane told his hosts the story of the mad ride through the streets of Moscow, stressing the humour of their driver trying to shake off his chauffeur, who loved nothing more than driving fast. After having thought about this through the dinner, Fitin explained that Deane was taken in such a roundabout way to the meeting place because his driver knew that he was going to be late for the appointment and did not wish his guest to be embarrassed by arriving there first. Deane remarked that they had gone at a tremendous rate of speed in trying to be late; and why, he wondered, did Soviet officials all have their cars fitted out with heavy black curtains? "Fitin's reply was that the curtains prevented the occupants from becoming sunburned, and with that I surrendered."

The dinner was wonderful, but Deane could not help wondering throughout what motives the NKVD officials had in mind. He found out after dinner, when Ossipov took him into a corner and whispered that he had some very important information for him: Soviet agents had overheard some American engineers who were assisting in the construction of an oil refinery in Baku discussing the forthcoming election in the United States. One of them had described Roosevelt as a "son of a bitch who should be taken out and shot." Deane thanked them profusely and gave them his assurance that corrective action would be taken, but attempted also to explain that Americans didn't usually take such talk very seriously.

Afterwards, he was sorely tempted "to cable the story to President Roosevelt and thank him for being the inspiration of the most delicious dinner we had thus far had in Moscow."

Source: John R. Deane, *The Strange Alliance: The Story of Our Efforts at Wartime Co-operation with Russia*, pp. 50-59.

*   *   *

Clandestine diplomacy need not necessarily revolve around spies, secret agents and fifth-columnists. It sometimes occurs at the highest levels of diplomacy and politics—which can make the arrangements all the more complicated and challenging.

The Secretive Diplomat

In February 1970 the North Vietnamese, after considerable hesitation, responded favourably to an American suggestion that the two sides should hold secret discussions, away from the public limelight of the formal peace talks in Paris. It had already been announced that Le Duc Tho, a member of the North Vietnamese Politburo, fifth man in the political hierarchy, and their principal diplomatic negotiator (in spite of his misleading status as "Special Adviser" to Xuan Thuy, the chief of North Vietnam's delegation to the Paris peace talks) would be in Paris to attend the forthcoming French Communist Party Congress. Although it would not seem of any particular significance that he was in Paris, getting Henry Kissinger, the American negotiator, there without causing a stir was going to be more challenging.

The arrangements for Kissinger were left to General Vernon Walters, the US defense attaché in Paris, who delighted in arranging clandestine meetings. Kissinger left from Andrews Air Force Base near Washington on a weekend or on a holiday, to provide better cover. He took one of the Presidential fleet of Boeing 707s, accompanied only by a secretary and one or two members of his staff; the plane's manifest recorded the trip as a training flight to check out itineraries for Presidential travel. The 707 landed at a French Air Force base in central France, where Mirage fighters and KC-135 tankers roughly resembled the President's plane. The plane carrying Kissinger touched down only long enough to let him off, and his secretary carried on to Frankfurt; the plane disappeared from radar screens for no more than twenty-five minutes. Kissinger and his staff then boarded a Mystère-20 executive jet belonging to President Pompidou and headed for a small airport used by private airplanes near Paris.

General Walters met the Kissinger team at the private airport and led them to an unmarked, rented Citroën. This particular part of the plan introduced a bureaucratic complication: no funds were available to reimburse Walters for a trip that could not be accounted for by the Paris Embassy. The General drove the team to his apartment building in the Neuilly section, entered by the underground garage, and took the elevator up to the apartment, where Kissinger would be introduced to the housekeeper as a visiting American general, "Harold A. Kirschman".

After spending the night in Walters' apartment, the group headed off the next day in the Citroën to a house in a lower middle-class neighbourhood on the outskirts of Paris. The house might have been owned by a foreman who worked in one of the factories located nearby: there was a small living room that connected to an even smaller dining room, which opened onto a garden. And there the negotiators secretly sat, in two rows of red-upholstered easy chairs, six North Vietnamese facing four Americans. And there they continued to sit, at intervals, for the next year and a half while they decided the fate of Vietnam.

Only once did the plan fail to work smoothly. While flying over for a meeting in March, the pilots of Kissinger's plane noticed that the hydraulic system for the landing gear was not working; this necessitated a landing at a spot other than the French air force base in order for repairs to be done. They were forced to fly into Frankfurt to land at the Rhein-Main airport; but no one there was expecting their arrival and, as the State Department had not been told of the trip, they could not contact the German authorities to arrange for the French plane to come and pick them up. Communications saved the day: one of Kissinger's assistants managed to make contact with Walters in Paris via a radio hookup through Washington.

Walters went to the Elysée Palace, where President Pompidou himself gave the authority for his jet to meet Kissinger in Germany. By the time the American plane arrived in Frankfurt, the French jet was already there and waiting for them; they landed, switched planes and were airborne again within ten minutes. Kissinger later explained that "Walters claimed that West German cooperation was speeded up by their belief, encouraged by him, that the passenger was a secret girlfriend of Pompidou's." National stereotyping can sometimes be helpful, even in conducting clandestine diplomacy.

Source: Henry Kissinger, *White House Years*, pp. 438-40.

*　　　　*　　　　*

Readers who remember the Kissinger era in American diplomacy might be inclined to regard the clandestine meetings between political opponents as representative of his singular obsession with subterfuge rather than of a recurring phenomenon in the behaviour of high officials. But in fact long before Kissinger, and well before the days of jet-travel and satellite communication, more than one precedent had been set—as an episode concerning Under-Secretary of State Sumner Welles will illustrate.

a.k.a. "Henry Smith"

In the desperate days at the beginning of the Second World War, the people of Belgium were facing the future with a sickening apprehension of what was about to happen. Although fighting had yet to break out in the west, they could hardly help but anticipate that the German armies would once again traverse their territory in order to strike at France. Thus, when it was announced that Sumner Welles would visit Rome, Berlin, Paris and London as a special emissary of President Roosevelt, the Belgians desperately regarded the announcement as a sign of hope that the timely diplomatic intervention of the United States might succeed in forestalling an invasion. When the White House made the announcement of the mission, it became the most significant news story of the day.

King Leopold immediately contacted the US Ambassador to Belgium, John Cudahy, pleading for Belgium to be included in the Welles itinerary. But the Ambassador pointed out that it would be impossible to arrange this without slighting the other small states of western Europe. The King suggested a compromise: would the Ambassador meet with Welles before he went to Berlin, and convey a message to him from the King? Cudahy promised to try; he called Rome and it was agreed that Welles would interrupt his journey to Berlin in Zurich. They also agreed that it would create a sensation in the press of Europe if it were discovered that the American Under-Secretary of State was breaking off his trip to Berlin in order to confer with the American Ambassador to Belgium, and they feared the consequences of creating false illusions and unrealistic hopes that might be conjured up by journalistic imagination.

Thus it was that the Under-Secretary of State two days later registered at the Bord du Lac Hotel in Zurich under the name of "Henry Smith". When the incognito diplomat emerged from the hotel during the course of the afternoon, to go for a stroll along the shores of Lake Zurich with the Consul General, he was disguised in dark glasses, "like a fleeing fugitive of the law." When Welles was ready to meet with Cudahy, he sent his secretary up to the Ambassador's room; only after he was able to give the password did Cudahy admit him into the room; the secretary undertook a careful reconnaissance of the stairs before calling for the Ambassador to dash down to see the Under-Secretary on the floor below. The two diplomats spent several hours discussing the European situation before Cudahy secretively returned to his room.

Early the next morning, long before the other guests had arisen, the mysterious guest boarded the train to Brussels. Every possible precaution had been taken to keep the meeting of the night before a secret. Nevertheless, the following day the Paris *Soir* confidently announced that a conference had taken place between the American Ambassador to Belgium and Mr. Sumner Welles in Zurich; the news broke just as Welles arrived in Berlin.

> Source: John Cudahy, *The Armies March: A Personal Report*, pp. 67-68.

*　　　　　*　　　　　*

A somewhat less cinematic example of the secretive aspects of diplomacy took place in London during the Second World War.

Strange Encounters

On 10 February 1944 an emissary from the Polish Underground Army found himself in London, standing in front of 10 Downing Street, deeply impressed by the fact that the head of government in Britain lived in an ordinary house of its period, with a brass knocker and guarded by only one policeman, armed with no more than a rubber truncheon. Lieutenant Jan Nowak was struck by the difference between this building and Hitler's monumental chancellery, which was surrounded by bunkers and barbed wire. Having spent most of the war underground, working as a courier and emissary, he was thrilled to find himself at the nerve-centre of the Allied war effort against Nazi Germany.

Nowak brought with him an important message from Warsaw for the Prime Minister, but he was first taken to meet Churchill's special adviser, Major Desmond Morton, who asked him to explain the contents of the message. Nowak mentioned three things: he was to convey to Churchill the hope and the confidence that the Polish people placed in him; he was to explain the reasons for the drops of arms and equipment that they had requested; and he was to hand him an anti-German pamphlet that the underground had dedicated to him.

Morton explained that the Prime Minister was probably too busy to receive the Polish emissary and, in any event, requests for arms and equipment ought to be directed through the proper channels. Josef Zaranski, Prime Minister Mikolajczyk's political adviser, who had accompanied Nowak to Downing Street, assured Morton that Nowak was serving in an official capacity as an emissary of the Polish underground army, and that their Prime Minister had asked that Nowak be given an audience because he believed it would be useful for Churchill to hear first-hand a description of the situation inside Poland. Morton replied noncommittally.

The Poles and Churchill's adviser then began a long discussion of the Home Army. Morton wanted details of the underground's strength, its deployment, its arms and equipment, the tactics it was using and its plans for the future. Nowak replied as best he could, but suggested that full and accurate information would best be obtained from Section Six of the Polish general staff in London. Morton's reply was rather surprising: he complained that while France, Yugoslavia, Greece, Czechoslovakia and Bulgaria had provided full information concerning the activities of their underground movements, Poland had supplied none. Nowak and Zaranski were astonished. Morton explained that only four days ago a meeting of the chiefs of staff had been held, which was presided over by Churchill himself; they discussed how they might help the various underground organizations in occupied countries, but they could arrive at no decisions concerning assistance to Poland because the Polish government had not supplied the necessary data.

The Poles left the meeting badly shaken. They knew that their Section Six provided answers to any questions asked by the Special Operations Executive concerning their underground operations, and that detailed reports were then passed on by the SOE to the government. Why, then, had Morton made such strange accusations?

The next day Nowak was summoned to meet with his superiors: he was to take a taxi and report to Upper Belgrave Street. There a worried and irritated Colonel Protasewicz immediately asked him, "What have you done, Lieutenant?" Nowak simply replied that he had no idea what the Colonel was talking about.

A representative from the SOE, Colonel Perkins, explained that Major Morton had telephoned their office to complain that the emissary of the Polish underground army had disavowed all the data that had previously been supplied by the Polish staff. According to Morton, he had, during their meeting, spread out a map that had been supplied by the Polish Section Six to the SOE; the map, which claimed to show the disposition and numerical strengths of the units of the Home Army had been declared by Nowak to be "sheer fantasy".

Futhermore, Nowak was reported to have argued that in the present political situation the Polish underground movement would have to limit itself to self-defense.

Nowak pleaded with them that Zaranski ought to be summoned to corroborate his side of the story. He arrived before long, listened to Perkins' story, and was utterly confused: "In my whole career," he cried, "I have never heard anything like this."

They decided to consult with Mikolajczyk and their Chief of Staff, who advised them that Zaranski should demand a minute of the conversation from Morton and send him a copy of his own version. Everyone involved in this curious affair was at a loss to understand what was at the bottom of the intrigue.

Nowak was taken by Zaranski to see Mikolajczyk, who, after listening to their report, gloomily told them that, "If Morton's reply to the letter and minutes do not settle the matter, you must go to Ambassador O'Malley and ask for an explanation of what all this means." He then muttered something to the effect that, "This was the worst possible moment."

After they left, Nowak asked Zaranski what this last remark had meant. "He was probably thinking about his last conversation with Churchill and Eden at Chequers a few days ago," Zaranski replied. Although he had not actually been present, he had heard that Churchill had once more insisted on the Curzon line as the basis for negotiation of the Polish-Soviet border, as well as some personnel changes in the Polish government to meet Stalin's wishes. "Otherwise, he threatened, Britain herself, without Polish participation, would come to an understanding with Moscow. He was quite brutal at times. Mikolajczyk refused, but did not reject the possibility of a compromise. Polish-British relations are tense at present."

When Morton received Zaranski's minute of their controversial conversation, he refused to respond in kind; although he had been pleased to meet with Nowak, "I hardly feel that what he had to say was of sufficient importance to warrant an agreed record."

Zaranski's report was sent to O'Malley, the British Ambassador to the Polish government-in-exile, who was visibly upset by it and promised to do what he could to clarify the situation. A few days later he admitted that he had not been able to learn anything about it at the Foreign Office.

Nowak, who had come to know O'Malley and his family quite well on his trips to London, was visiting their house on the Chelsea Embankment one day afterwards when he asked if the Ambassador could, confidentially, explain to him what Morton's strange behaviour might mean. O'Malley admitted that he could only guess, that he did not really understand it himself. In Churchill's entourage, he said, were a few close friends from prewar days whose attitude to Poland was unfriendly, or even hostile: Lord Beaverbrook, Brendan Bracken and Lord Cherwell. Morton, who had worked in War Office Intelligence before the war and had supplied Churchill with confidential information with which to attack Chamberlain's policy, belonged to this group. A couple of weeks later Nowak became involved in another episode that tended to confirm that O'Malley's guess had been accurate. Section Six called him in to verify the identity of an Englishman who claimed to know him and to have had contacts with the Home Army in Poland. Nowak was surprised, but delighted, to see that the man was Ronald Jeffery; he was able to confirm that Jeffery had proven himself to be an extremely courageous and intelligent corporal who had engaged in commando activities against the Germans, learned Polish and German, and undertaken various missions to Germany. O'Malley invited Jeffery to tea and was so impressed by his reports that he arranged an audience for him with Churchill and Eden. Jeffery confirmed all that the Poles had told the British about Poland's situation.

The appointment with Eden had already been arranged when British counter-intelligence intervened and asked for a postponement. They demanded that Jeffery give them a detailed explanation of how he had escaped from Poland; until he did so he was to refrain from contacts with the press and the public. The interrogation continued for several months, after which he was given a military assignment outside London. The meetings with Eden and Churchill never took place.

In the meantime, Nowak attended a session of the House of Commons on 22 February at which Churchill was scheduled to give a major address on the conduct of the war and on foreign policy. Nowak knew that for days prior to the speech, Polish diplomats had been urging the Prime Minister not to touch upon Polish affairs and not to express support for Stalin's demands in public. "I waited, tense and excited, for the arrival of one of the greatest statesmen of our century."

When Churchill finally began to speak, he announced that Germany was still strong, that there was no reason to believe that she was ready to collapse, and that the Allies were preparing to throw all their forces into a combined offensive that would open a second front in the spring or the summer. But he then went on to state that during the war all ideological differences between the Allies must be subordinated to the joint effort to defeat the common enemy. In conjunction with this, he launched into a denunciation of Mihajlovic, the leader of the Chetniks in Yugoslavia, while praising the efforts of Tito and his partisans. On the other hand, Churchill declared that the communist partisans in Greece were not concentrating on the defeat of their German occupiers, but were interested only in getting power for themselves.

The Polish observers in the House of Commons were deeply worried by the time Churchill began to discuss Poland. After praising the efforts of the valiant Poles and reminding the House that it was in Poland's defense that Britain had entered the war, he turned to the subject of Polish frontiers. The Prime Minister declared his support for the Russian annexation of Polish territories up to the Curzon line; Poland never had any right to these territories, which she had seized by force. Moreover, Russia had twice been attacked through Poland

and she had the right to safeguard her western border. Poland could be compensated for these losses with territories in the west. Churchill declared that he had Stalin's promise that Poland would be reinstituted as an independent state.

Nowak turned to see the response of the Soviet press attaché and the TASS correspondent. They were listening attentively and smiling, while an embassy official feverishly took notes. The emissary from the underground, who had arrived in London with such high hopes and with good news concerning the successes of the resistance, now saw that Stalin had been given the green light: Poland was open and waiting for him; he could do as he wished there without fear of conflict with the Allies.

It now became clear why Morton and the Prime Minister's office had resisted receiving the information provided by Nowak and Jeffery, and why they used their appearance in London to create the impression that the Poles were not cooperating sincerely with the Allies: they had no intention of lending credibility to the Polish case. After Churchill's speech, Nowak met Zaranski in the hallway. "What do you think about it all?" he asked.

Zaranski explained: "Churchill has repeated all that he and Eden have been telling Mikolajczyk at every meeting they have had since Teheran. The difference—unfortunately a very important one—is that he has now said it all in public."

Source: Jan Nowak, *Courier from Warsaw*, pp. 260-69.

*   *   *

*T*he connections between diplomacy and intelligence are numerous, but one recurring phenomenon is that of the "friendly" agent of a foreign government who, for political, ideological or personal reasons is prepared to pass along useful information. One such story involves a Second Secretary of the German Embassy and the negotiations leading to the Nazi-Soviet Pact between Hitler and Stalin in 1939.

Against the Grain

Hans Heinrich Herwarth von Bittenfeld, known to his friends as "Johnny" Herwarth, came to be very friendly with a member of the American Embassy staff in Moscow, Charles Bohlen. The two families spent many weekends together, skating, riding and, naturally, talking. "Johnny" had always been very frank in discussing international affairs with Bohlen, but the American was nevertheless rather surprised when, on 16 May 1939, the German passed along some secret information to him. Johnny had recently returned from a trip to Teheran, where he had accompanied the German Ambassador to Moscow, Werner von der Schulenberg, to the wedding of the Shah's daughter. While in Teheran, Johnny said, Schulenberg had been suddenly recalled to Berlin for a consultation with Hitler; although he did not know what was discussed or being envisioned, he anticipated that it meant some significant shift in German policy toward the Soviet Union.

Further evidence that "something was up" was indicated by the recall of the German military attaché to Berlin in the week previous to this, where he was asked whether the Soviet Union was militarily stronger than in September 1938. The Germans seemed to be assessing the prospect of a Soviet counter-attack should they decide to attack Poland.

Bohlen was already aware that Johnny opposed Nazi policy, although the German was careful to avoid saying so in public. Nevertheless, he did not understand why he was passing along this information when he knew that the government Bohlen represented was unfriendly to his own. Given the German diplomat's reputation for being a forthright and honest man, however, Bohlen decided to discuss the information with the new Chargé d'affaires, Grummon. As a result, a telegram was sent to the State Department in Washington; in the meantime, he resolved to stay in close contact with Johnny.

A few days later Bohlen was told by Johnny that Ribbentrop, the German Minister for Foreign Affairs, had instructed Ambassador Schulenberg to feel out the Soviets on the possibility of closer relations. On 20 May the American Embassy wired Washington that Ribbentrop, clearly reflecting Hitler's own views, had informed Schulenberg that "Communism had ceased to exist in the Soviet

Union; that the Communist International was no longer a factor of importance in Soviet foreign relations, and that consequently…no real ideological barrier remained between Germany and Russia." The German Ambassador had been warned to be extremely cautious in making his approach to the Soviets, as the German government feared alarming Japan. Without committing Germany to anything specific, the Ambassador was to convey this change in attitude; although this move could not be seen as a definite proposal to the Soviet Union, it might well be the prelude to one. Moreover, Bohlen reported, some Soviet officials in Berlin had recently been reported as conveying to the Germans that their own foreign policy "was now on a new basis".

Bohlen attempted to be as circumspect as he could in protecting the source of his information. He did not make notes during his discussions with Johnny, but later jotted down specific facts on a scrap of paper or on the back of an envelope. He wrote the telegrams to Washington in longhand himself. He would not risk dictating the telegrams, fearing that the embassy offices might be bugged. In Moscow, the only people who knew about Johnny and the information he was passing along were Bohlen and his wife, Grummon, and later, the new Ambassador, Laurence Steinhardt (who arrived in August). In Washington, the encoded reports went directly to the Secretary of State, Cordell Hull. Bohlen would not jeopardize his source by informing British and French diplomats in Moscow; Hull, however, called in their ambassadors in Washington and gave them the details of what was going on.

A few days after Schulenberg's meetings with Molotov, the Soviet Commissar for Foreign Affairs, and Potemkin, Molotov's deputy, Johnny met Bohlen and passed along the essence of the conversations. It seemed that nothing much had been achieved, as Molotov was unwilling to commit the Soviet Union to anything, and seemed to imply that the Soviets would consider only specific proposals from the Germans; given the German fear of alienating Japan, Johnny assumed that nothing more would be done until the current discussions between Germany and Japan had reached a conclusion. His assumption proved correct; Schulenberg was instructed to make no further approaches to the Soviets.

Meanwhile, the diplomatic community in Moscow was feverishly speculating on the possibility of a Nazi-Soviet *rapprochement*. Opinion was divided between those who believed that the Soviets were attempting to use the prospect as a method of putting pressure on the British and the French for a specific, binding guarantee of the Soviet Union's western frontier, and those who believed that the desire for *rapprochement* was genuine. Nothing much happened throughout June, as Ribbentrop continued to pursue his aim of drawing Japan into the Anti-Comintern Pact; but Bohlen learned from Johnny that, although Schulenberg had been instructed to put the discussions with the Soviets on ice, he had exceeded his instructions and kept the idea of a deal alive by maintaining his contacts with Molotov.

On June 28, following a trip to Berlin, Schulenberg again approached Molotov, and a few days later Johnny filled Bohlen in on the gist of their discussions, which Bohlen immediately reported to Washington. In essence, Schulenberg suggested that the new German attitude was symbolized by the disappearance in their press of any anti-Soviet articles. He indicated that his government still adhered to the 1926 nonaggression treaty with the Soviet Union, and was prepared to give new confirmation of this; Molotov, on his part, seemed more receptive to these advances than he had during May.

Bohlen remained uneasy about Johnny's role in this affair: why was he continuing to feed this information to an American? Their two countries were antagonistic toward one another, and Bohlen was giving him nothing in return. Moreover, Johnny was not behaving in the manner that might be expected of a conspirator: there were no whispered conversations, no guarded telephone calls, merely natural discussions while riding, playing tennis or having a drink.

Still, the information continued to come. Johnny told him that members of the German Embassy were confident that the Soviets would not reach an agreement with Britain and France because of their fear of antagonizing Hitler. Then, on 5 August, he reported that the Germans were now convinced that Molotov was serious about the prospect of an agreement with them. Schulenberg was doing everything in his power to convince Molotov that the anti-Comintern Pact was no longer operative, as the Soviet Union was no longer a "revolutionary" state. The Germans, he assured him, had no aggressive designs against the Soviet Union, via the Balkans or elsewhere, and they prepared to recognize the validity of Soviet interests in the Baltic, including Lithuania. Johnny nevertheless anticipated that it would take a considerable time to work out the details of any Nazi-Soviet agreement.

He was wrong. Arriving at a ball given at the German Embassy on August 15, Bohlen spotted Johnny standing in a corner and immediately approached him. Johnny pointed out that Schulenberg was not present; he had left for the Soviet Foreign Office following receipt of instructions from Hitler himself. Although he had not seen the instructions, Johnny heard that they went far in meeting the wishes of the Soviets. Bohlen later recalled thinking "that a momentous event was taking place at the Kremlin while I was eating pâté de foie gras and drinking champagne at the German Embassy." He whiled away the time by dancing and drinking, but tried to keep a clear head in order to transmit the new information to Washington after the party.

In the meantime Schulenberg appeared, urbane and smiling, and yet managing to avoid giving the impression that "he had just pulled off one of the greatest coups in modern diplomatic history." Johnny and Bohlen went off into a corner and, while they drank champagne and the music played, Johnny outlined the general nature of the agreement that had just been reached. If Bohlen could drop by the embassy tomorrow, Johnny promised to give him all the details.

When Bohlen came by the next day, Johnny said that he was now certain that there would be a pact, and that this would mean a quick attack on Poland. The Germans wanted the treaty signed quickly in order to begin their attack during the good autumn weather. Bohlen, although he was certain that the information was reliable, hedged slightly in communicating with Washington, as an agreement had not yet been signed and there was still the possibility of last-minute changes. When Bohlen's telegram arrived in Washington, the State Department took a sceptical view of it, as it seemed doubtful that a Marxist state could reach an agreement with such a deeply-despised enemy. Nevertheless, Cordell Hull called in the British and French ambassadors and conveyed a summary to them.

Ribbentrop arrived in Moscow a week later. His sudden arrival created some difficulties for the Soviets in providing a proper reception for him. They had no Nazi flags, and had to borrow some from a film studio that had been engaged in making anti-Nazi propaganda films. A band had to quickly learn the *"Horst Wessel"* song, which they then played at the airport, along with the *"Internationale"*. By 2 a.m. the next day the Nazi-Soviet Pact had been signed.

Bohlen's informant provided him with all the details of the agreement, including the secret protocol, in which eastern Poland, Estonia, Latvia, and Bessarabia were recognized as coming within the Soviet sphere of influence, while western Poland was recognized as within the German sphere. Johnny, sitting in his dark, panelled office in the German Chancery while he recited the details to Bohlen, became deeply depressed and said that he intended to go back to Germany to rejoin his regiment.

After the war Bohlen learned why Johnny Herwarth had run the risks involved in passing on secret information to the representative of a foreign government. Johnny, who was one-quarter Jewish, explained that even in the spring of 1939 he had been a member of an upper-class group pledged to resist the Nazi regime. He had hoped that, by placing information with western authorities concerning the possibility of a Nazi-Soviet accommodation, they might somehow succeed in preventing it. He recognized, however, that Germany enjoyed a number of advantages over Britain and France when it came to offering the Soviets a deal, and he had not been unduly optimistic that his information would have the desired effect. The resistance movement in which he participated was mainly sentimental; it was not well organized, and the plot to kill Hitler had yet to be conceived.

Johnny fought in the German army throughout the war, participating in the invasion of Poland, the invasion of France and the invasion of the Soviet Union. He came through without a scratch. He was temporarily out of Berlin, and in the Balkans, at the time of the attempt on Hitler's life, which was led by Count von Stauffenberg. When he returned to his office he found five memos from his secretary telling him that Stauffenberg had called him urgently on the day of the *coup*. "Johnny told me that this was the only time he lost his nerve. His legs gave way and he slumped to the floor." He realized that if the Gestapo had discovered these memos he would certainly have been executed.

When the war ended, Herwarth re-entered the diplomatic service. He became the first Ambassador to London appointed by the new government of West Germany.

Source: Charles E. Bohlen, *Witness to History, 1929-1969*, pp. 68-87.

The Diplomat as Warrior

*W*artime *conditions impose unusual pressures and difficulties on diplomats, who may find themselves interned, imprisoned, isolated or shipped off to unknown destinations. Like men under fire at the front, these conditions sometimes throw aspects of individual character into bolder relief than in peacetime. Some discover that they are able to make the best of a bad situation; others demonstrate a capacity for making a bad situation worse.*

The Greater East Asia Golf & Country Club

On 8 December, 1941, following the attack on Pearl Harbor, the Japanese government ordered the functions of the United States Embassy and Consulates to be suspended. It was "recommended" that all members of the embassy be congregated in the embassy compound in order that they might be accorded protection and living facilities. All communication with the outside was to cease, and permission had to be sought from the Japanese authorities before anyone could leave.

Under these circumstances, the Ambassador, Joseph C. Grew, wished to do whatever he could to keep up the spirits of those confined to the compound without giving the appearance of taking the whole situation too lightly. Thus, he felt that he had to deny permission to hold a dance in the community room of the chancery.

As Mrs. Grew was an enthusiastic bridge player, he did encourage daily bridge parties at their residence after lunch and, as a keen golfer, he could not resist the suggestion of the Assistant Naval Attaché that he be permitted to construct a golf course for chip shots and putts in the lower compound. The course was quickly christened *"The Greater East Asia Black Sulphur Springs Championship Golf Course"*—an allusion to a report that the Japanese in Washington had been interned in White Sulphur Springs—and opened on 13 December with a ceremony and a tournament, which was won by the future Ambassador to the Soviet Union, and Deputy Undersecretary of State, Charles "Chip" Bohlen.

In the diary that he kept throughout the confinement, Ambassador Grew, like any keen golfer, recorded many of his triumphs on the imaginatively-constructed course, which consisted of nine holes over 422 yards, with small putting greens "and everything". The most challenging hole forced the players to go around, or over, one of the apartment houses; the daring player who chose to go over the house obviously ran some risk in doing so, but after three weeks of play Grew was able to record that "only one window has been broken so far". Meanwhile, the fish in the reflection pool were having a lovely time, "if they like old golf balls". The Ambassador spent an hour golfing each day, and proudly recorded his first hole-in-one on 4 January, 1942.

Source: Joseph C. Grew, *Ten Years in Japan*, pp. 501-510.

*   *   *

The life of diplomats in wartime can certainly be more hazardous, and considerably less comfortable than the conditions described by Grew. They may be used as hostages, or they may be easy targets for carrying out reprisals for the unwelcome actions of their government.

The Prisoner of Sofia

Such was the case in Bulgaria during the First World War. Britain and France had landed forces at Salonika, in Greece, which had remained neutral. Worrying that the consuls of Germany, Austria-Hungary and Bulgaria would be in a position to report military movements to their governments, the British and the French, quite illegally, arrested the consuls and sent them away, in a warship, to an unknown destination.

When the Bulgarian government received word of this mistreatment of their consul, orders were immediately given to return the favour by arresting the French Consul and the British Vice-Consul. The Frenchman was promptly incarcerated, but Hurst, the Englishman, happened to walk into the rooms of the American Consul just as the order for his arrest was issued.

The American Consul, Lewis Einstein, decided to call on the Secretary-General of the Bulgarian Foreign Office, General Kosseff in order to clarify the situation. Kosseff insisted that they wished to arrest Hurst in order to protect him from an outraged populace; the Bulgarian people were so angered by the illegal act of the British in Greece that it would be necessary to shield him from a mob. Einstein replied that he did not believe that Hurst was in any danger, that he was prepared to run the risk involved by keeping him as his guest; if the Bulgarians attempted to arrest him, they could only do so by violating the American Legation. The Bulgarian General was not pleased and made no effort to hide the fierce hatred that he suddenly felt for the American.

There were some practical difficulties involved in attempting to offer asylum to the British Vice-Consul. To begin with, the American Legation was lodged in a hotel, and consisted of no more than two fair-sized rooms, one of which was Einstein's bedroom, the other an office; a third small room was used for keeping records, and it was here that he installed a bed for Hurst. What made things particularly awkward was that a small corridor separated the small room from the other two.

The day after the attempt to arrest Hurst, Einstein awoke to discover a number of plainclothes policemen loitering in the corridor. Their intention was clear: Hurst would be arrested the moment he set foot in the passage. Einstein dispatched a formal note to the Prime Minister of Bulgaria insisting that, although this corridor led to the hotel dining room, it was, nevertheless, an essential part of the Legation and, as such, the rules of extraterritoriality applied there as well: it was to be treated as American soil.

Despite the rather doubtful nature of this diplomatic theology, which argued the dual nature of a hallway, the Bulgarian Prime Minister apparently decided that it would be best to avoid an unpleasant incident with the government of the United States, and called off his sleuths.

But then an unexpected bombshell hit. Einstein received from Lansing, the U.S. Secretary of State, a telegram that read: "You may make strong representations in favour of Hurst but if the Bulgarian Government insists upon arresting him you will not continue to give him shelter in the American Legation." To make matters worse, this telegram had not been sent in cipher, but in the open, which almost certainly meant that the Bulgarian government had read the text before Einstein received it.

Einstein responded by sending a dispatch to Washington, refusing to participate in such a disgraceful surrender, and asking that if the State Department continued to insist that he submit, his resignation should be accepted at once. He did not, however, communicate this by telegram, sending it by diplomatic pouch instead, knowing that his refusal to carry out the order would not be received in Washington for several weeks.

The Bulgarian government, recognizing the shakiness of Einstein's position, resumed their earlier tactics. The plainclothes policemen reappeared in the corridor the next day, waiting to arrest Hurst whenever nature should compel him to leave his room. New tactics were called for: when such occasions occurred, Einstein was informed in order that he might take up a position at the head of a triangular bodyguard, the other members of which consisted of an Armenian clerk and a Macedonian messenger who had once been a rabbinical student. "The three of us would solemnly stand outside the door of the toilet until the Vice-Consul was able to return under our joint protection to the sanctuary of the bedroom."

The next logical step for the Bulgarians was to cut off the food supply to Hurst from the hotel; this was countered by Einstein sending the Macedonian messenger out into the town to forage for provisions. Then the hotel-keeper announced that his guests were so indignant at the action of the American Consul in harbouring an enemy subject that they threatened to leave his hotel; he therefore gave notice that he had let the rooms occupied by the legation, and that they had three days in which to clear out. Einstein ignored the notice. "After the three days were up, a Bulgarian lieutenant in uniform asked to see me. He was followed by a picket of eight men with bayonets on their rifles."

Clicking his heels and saluting the American Consul, the Bulgarian officer announced that he came on the order of the General Commandant of Sofia, who wished to put certain questions to Hurst. He guaranteed that no harm would befall the British Vice-Consul. Einstein in turn assured him that he had confidence in the guarantee of the Commandant, but asked for a simple statement in writing to the effect that Hurst would be returned to the American Legation in the same condition in which he had left it. While the officer considered this unforeseen request, the German hotel keeper peeked through the bayonets, and piped up to say, "Excuse me, Excellency, but you have not yet left your room, although the three days are over."

"Go to hell" was the American's terse reply.

The hotel keeper fled, followed by the Bulgarian officer, who clicked his heels once again, saluted and left. The next day the official Bulgarian agency at Bucharest reported that Hurst had been arrested. In reality, after this episode, Einstein was left in peace. Five weeks after the affair had begun, the Bulgarian Consul at Salonika was allowed to cross the frontier into Switzerland. The American Consul accompanied the British Vice-Consul back to the British Legation. They walked through the streets unnoticed.

Three months after the affair ended, Einstein received an instruction from Washington that his action, which had brought up several interesting new points of international law, had been officially approved.

Source: Lewis Einstein, *A Diplomat Looks Back*, pp. 158-164.

*   *   *

No doubt the British Vice-Consul found his experience of confinement less amusing than it appears in retrospect. Diplomats, although they have custom and law to protect them in otherwise perilous situations, are really at the mercy of their hosts—the extent of which might well depend on the threat of reprisal. The experience of confinement, isolation or internment may prove to be an enlight-

ening one in a number of ways, particularly when it seems demon-
strable that the state and the people that one is meant to be serving
apparently have such little regard for their loyal servants.

The Education of a Diplomat

Following the American declaration of war on Germany, George
Kennan—at that time serving in the embassy in Berlin—was summoned to the Foreign Office on a Saturday afternoon in the middle
of December to be told that all American personnel were required to
liquidate their residential establishments immediately and to report
in by eight o'clock the next morning, bringing with them no more
than two pieces of hand luggage. After a busy and sleepless night,
the staff gathered at the embassy "only to find the building, inside
and out, already guarded by members of the Gestapo, and ourselves
their prisoners."

The prisoners were taken in buses to the station, where they were
packed into two special trains and sent away for five months of
confinement under armed guard in a building on the outskirts of Bad
Nauheim; a few additional American officials and journalists, picked
up from other parts of Europe, were added to the company, which
eventually totalled 130. More than four months passed before their
government made any effort to communicate with them, which,
apparently, they could have done quite easily through the Swiss.

The experience was an educational one for Kennan, who bore the
immediate responsibility for disciplinary control of this group of
hungry, cold, and worried prisoners, as well as for their liaison with
their German captors. Every moment of his day was filled with the
cares, quarrels, jealousies and complaints of his colleagues, about
whom he learned a great deal: "the untrustworthiness and failure of
a minority at one end of the human spectrum; the rather passive
response to leadership on the part of a majority in the middle; the
extraordinary faithfulness, courage, and general excellence of a few."

He found the constant complaints about the food particularly
disillusioning. It was true that the interned diplomats received less
than ordinary prisoners of war were entitled to, and that they had none
of the Red Cross parcels that such prisoners received; but it was also

true that they received the rations of German civilians. "We were, by consequence, appreciably less well fed than the prisoners were, and most of us were emaciated when we emerged from the experience. But we were not the only people in Europe who were hungry at that time..."

Their captivity ended in the middle of May when they were sent to Lisbon to be exchanged for a similar group of Germans. They left Germany in two special trains, traversing Spain by night, where Kennan, in charge of the first train, had to lock the doors to keep members of the group (especially the journalists) from disappearing into the crowded stations in search of liquor and then getting left behind. Kennan was up all night trying to keep his people together.

At last they reached a little mountain station at the Portuguese frontier early in the morning. An assistant naval attaché had arrived there from Lisbon, and Kennan left the train to meet him. After the greetings were completed, Kennan asked if breakfast was available at the station; the answer was yes. "Thereupon I, who had been for five months on the receiving end of the food complaints, took final revenge upon my fellow internees by repairing to the station buffet and eating a breakfast of several eggs, leaving the rest of them to nurse their empty bellies..." Six or seven hours later they were in Lisbon, where they immediately made themselves sick on the rich fare that was suddenly available.

Equally educational was the behaviour of the State Department throughout this affair. "When the department did finally take cognizance of our plight and consent to communicate with us by telegram for the first time...it did so only for the purpose of informing us that by decision of the comptroller general...none of us were to be paid for the months we had been in confinement: we had not, you see, been working." This telegram was soon followed by another, which informed them that half of the group was to be left behind in German custody, in order to make space available on the exchange vessel for Jewish refugees. Some congressmen, it seems, were anxious to please their constituents by bringing in these refugees, and the State Department gave in to the pressure. "The department was obviously more concerned to relieve itself of congressional pressures than to worry about a group of its own employees, many with long and creditable records, whose fidelity to duty, and to duty in peculiarly difficult circumstances, had caused them to fall into enemy hands."

In the end, the State Department reversed these decisions, but the initial attitude left a lasting impression. When they arrived at Lisbon, "we found awaiting us telegrams curtly assigning some of our most valuable people to service on the Iberian peninsula, and telling them to go to work the following day." It was quite clear that the department had no comprehension of the condition of its employees after their months of confinement. Kennan could not recall afterwards that the government either then, or when its employees returned to the United States, ever expressed its appreciation for their services or for the rigors of the confinement that they had endured.

Kennan found this attitude to the Foreign Service widely reflected in a variety of practises and institutions. The State Department advised officers in the Service that their experience and qualifications were more urgently needed there than in the armed forces, and that they should therefore apply for deferment of the draft call. But the Department was itself unwilling to approach draft boards with such a request, fearing that this would provoke congressional disapproval. This procedure obviously left those in the Service vulnerable to charges of having dodged the draft—in spite of the fact that many of them performed duties in wartime that involved dangers and hardships similar to those faced by men in the armed forces.

Foreign Service officers were constantly reminded of their civilian status throughout the war, and in Allied countries they were denied even the modest privileges that were available to the lowest ranks of armed forces personnel. Later in the war, when he was serving in London, Kennan had an assistant "who had seen combat as a regular soldier in France during the First World War. He was denied access to the great military mess in Grosvenor House, only two blocks from our office, and had to seek his lunches alone in the greasy spoons along Oxford Street..." On another occasion, when he approached a chief of mission to request leaves on behalf of some obviously tired and overworked officers, the request was denied and, "the refusal was accompanied by the observation that they ought all to be in uniform anyway. This observation cut to the heart, and I never forgot it."

Source: George F. Kennan, *Memoirs, 1925-1950*, pp. 136-141.

*   *   *

*O*ccasionally, diplomats become directly involved in the hostilities,
leading to some unexpected scenes.

The League of Consuls

In 1912, when war broke out in the Balkans, Andrew Kalmykow,
the Russian Consul in Uskub, Macedonia, found things got quite
exciting when news reached the town that the Serbs, who were at
war with the Turks, were nearby. When the cry, "the infidels are
coming," was heard, the Turkish soldiers quickly began to disappear
from the town. Before long there was a knock at the door of the
Consul's study: the Vali (the Turkish Governor-General) was there,
accompanied by a single policeman; they were, it turned out, the only
remaining vestiges of Turkish rule in the town.

The Vali quickly described the desperate situation in which he
found himself: "The commander in chief left the town without even
informing me of his departure. Some officers took my carriage. Can
you find me one, as I want to leave also?"

"Certainly," the Consul answered. "It will be ready in a moment."

The Vali took the carriage and left to collect some of his things
from his house, which was nearby. A few minutes later Kalmykow
heard shots being fired in the street; grabbing a revolver he rushed
outside, where he met the Vali, his hands covered in blood. "I am not
hurt," the Turk reassured him. "But my secretary, who sat next to
me, is killed, and your coachman is wounded."

An Albanian had fired at the Vali but missed him, killing the
secretary and wounding the Consul's driver. Kalmykow offered to
give the Vali refuge in his house and went looking for his driver. "I
saw him walking back with his arm hanging limp and dripping blood,
which left a winding trail in the dust. The horses with the empty
carriage followed the wounded driver." A doctor was sent for to attend
to the driver; the Vali was taken up to the children's nursery where
he cleaned up. A servant brought in two elegant leather bags, which

were deposited in the corner. "Can I leave them here?" asked the Vali. "There is money in them." Kalmykow readily agreed.

The Vali decided that he would take the train to Salonika rather than risk the coach again. But the servants warned him that there were no police left in the town, and that it would be extremely dangerous to attempt to reach the station. He went upstairs to rest.

The servants began closing the shutters, explaining that it was known throughout the town that the Vali had taken refuge there. "Give us guns," they said. "It is time to be armed." The Consul handed out seven rifles; heavy cartridge boxes were brought into the dining room and opened; Kalmykow himself sat in an armchair in the darkened room, a rifle on his lap, watching the grim preparations of his servants.

No attack came during the day, and that evening, after darkness fell, they decided to risk the walk to the railway station. They succeeded in getting the Vali onto the last train for Salonika. As Kalmykow, feeling sad and lonely, walked back from the station through the deserted streets, he came across the French Consul, who bravely announced that he was patrolling the Christian quarter. "There are no police, and I am disarming the people I meet."

"Good gracious!" Kalmykow exclaimed. "Why don't you go home also? Let things take care of themselves. You will be murdered if you stay out all night." But the Frenchman had no sense of fear. Kalmykow, wishing that he could act as bravely as his colleague, continued the long walk home.

When he got there, he found a delegation of Albanians, led by the mayor, waiting for him. They wanted to know if the Serbs would bombard them. He assured them that they would not, if the Albanians made no attempt to defend the town. "Will you go with us tomorrow morning to meet the Serbs and tell them that the army is gone?" they asked. He agreed that he would.

The next morning the mayor called for him. The Consul donned his dress uniform and was preparing to go out to meet the invading Serbs when the other three consuls at Uskub, the Frenchman, an Englishman and an Austrian arrived. Seeing what the Russian was preparing to do, they decided to join him if he would permit them to do so; he agreed and waited for them while they returned to their houses to fetch their uniforms. When they returned, the concert of nations was complete. They prepared a white flag and a trumpet, but supplied themselves with loaded rifles as well.

"The procession started. A man with a flag and the trumpet rode first, then an escort of mounted cavasses of the four nations, and finally the carriages. A Serbian priest on horseback appeared from nowhere and joined us." They left the city, dead as a cemetery, while the inhabitants watched them from peepholes. Not long after leaving the city they spotted a file of Serbian cavalry, and before they knew it, the procession was surrounded.

They attempted to explain their mission, but the officer in charge ordered them to step out of their carriages. Their rifles and their ceremonial swords were taken from them; their eyes were bound and they were commanded to march. "We heard the stamping of hoofs around us as we moved, holding each other's hands in order not to be separated. It was evident that we were out of the diplomatic sphere and in purely military surroundings."

They began to slowly make their way up a mountain road when it began to rain. With no overcoats, their uniforms were soon soaking as they slipped their way along. "The situation," Kalmykov writes, "was decidedly unpleasant."

When they were finally ordered to stop and permitted to take off their blindfolds, they found themselves at the top of a mountain pass, surrounded by swarming soldiers. They explained to the general who approached them that the town of Uskub, which could be seen in the distance, was defenceless; he brusquely asked them what guarantees they could offer—but they could offer none. With their civilian mentalities, the consuls had expected the Serbs to be relieved to avoid a battle; they had failed to anticipate that they would be depriving men like the general a chance of glorious combat. The Serbs, following their earlier victory at Kumanovo, assumed that the retreating Turks had made a strategic withdrawal to Uskub, where they would dig in and make a stand. They had not realized that the Turks were completely demoralized, the army in disarray, and that the entire western Turkish front had collapsed at once.

Crown Prince Alexander himself, the future king of Yugoslavia, thundered up on horseback to the wet, muddy and pitiable consuls. Unlike the brusque general, he listened attentively to their description of the situation and appeared to be relieved that a further battle would be unnecessary; his concern was that the Christians of the town would now be defenceless; he decided to move to their rescue immediately.

Thus, the consuls soon found themselves in a carriage once more, wet and hungry but drinking wine from the personal flask of the prince, and this time travelling back to Uskub at the head of 40,000 Serbian soldiers. The sun was setting as they approached the city across an open field. "Suddenly a flood of humanity burst out of the town. People wild with joy were running, shouting, and throwing their hats in the air. It was the Christian population of Uskub welcoming the prince and the army." The danger had passed and a new era began.

Source: Andrew D. Kalmykow, *Memoirs of a Russian Diplomat: Outposts of the Empire, 1893-1917*, pp. 234-40.

*　　　　*　　　　*

War creates havoc and dangers for diplomats, but the dangers and the complications become even more complicated when fused with the upheavals of domestic revolution and the disintegration of the state.

"Special Project"

Certainly there have been few situations more complicated than the breakdown of the Habsburg Empire at the end of the First World War. When the Emperor Franz Josef died in 1916, was succeeded by his grand nephew, Charles who, in November 1918, was compelled to flee Austria-Hungary, which was in the process of breaking up into its various national components, for refuge in Switzerland. The Allied Powers ceased to recognize the Habsburg Empire as a sovereign state, recognizing instead the republican successor states of Austria, Czechoslovakia, Poland, and the "Triune Kingdom" of Serbs, Croats and Slovenes that would come to be known as Yugoslavia. Hungary itself was left a shrivelled rump in the hands of foreign troops and communists led by Bela Kun. The Emperor

Charles refused to abdicate, however, and from Switzerland he attempted to organize a successful return to the throne.

One of the Emperor's loyal supporters, Prince Lajos Windischgraetz, a Magyar magnate who had been serving as "Special Purposes Assistant" to the Minister of Foreign Affairs during the last days of the Empire, continued to serve Charles as a diplomatic emissary in a way that makes "Special Purposes" seem a most appropriate title. The Emperor, who was installed in the château of Prangins, bordering on Lake Geneva, needed to be able to enjoy confidential contact with his key supporters. Windischgraetz made the acquaintance of an old bachelor who owned a house on the Lausanne-Prangins road and was prepared to lend two rooms; thus, the Emperor could slip through a back door in the park of the château, walk a few hundred yards on a track that wound through the vineyards and meet with supporters out of sight of the horde of detectives and journalists who were constantly watching him.

Representatives of the new Austrian, Czechoslovak, Polish and Yugoslav governments appeared in Switzerland to offer the Emperor a deal: 184 million Swiss francs paid over four years in commutation of all assets at home and abroad. In return, he was to undertake not to set foot inside the former monarchy for twenty-five years and to relinquish all claims to the throne on behalf of himself and his heirs. He refused to make the deal. Instead, he chose to draw upon the several million Swiss francs that had been placed at his disposal by a wealthy Austrian industrialist to create a "news agency" registered as a Danish trading corporation, which would maintain contacts with the Emperor's supporters in what he still regarded as his domains.

Some of the articles in this journal apparently succeeded in catching the eye of the French Minister of Foreign Affairs, Aristide Briand; evidently, he was already beginning to regret the wartime policy of allowing the Dual Monarchy to be eradicated. Prince Windischgraetz, who had cut his teeth on clandestine activities before the war by disguising himself as a waiter in Serbia and drawing sketches of their fortifications, was ordered to go to Paris to meet with the French Minister.

The two men met in the private room of a restaurant close to the Madeleine. Briand came straight to the point: "As I understand it," he said, "the Emperor is interested in an operation which, though not of a Legitimist character, is taking shape at Szeged against Bela Kun's regime. Well, what is it that you want?" Windischgraetz replied that they needed arms to supply the several thousand Hungarian soldiers gathered at Szeged under the command of Admiral Horthy; so supplied, they would march on Budapest, where they would undoubtedly be joined by masses of loyal soldiers currently serving under the Communist flag. Briand was ready to support the idea. That evening a French General Staff officer appeared at the Hotel Wagram to promise that the French Occupation Forces would supply Horthy with 6,000 rifles, 28 machine guns and an appropriate supply of ammunition. Windischgraetz was then escorted to the Swiss frontier during the dead of night.

The armed resistance to the new regime went so well that the Emperor decided he could re-establish the monarchy in Hungary, and to this end he sent Windischgraetz to Budapest in November, who arrived just before the triumphal entry of Horthy on the 16th. The Emperor's emissary was surprised to discover, when he arrived at the Admiral's suite in the luxurious Hotel Gellert, that Horthy regarded his triumph as a personal one. After reading the letter that Windischgraetz brought for him from the Emperor, Horthy remarked that, "His restoration is going to be terribly difficult. He has so many enemies here." He refused to agree to the Emperor's suggestion that Windischgraetz should accompany the Hungarian mission to the peace negotiations at Paris as one of its senior delegates.

Windischgraetz was not easily denied, however. He had just been elected head of the "Upper Hungarian War Veterans," the practical importance of which was to place him in control of men equipped with 15,000 rifles and 64 machine guns—the best-armed military organization in Hungary. This was no accident: he had managed to purchase the weapons with German assistance and then had them smuggled on tugs down the Danube. Few diplomats have negotiated with the force of a private army behind them. So fortified, he went off to Paris in spite of Horthy, and again met with Briand.

Windischgraetz wanted to know how France and the Allies would react to a royal restoration in Hungary. Briand replied that if Charles could succeed in this project without provoking the armed intervention of the newly-formed states in the region, "a union of Hungary with Austria could prevent accession of the latter to Germany. That would render the tenure of Imperial authority in Central Europe not merely possible but even desirable. France could of course not officially support such a manifestly monarchical enterprise." In other words, the Emperor and his supporters were free to attempt a restoration; they would not be opposed by the French.

In March 1921 Charles had himself bandaged up, disguised as an invalid and boarded a train for Hungary; he made his way to his former palace in Budapest where he confronted Horthy in what had once been his own study. The Admiral refused to cede to Charles, maintaining that he had rendered an oath to the new National Assembly, and that he could not break his word. The Emperor was forced to flee to Switzerland once more, where Windischgraetz met him in July. Charles was undaunted by his failure: "Now that I have been back once, I shall return a second, a third, a fourth, a fifth, a tenth time and try again and again to put myself at the head of popular movements to restore Danubian unity." If the restoration failed to take place, he predicted, a terrible fate would be in store for his people. "German power will be resuscitated more strongly than before and in the east the Soviets will menace European civilisation as a whole. Unless they find a way of co-operating peacefully, the small nations of Central Europe are going to be enslaved and destroyed by these two giants."

By October the Emperor was ready to try again. This time he and the Empress arrived at Sopron on the Austro-Hungarian border, where they were accorded a tumultuous welcome. But soon afterwards, Windischgraetz, who was in Paris staying at the Hungarian Legation, was called to the Quai d'Orsay where he was warned that news from Czechoslovakia and Yugoslavia was bad; he ought to go to Hungary immediately and bring the Emperor to some neutral spot. The French would provide him with an airplane to accomplish this mission.

Flying over the Ardennes, they ran into a gale. The pilot made a detour to the north to avoid the storm, but near Hof, close to the German-Czechoslovak border, they ran into engine trouble and were forced to land in a stubble-field. Nevertheless, the intrepid Windischgraetz managed to hop the night express to Prague. When he arrived there, he stepped onto the platform in order to change trains and was immediately arrested. He was informed that the Czechoslovak government was taking this action for the sake of his personal safety, in order to prevent him from making his way to the scene of the hostilities in Hungary. He was taken, under guard, to a hotel. He immediately sent a note to the Foreign Minister protesting against this interference with a diplomatic functionary travelling legally on a courier's passport.

The next morning two detectives took him to Bratislava by train: "On approaching our destination, my escort (who had been at great pains to be pleasant) suddenly disappeared. Inside the station a posse of gendarmes fell on me, relieved me of my luggage, and even deemed it prudent to manacle me hand and foot." The unfortunate emissary was imprisoned for the next two months.

When he was finally taken to the Hungarian frontier in December, he discovered that all had been lost. The Emperor had been arrested and deported to Madeira; within four months he was dead. Windischgraetz's career as a "Special Projects" diplomat on behalf of his emperor had ended.

Source: Lajos Windischgraetz, *My Adventures and Misadventures*, pp. 115-127.

*   *   *

From neutrality to alliance; from communicating with former friendly powers to being detained and arrested: these are some of the upheavals that diplomats may expect to occur in wartime. Such sudden changes in fortune are always make life difficult, and few changes can have created more ironies than those caused by the reversal of fortunes in eastern Europe that saw the Nazi-Soviet Pact break down and the unexpected transformation of Poland into an ally of the Soviet Union.

Our People are Missing

In December 1941 General Sikorski, Premier of the Polish government-in-exile left London on a journey to the Soviet Union. Travelling via Cairo and Teheran, he arrived in Kuibyshev on a cold and dreary evening, where he was nevertheless given a full-dress state reception at the airport. Vodka and hors d'oeuvres were provided for the party in the wooden shack used as a waiting room. Continuing his journey to Moscow to meet with Stalin the next day, his plane was escorted by Soviet fighter planes; the Germans were fighting in the streets of Rostov and the Soviet front was only twenty miles from the city.

On the evening of 3 December, the General and the Polish Ambassador to the Soviet Union were taken through the blacked-out, deserted and frozen streets of Moscow (it was thirty-two degrees below freezing) to meet with Stalin and Molotov, the Commissar for Foreign Affairs, in the Kremlin. Outside, they could hear the guns pounding away.

Sikorsky began by expressing his admiration for the heroic efforts of the Red Army and for Stalin's brilliance as a military strategist. Having attempted to create a mood in which business might be effectively transacted, he moved on to more difficult matters: the abuse of the Poles in the Soviet Union must cease, and it was up to Stalin to see that they did. He assured Stalin that he fully appreciated the difficulties of the situation confronting him: "I know that the German Reich has attacked you with four fifths of all its armed might." He went on to assure him that he had ardently advocated the Soviet cause in London. "I submitted to Churchill some time ago military facts and figures proving the necessity of the speedy creation of a second front."

"That is good. I thank you, Mr. Prime Minister," replied Stalin, nodding.

But, Sikorski continued, Stalin would have to appreciate the difficulties involved in launching an invasion of Europe, which required careful planning as well as huge numbers of troops and the acquisition of a tremendous amount of matériel.

"You are right," interjected Molotov. "If the invasion were unsuccessful, the moral effect would be detrimental."

Having done his best to establish himself as an admirer of Stalin and as an advocate of the second front, Sikorski then turned to the real business that he had come to discuss. "I regret to say that the amnesty granted by you to our people is not being carried out. Many of our most valuable men are still in labor camps or in prisons."

Stalin, who was jotting down a few notes while Sikorski spoke, denied that this could be so: "That cannot be correct, since the amnesty was to embrace all, and all the Poles are liberated by now."

One of Sikorski's aides responded to the denial by reading out a number of depositions from liberated Poles, testifying to the fact that many of their colleagues who had been in camp with them were still being detained. He provided a practical reason for this: many of the commanders of the detention camps had to carry out a production plan and thus did not wish to deprive themselves of workmen, without whom they might find it impossible to meet the production quotas required of them. Molotov smilingly responded to this suggestion: "I think that may be so."

The Poles pointed out that these camp commanders appeared not to appreciate how much their common cause was suffering as a result of their failure to free the detainees. "Such commanders should be punished," came Stalin's grim reply.

Sikorski complained that the Polish Government had never been informed who had been deported to the Soviet Union, or why. But he did have with him a list of about 4,000 Polish officers who had been taken prisoner in Poland but had never appeared in the military camps. "Not one of these officers—and their number is probably at least twice as large as the 4,000 shown on my list—has turned up as yet."

"That is impossible," snapped Stalin. "They must have escaped somewhere."

Where, Stalin was asked, could the missing Poles possibly have escaped to?

"Well, to Manchuria, maybe," answered Stalin.

The Poles denied that all of these officers could possibly have escaped. Besides, all correspondence between the missing officers and their families had abruptly ceased in April and May 1940, when they were transferred from their three former prison camps to an unknown destination. Amongst those missing were many high-ranking staff officers, physicians and surgeons, who the Polish army now needed very badly.

"Unquestionably they were liberated," insisted Stalin, "but they have not yet reached your quarters."

"I know that Russia is enormous," interjected Sikorski, "but is it possible that several thousand officers could escape or disappear without even one of them being accounted for?"

The discussion eventually turned to the more productive subject of how the two nations could assist one another in the war effort against the common enemy.

Two years later, in June 1943, German radio announced that the bodies of thousands of Poles had been discovered in a mass grave in the forest of Katyn, all of whom had been shot in the back of the neck. Although the majority of those who had been killed were officers, among the dead were 21 university professors, 300 doctors, 200 lawyers, 300 engineers, hundreds of school teachers and a number of journalists and writers. The Germans immediately accused the Russians of the crime, who steadfastly denied it, insisting that the Germans were themselves responsible. The "mystery" of the missing Polish officers continued for almost half a century until, after the launching of *perestroika* the truth of the horrors hidden in the Katyn forest were finally revealed.

Source: Jan Ciechanowski, *Defeat in Victory*, pp. 66-69.

*　　　　*　　　　*

*W*artime diplomacy reveals many things, some horrifying, some disillusioning.

The End of Solidarity

When Angelica Balabanoff arrived in Belgium in July 1914 as the Italian representative to the Communist International, she was determined to do what she could to contribute to the international solidarity of the proletariat. The Executive Committee on which she sat must lead the workers' in refusing to follow the orders of their governments to take up arms against one another. But the young woman found the discussions with some of the leading figures of international socialism to be sadly disillusioning and disheartening.

Following the meeting in Brussels, she received an urgent letter from Plekhanov, the great Russian Marxist philosopher, asking her to visit him in Geneva. As soon as she arrived there he abruptly asked her: "What is your and your Party's attitude towards the war?"

She was amazed by the question; surely the answer was implicit in the philosophy to which they both adhered, and of which he was a leading theorist. "We will do our utmost to prevent Italy from entering the war and to end the war as soon as possible," she simply replied. "As far as I am concerned, I shall naturally do all in my power to assist the Party."

Her reply angered the great man: "So you would prevent Italy from entering the war. How about Belgium? Where is your love for Russia?"

She could not understand the point of these questions: "What do you mean—my love for Russia? Must my attitude towards war change because Russia is involved? Would other imperialist governments not act as Germany has done in Belgium if it were necessary to gain their ends?" But surely Plekhanov, being the great theorist that he was, must understand this as well as she: "Wasn't it you who taught me the real causes of war? Didn't you warn us that this slaughter was being prepared and that we must oppose it?"

His answer shocked her. "So far as I am concerned," he said, "if I were not old and sick I would join the army. To bayonet your German comrades would give me great pleasure."

Why, she wanted to know, did he call them *her* German colleagues? "Are they not yours as well? Who, if not you, taught us to understand and appreciate German philosophy, German Socialism—Hegel, Marx, Engels?" She left that evening to return to Milan. "Never, in all my life, have I travelled with such a heavy heart."

Source: Angelica Balabanoff, *My Life as a Rebel*, pp. 120-121

*   *   *

*W**ar always surprises, creating confusion and strange scenes. One of the strangest concerns the story of the flight of the Belgian Foreign Minister, Premier and Cabinet following the German invasion of Belgium in 1940.*

In Diplomatic No Man's Land

In May 1940, the entire Belgian Cabinet took refuge in France following the occupation of their country by the German army. The French Premier, Paul Reynaud, who went on radio on 28 May to announce that the Belgian army had surrendered and that King Leopold had offered himself as a prisoner, was furious with the Belgians for their military collapse and their refusal to continue the fight. But the members of the Cabinet had little choice: their army had been defeated and the King, unconstitutionally in their opinion, had signified his determination to end the futile fighting. They found themselves isolated in Paris, separated from their Head of State and in a country whose Premier treated them like guilty men.

The following day, Pierlot, the Belgian Premier-in-exile went on the radio to respond to the declaration. He announced that the government had broken with the King, that they wished to continue the war, that they were assuming all executive powers, and that the military henceforth owed allegiance to them alone and were thus released from their oath of allegiance to the King. By mid-June, however, France had also been defeated and the Belgian government was forced to decide what to do. The British offered them an aircraft with eighteen seats, which was insufficient to convey the whole party, and the Defense Minister was still responsible for what remained of the Belgian army, while the Minister of the Interior was acting on behalf of the refugees who had escaped to France. Rather than split up the government and abandon those who were continuing to follow their lead, they declined the British offer and decided to throw in their lot with the French.

On 18 June the Belgians arrived in Bordeaux, where the French government had installed itself, and found lodgings in a modest house in the Rue Blanc-du-Trouille (ironically, the street "white with fear"). There the Belgian government continued to meet, in a dusty room filled with ill-assorted furniture, some of them sitting on packing-cases. The Foreign Minister, Paul-Henri Spaak, quickly became accustomed to sitting for hours in the Foreign Ministry while waiting for his French counterpart to speak with him; his lack of influence was readily apparent to all concerned.

When the new French government under Pétain was formed, the Belgians moved from their house and took refuge on the *Baudouin-ville*, a Belgian steamer anchored in the Gironde Estuary. There they continued to debate whether or not they should attempt to reach England. In the meantime they had completely lost contact with their embassies abroad, while news reached them from Belgium that the overwhelming majority of their people supported the King and that their own unpopularity was complete. Still, their policy had seemed rather clear-cut to them as long as France and Britain stood together; but with the defeat of France they did not know what to do. How could they continue the war when they were diplomatically isolated, discredited at home, without resources and scarcely recognized in France as a legitimate government?

The government-in-exile's ambassador in London managed to get word to them that Britain had no intention of submitting to the Germans; on the contrary, the British government urged them to leave France. This clarified the issue for the Ministers, who agreed that it was now their duty to give whatever services they could offer to the common cause. It was decided that Spaak, Pierlot and the Ministers of Defense and Colonies should make their way to London, where they would comprise the government; those who remained in France would tender their resignations, to avoid the appearance of a split. But this arrangement was not easily accomplished: the French government was opposed to their departure, while the Spanish government was not prepared to grant them transit visas. Nevertheless, a party of twelve set out from Vichy on 24 August: Pierlot, his wife, his seven children, his principal private secretary, a governess, and Spaak.

At the end of their first day's travel, they were stopped by French gendarmes who, after checking their identity papers, asked them to return to Vichy. They were taken to the Préfet of the Département, who told them that "The French Government will not permit you to cross the frontier unless you first give a written undertaking not to go to Britain for the duration of the war." Spaak wanted to sign the undertaking provided and then pay no attention to it, on the ground that it had been given under duress; but Pierlot insisted that such a procedure would be dishonourable, that even under the circumstances he was not prepared to give his word to something when he knew that he had no intention of abiding by it. Instead, he telephoned the Vichy Minister of the Interior: "M. Pierlot gave the minister a piece of his mind. He reminded him that we had entered France of our own free will as friends and allies and that it was unthinkable that we should be prevented from leaving by the imposition of unacceptable conditions." Spaak sceptically listened to the conversation, impressed by his Premier's invocation of the highest moral principles and fine sentiments, but quite certain that they would have no effect. He was wrong. The Vichy Minister agreed that they could continue their journey without giving the undertaking that had been demanded.

Relieved, the Belgians continued their journey, arriving at the Spanish frontier in the middle of the night. Now they were prevented from entering Spain because neither Spaak nor Pierlot had the required visas. After prolonged discussion, the police officer in charge, perhaps feeling sorry for the children, permitted them to cross the frontier on the condition that they should be arrested at La Junquera, the first village on the Spanish side; they would not be permitted to go further than this until the government in Madrid had decided what to do with them. The Belgians agreed, with the result that they spent the next few days at the village inn, while their Ambassador in Madrid argued their case.

The police officer who had allowed them to enter Spain finally came to see them one evening. His news was bad. They would have to return to France: "I took a great deal upon myself when I allowed you to cross into Spain and my career is in danger. Please do as I ask." What were they to do? They did not feel that they could turn a deaf ear to the pleas of one who had been so kind to them, yet if they returned to France they were convinced that they would never get out. They compromised. They agreed to leave the village, but not to re-enter France: they would stay in the no-man's-land between the two customs posts.

And thus it was that the Belgian Premier and his Foreign Minister settled down in the middle of the road between France and Spain at the foot of a statue put up to honour the glory of General Franco. The sight of the Premier, his wife, their seven children and the Foreign Minister seeking shelter from the sweltering sun by moving round and round the statue in order to remain in the shade provided by the General must have been a peculiar one indeed. Spaak had had the foresight to acquire provisions before they settled down in this diplomatic no-man's-land; so they ate in the shadows, slept in their cars and used water from a nearby fountain for drinking and washing. After three days of this, the Spanish government finally gave way and permitted them to proceed to Gerona, where they were to be arrested.

Spaak and Pierlot now decided that the time had come to separate themselves from the family, as they might well have to make a run for it if they were to get to Britain. Mme. Pierlot, the children, their governess, and the Premier's private secretary struck off on their own for Lisbon. The two men were taken under guard from Gerona to Barcelona; when they arrived at police headquarters they were required to give their personal details to the clerk, and Spaak could still hear in his mind years later his Premier saying that his name was "Pierlot, Hubert" and, with an air of solemnity, that his occupation was that of "Belgian Prime Minister". From the police station they were taken to a hotel, which they were permitted to leave during the day, but always with a police escort.

Managing to contact the Belgian Consul in Madrid, they soon set about designing an escape plan, with the assistance of two Belgians who were living there. They got hold of a van in which they had a secret compartment installed behind the driver's seat, just large enough to hold two people. In the meantime, they became quite friendly with their guards who, one Saturday afternoon, told them that, although they wished to go to a football game, they could not do so unless their "prisoners" first promised not to run away. The Belgians gave them their word, along with a little money to help them enjoy the afternoon. Although this helped to establish a relationship of trust, the two men were still reluctant to make their escape, as they faced a journey of some fifteen hours through the mountains; if their absence were detected, there was every likelihood that the frontier posts would be alerted, and that they would be captured and returned to Madrid where they would enjoy much less favourable conditions than they faced at the moment.

They decided that the time had come to make a break for it when they learned that Himmler was to visit Madrid; it seemed quite possible that he would demand that the Belgians be handed over to the Germans, or that they should really be imprisoned.

Early one Saturday afternoon, when their guards had again gone off to a football game, they executed their plan. Abandoning their luggage in a prominent location in the hotel, they went off to the consulate, where they slipped into the secret compartment of the van. The Premier immediately took out his rosary and began saying his prayers; Spaak at the same time, "called upon all the gods and prophets that I could think of, including Mohammed, Confucius and Buddha. I took the view that if I was going to take out an insurance policy at all I might as well have maximum cover."

Fortunately, their guards failed to return that day. When they came to the hotel on Sunday morning to find the Belgians gone, they at first assumed that they were attending mass. When they realized their mistake they finally gave the alarm, but the head of police by that time happened to be attending a bullfight and refused to attend to business until after the *corrida*. The extra time that they gained turned out to be precious: the journey took them not fifteen hours, but twenty-four, during which time their driver never left his seat. When they arrived at the Portuguese border, the customs officers opened the van and began searching through the heap of old tires that were piled up in the back. But the Premier and the Foreign Minister, praying silently in their tiny compartment, remained undetected. They were allowed to proceed. They thought they were safe.

They had travelled only a few hundred yards from the customs post when the van stopped and they heard the sound of footsteps approaching. "We did not move an inch. Heavy beads of sweat ran down my face and I had pins and needles in my legs. The Premier remained motionless.... We looked at one another full of fear and neither of us said a word. Then the van moved off again." In their anxiety, they had forgotten that they also had to pass the Portuguese post. A few miles later they crawled out of their hiding place and stepped into the bright sunlight.

As soon as they could, they called Lisbon to give the Belgian Minister a coded message signifying their arrival. He told them that Mme. Pierlot was already on her way from Lisbon to join them. Before long she appeared, and when the joyful greetings were over, Spaak asked her: "Are you not surprised to see us?"

"Not at all," she replied. "This morning, at Mass I came upon a passage in my missal which begins with the words 'The captives shall be delivered.' So, you see, I knew you were coming."

A flying boat took the Belgians to Britain, where they spent the next four years. Spaak, who had been a convinced neutralist before the war, became an equally dedicated advocate of the alliance to defeat Hitler, and of positive European co-operation following the defeat of Nazi Germany.

Source: Paul-Henri Spaak, *The Continuing Battle: Memoirs of a European, 1936-1966*, pp. 48-65.

*   *   *

Even in wartime diplomats are apt to be confronted with strange requests, and some diplomats are able to retain their sense of humour, in spite of the depressing circumstances.

Who's Speaking?

During the Second World War, Lord Halifax, the British Ambassador in Washington, received a telephone call asking for his help; the request was handled by his personal assistant, Angus McDonnell. The earnest young man making the call wished to enlist the aid of the embassy in transporting a young male hippopotamus from Kenya to Chicago. McDonnell's first response, in the best diplomatic tradition, was to give a polite, but neutral reply.

When the young man continued to press his request, however, the Ambassador's assistant was led to ask: "Whoever could want to transport a young male hippopotamus half way round the world in today's circumstances? Unless it was a young female hippopotamus. I am not, by any chance, speaking to a young female hippopotamus, am I?"

Source: Lord Casey, *Personal Experience, 1939-1946*, p. 88.

*   *   *

Occasionally, clandestine diplomatic intrigues during wartime are initiated to serve the wishes of eccentric political leaders.

Precious Stones

The eccentricities of Mackenzie King, Prime Minister of Canada for some twenty years, are well-known: he patronized prostitutes with a view to rehabilitating them; attended seances believing himself to be in touch with the spirits of his mother and his beloved dog, Spot; and constructed over the course of several years an artificial ruins at his Kingsmere estate, collecting the raw materials from a variety of sources.

His oddity emerged in dealing with his diplomatic corps in the darkest days of the war in 1940. On the day after Westminster Hall had been bombed, a telegram marked 'Secret and Most Immediate' was received at Canada House in London. The telegram from the Prime Minister requested that, as a matter of the highest priority, a few stones from the rubble of Westminster be dispatched to him personally. It fell to future Prime Minister 'Mike' Pearson, then a diplomat at Canada House, to arrange for the shipment. Remarkably, the Office of Works complied with the request promptly and, as Pearson puts it in his Memoirs, "this historic and heavy freight was shipped safely through submarines to add a new distinction to Mr. King's ruins at Kingsmere."

Source: Lester B. Pearson, *Mike: The Memoirs of the Rt. Honourable Lester B. Pearson*, pp. 178-79.

The Munich Crisis

It would be a futile exercise to attempt to determine when any crisis begins, but this is particularly so in the case of the "Munich" crisis of 1938. In a sense, the crisis began with the dissolution of the Habsburg Empire in Austria-Hungary in 1918-1919, and the creation of the independent state of Czechoslovakia. Three neighbouring states had grievances against the new state simply by virtue of its creation: Hungary was determinedly "revisionist" and believed that territory in southern Czechoslovakia ought to be hers; Poland felt aggrieved that the Polish-speaking area of Teschen had been awarded to Czechoslovakia; Germany complained that the principle of national self-determination had been clearly violated by including the Germans of the Sudetenland in the new state. Still, the crisis remained latent throughout most of the interwar period until the Anschluss between Germany and Austria was declared by Hitler in March, 1938.

The creation of a "national" German state, and the breakdown of one of the essential provisions of the Treaty of Versailles led immediately to demands from German people in the Sudetenland that they too should have the opportunity to join the greater German Reich. On 28 March Hitler entertained representatives from the Sudetenland, and appointed their leader, Henlein, his "viceroy" there. Negotiations were to be initiated with the Czechoslovak government, but they were to see to it that their demands were such that they could not possibly be satisfied. On 24 April Henlein gave a speech in which he demanded the transformation of Czechoslovakia into a "state of nationalities" and a change in her foreign policy that would, in effect, turn her into a satellite of Germany.

In the spring of 1938, the Czechoslovakian question was placed on the agenda of European diplomacy. Discussions were held between the British and the French; the Poles and the Hungarians began formulating their demands; Hitler publicly denounced the Czech frontiers imposed in 1919 and demanded that the problem of the German minority be solved. On 20 May Czechoslovakia called up its reservists and manned the frontier posts along the border with Germany.

The British decided that Hitler aimed to achieve his "solution" of the Sudeten problem by 12 September, the last day of the annual Nazi Party rally that was scheduled to be held in Nuremberg. If the crisis were to be resolved peacefully, something would have to be done before this date. At the end of July the British government sent Lord Runciman to Czechoslovakia as an independent "mediator" to find a solution to the problem. This proved to be unnecessary as Benes, the president of Czechoslovakia, short-circuited the mediation process by accepting everything that the Sudeten leaders were asking for.

At the Nuremberg rally, Hitler listed the usual grievances and proclaimed that the Czechoslovak government must remedy them. The next day the Sudeten leaders broke off negotiations with Benes. In London, the government was convinced that war was near. The Prime Minister, Neville Chamberlain, decided to take the initiative.

Hitler's interpreter, Dr. Paul Schmidt, tells the first part of the story.

At Berchtesgaden

"On the morning of September 14th events took a dramatic and sensational turn. I had to translate for Hitler a seven-line message: 'Having regard to the increasingly critical situation, I propose to visit you immediately in order to make an attempt to find a peaceful solution. I could come to you by air and am ready to leave tomorrow. Please inform me of the earliest time you can receive me, and tell me the place of meeting. I should be grateful for a very early reply. Neville Chamberlain.'

"That same evening I left for Munich in a special train, without uniforms, feeling that this time I was not going to act as an extra in an international show, but to play a modest, if not unimportant, part in a real historical drama. 'Keep your mind quite clear,' von Weizsäcker, the Foreign Office head, said to me in the train. 'Tomorrow at Berchtesgaden it will be a matter of war or peace.'

"Next day at noon I met Chamberlain at the Munich airport with Ribbentrop [the German Minister of Foreign Affairs], whom Hitler had sent for the purpose. As he got out of the plane, Chamberlain said to Ribbentrop: 'I stood the passage very well, although we had bad weather part of the way, and I had never been in an aeroplane before.'

"With Chamberlain were Sir Horace Wilson, the Prime Minister's most intimate adviser on all political questions, and Sir William Strang, head of the Central European section of the Foreign Office. As we drove in open cars through Munich to the station, the people greeted Chamberlain very warmly—considerably more so, as it seemed to me, than they had Mussolini the year before.

"We lunched in Hitler's dining car on the way to Berchtesgaden. The scene is still very clear in my memory. During almost the whole of the three hour journey troop transports rolled past, making a dramatic background, with soldiers in new uniforms and gun barrels pointing skywards. 'Peace Envoy Chamberlain,' as he was then called in Germany, formed a curious contrast to this warlike picture.

"Shortly before we reached Berchtesgaden it began to rain, and as we drove up with Chamberlain to the Berghof the sky darkened and clouds hid the mountains. Hitler received his guests at the foot of the steps leading up to the house. After greetings, hand shakings, introductions, we all sat down round the tea table in the large room with the view towards the Untersberg in which Hitler had received Lloyd George and the Duke of Windsor. Not only was the weather threatening—indoors the tension was noticeable. The protagonists, it was clear, were taking each other's measure for the ensuing conversation, at which the issue would be war or peace.

"After conventional remarks about the weather, the size of the room, the possibility of Hitler visiting England, and Chamberlain's journey, Chamberlain asked rather abruptly whether Hitler would speak to him alone or whether he wanted the support of his advisers. 'Of course Herr Schmidt must be there as interpreter,' said Hitler, 'but as an interpreter he is neutral, and forms part of neither group.' I already knew that Chamberlain would express the wish to speak to Hitler alone. With Hitler's knowledge this had been settled between the English and the Germans beforehand, behind Ribbentrop's back. Both sides felt that our Foreign Minister would prove a disturbing element in any endeavour to achieve a friendly settlement between England and Germany. Hitler too had noticed the wounded vanity aroused by the English in his former London Ambassador. He had therefore agreed to the plan to exclude him which had the approval of Henderson [the British Ambassador to Germany] and Weizsäcker and the warm support of Göring.

"Ribbentrop therefore remained angrily in the background, while I went with Hitler and Chamberlain to the office on the first floor. It was the same simple, almost bare, room in which Hitler and Halifax had got on so badly a year before. This conversation also, on which hung the issue of peace or war, was not conducted in an exactly serene atmosphere, and sometimes became quite stormy. It lasted nearly three hours. Hitler, the Party Rally just over, was apparently still attuned to long speeches, and from time to time he was so carried away by his rage against Benes and Czecho-Slovakia that his harangues went on interminably.

"Hitler began fairly quietly by presenting in full the list of complaints against Germany's neighbours which he always brought forward. The Versailles Treaty, the League of Nations, and disarmament were discussed in detail, as well as economic difficulties, unemployment and National Socialist reconstruction. Chamberlain was reproached in rising tone with the attitude of the British Press, with Britain's 'interference' in German affairs, and in the Reich's relations with South-East Europe, including Austria.

"Chamberlain listened attentively, looking frankly at Hitler. Nothing in his clear-cut, typically English features, with their bushy eyebrows, pointed nose and strong mouth, betrayed what went on behind his high forehead. His brother, Sir Austen, sitting opposite Stresemann at Locarno had always looked like that; but Neville Chamberlain had nothing of his brother's aloof frigidity. On the contrary, he dealt in lively manner with individual points brought up by Hitler, giving the stock answer about the freedom of the Press with a friendly, almost conciliatory smile. Then, looking Hitler full in the face, he emphasised that he was prepared to discuss every possibility of righting German grievances, but that in all circumstances the use of force must be excluded.

" 'Force!' Hitler exclaimed. 'Who speaks of force? Herr Benes applies force against my countrymen in the Sudetenland, Herr Benes mobilised in May, not I.' Outside it was pouring with rain, and the wind was howling. 'I shall not put up with this any longer. I shall settle this question in one way or another. I shall take matters into my own hands.' This was the first time, in a discussion with a foreign statesman, that the phrase 'in one way or another' had been used—a phrase which I observed then and later to be an extreme danger signal. I rightly translated it 'one way or another,' but its meaning now and on later occasions amounted to: 'Either the other side gives in, or a solution will be found by means of the application of force, invasion, or war.'

"Now Chamberlain, who had hitherto listened to everything that was said with serious calm, also became excited. 'If I have understood you aright,' he said, 'you are determined to proceed against Czecho-Slovakia in any case.' After pausing for a second, he added: 'If that is so, why did you let me come to Berchtesgaden? Under the circumstances it is best for me to return at once. Anything else now seems pointless.'

"Hitler hesitated. If he really wants it to come to war, I thought, now is the moment; and I looked at him in agonized suspense. At that moment the question of peace or war was really poised on a razor's edge. But the astonishing happened: Hitler recoiled.

" 'If, in considering the Sudeten question, you are prepared to recognise the principle of the right of peoples to self-determination,' he said in one of those sudden changes from raging to complete calm and collectedness, 'then we can continue the discussion in order to see how that principle can be applied in practice.'

"I thought that Chamberlain would immediately assent. The principle of self-determination had always played an important part in English political thought, and its relevance to the Sudeten question had been generally admitted by the British Press and by prominent British visitors to Germany. But Chamberlain at once raised an objection—though whether this was because he had been angered by Hitler's aggressive manner, or because, as a practical administrator, he recognised the complications in applying this principle to Czecho-Slovakia, it is difficult to say.

" 'If, in the application of the right of self-determination in Czecho-Slovakia, a plebiscite were held among the Sudeten Germans, the practical difficulties would be enormous,' he replied. Even so

Hitler did not get indignant. Had Chamberlain's threat to return home frightened him? Was he really recoiling from the prospect of a war?

" 'If I am to give you an answer on the question of self-determination,' said Chamberlain, 'I must first consult my colleagues. I therefore suggest that we break off our conversation at this point, and that I return to England immediately for consultation, and then meet you again.' When I translated these words about breaking off the discussion, Hitler looked up uneasily; but when he understood that Chamberlain would meet him again, he agreed with obvious relief. The atmosphere had suddenly become friendly again, and Chamberlain at once availed himself of this change to secure a promise from Hitler that in the interval no aggressive action would be taken against Czecho-Slovakia. Hitler unhesitatingly gave this assurance, but added that it would not apply if any particularly atrocious incident occurred.

"Thus the discussion ended. After Hitler's change of direction, the prospects for the maintenance of peace seemed to me more hopeful. I drove with the English to the Berchtesgaden hotel, where we dined and spent the night."

Source: Paul Schmidt, *Hitler's Interpreter*, pp. 90-94.

*   *   *

When Chamberlain returned from this initial meeting with Hitler, he felt that he had achieved something worthwhile in obtaining from him the statement that he had no further territorial ambitions once the Sudeten question had been settled. Before returning to Germany to resume the negotiations, the French Premier, Édouard Daladier, and the Foreign Minister, Georges Bonnet, were invited to a conference in Downing Street on 18 September. Although the French had already expressed their support for the direction taken by Chamberlain, both sides believed that it was important to maintain an Anglo-French front in the next round of negotiations. Sir Samuel Hoare, who was at the time the Home Secretary, has given us one version of the meeting.

The Anglo-French Meeting in London

"The meeting lasted for twelve hours, from eleven o'clock in the morning until eleven o'clock at night. The British were represented by four cabinet ministers, the French by two; six British civil servants were present, five French. They met in the Cabinet room, with the British sitting beside and behind the Prime Minister, the French opposite.

"Reading again the notes that I made after the meetings, and sorting my memories of what actually happened, I have again experienced the deep depression that possessed me throughout the many hours of these dismal talks. It was not only that I felt frustrated on our own account, but that I could see, and indeed feel, the emotional strain through which the French were passing. In front of me sat Daladier, square and squat, his face flushed redder than ever, the man who, as an artilleryman, had stubbornly fought through the First World War, and as a Minister, had faced the Paris mob. By his side was Bonnet, as white as Daladier was red, sensitive, and apparently on the verge of a *crise de nerfs*, with a mind that moved like quicksilver, made especially sensitive since he had discovered that there were no gas-masks in France. Behind them sat Léger, the very embodiment of the conservative traditions of the Quai d'Orsay, yellow-complexioned, silent, imperturbable and sphinx-like. Their faces, each in its own way, showed that they were confronted with questions to which all the answers were bad. As for ourselves, it was at least some comfort that, although we were under no treaty obligation to the Czechs, we had already acted, and Chamberlain's bold stroke had permitted us to retain a certain measure of hope.

"The French decisions were much more difficult than ours; they had let things drift, and lost the initiative for stopping a great calamity, and yet were still bound by a treaty that depended on military strength that they no longer possessed. [in 1925 France and Czechoslovakia had signed a treaty providing for mutual defense against aggression].

"It was a relief when Chamberlain, in his peculiarly incisive and matter-of-fact manner, began the conference with a detailed description of his three hours' talk with Hitler. It is always helpful to start a difficult discussion with the sedative of a long narrative. In this case, the full story was necessary to bring out the two overriding factors in the crisis—Hitler's set purpose to march at once, if no agreement was reached, and the separation of the Sudetenland from the Czechoslovak Republic as the one indispensable condition of any accommodation. As was only to be expected, the main burden of the discussion fell upon the two Premiers.

"The first session turned upon the danger of admitting the far-reaching principle of self-determination. Where would it stop in Hitler's hands? If plebiscites were accepted as the method of applying it, what of the Magyars and Slovaks in Czechoslovakia? What, nearer home, would be the reactions in Alsace? As I listened to Daladier's French logic, admirably expressed and accurately documented, I could not help wondering what the nineteenth-century Liberals and President Wilson would have thought of the Frankenstein monster of self-determination that they had so optimistically created at Versailles. Daladier soon convinced us that it was much too dangerous to base our attitude on any general proposition, and that in particular, plebiscites would put into Hitler's hands an irresistible lever for future revolutions. We therefore agreed to restrict any negotiation to the narrow point of the Sudetenland, and to consult the Cabinet upon the question of substituting the direct transfer of territory for Hitler's proposal of plebiscites.

"The discussion of these points brought us to the central issue. Should we or should we not press Benes to accept the loss of the Sudetenland? It was at this stage that we adjourned in order that the French Ministers should discuss between themselves the implications of this very grave question, and that we should obtain the Cabinet's approval of our provisional decisions.

"When we resumed the conference, Daladier informed us, as the prelude to further discussions, that he agreed with our proposal that the Czech Government should be advised to postpone mobilisation pending Chamberlain's further meeting with Hitler. He then reverted to his objections to a plebiscite, with the result that Chamberlain reluctantly, but with the authority of the Cabinet, accepted the alternative of a direct transfer of territory. There then arose the question of the future of the Czech Republic, when once it had lost the Moravian frontier and the line of fortifications that had been built along it. If Czechoslovakia was to continue at all, and equally, if France was to be compensated for the loss of a bastion against Germany in Central Europe, it was essential in Daladier's view for the British Government to join in an international guarantee of the weakened and attenuated state.

"It had always been a tradition of British Governments to refuse to undertake guarantees on the Continent that left the final decision of peace or war in hands other than our own. With the growth of the Dominions and their extreme reluctance to be involved in Continental commitments, the need for caution in undertaking European obligations had in recent years become increasingly important. When, therefore, Daladier pressed for a British guarantee, we had to consider very carefully the reaction on Dominion as well as British opinion, and it was only after a long meeting between ourselves that we were able to tell the French that we accepted their proposal.

"The ground was then cleared for the final act, the drafting of the telegram to Benes announcing our considered view that only the cession of the Sudetenland could avoid war, that we strongly pressed him to agree to it at once, and that if he agreed, we would join in an international guarantee of Czechoslovakia against unprovoked aggression.

"Daladier, in approving the draft, was obviously under an almost intolerable strain. He was sacrificing an ally, and weakening a strategic outpost of France in Central Europe. None the less, it seemed to be the only choice open to him. If war broke out, France was grievously unprepared, and would be forced to choose between the undisguised repudiation of the Franco-Czech Treaty and fighting in conditions that made the immediate defence of Czechoslovakia impossible. In these circumstances he felt bound to agree to the telegram that was sent to Prague on September 19 asking categorically for the Czech acceptance of self-determination for the Sudeten Germans.

"One question remained unanswered. What was to happen if Benes refused to cede the Sudetenland? Daladier brushed it aside on the ground that a refusal was unthinkable. I thought on the contrary that Benes was sure to refuse, if only to make it clear that he was acting under duress. I was also convinced that the French Ministers, having once accepted the separation of the Sudetenland, would sooner or later be forced to make it plain that the French would not go to war, if their advice was rejected.

"It was at this point that the conference ended. Between its termination and Chamberlain's second meeting with Hitler at Godesberg there were only three days. In this short time it was necessary to obtain Benes's agreement to the cession to Germany of the Sudetenland. The increasing gravity of Nazi incidents, and the news of German troop concentrations on the Czech frontier made any postponement of the Godesberg meeting very dangerous. Hour by hour, we awaited with deep anxiety the news of Benes's reply. Only if it was an acceptance of the Anglo-French proposals would it be possible for Chamberlain to resume his talks with Hitler and stop the German march with all its consequences into Czech territory. Telegrams from Prague, Paris and Berlin began immediately to arrive in quick succession. One of Henderson's from Berlin, in which he informed us that Ribbentrop had refused to let the Prime Minister have the shorthand note of the Berchtesgaden conversation, was anything but reassuring as to the prospects of the next meeting."

Source: Viscount Templewood, *Nine Troubled Years*, pp. 304-8.

*   *   *

The subject of a redefinition of Czechoslovakian frontiers instantly reinvigorated Polish and Hungarian claims on the territories of the state. Since Hitler's speech of February, a number of discussions had been held concerning how, and in what manner, Poland and Hungary might achieve their ambitions. Two days after the British and the French had met in London, the Polish Ambassador to Germany, Józef Lipski, met with Hitler and at Obersalzberg. Lipski reported their conversation, which lasted for more than two hours, to the Polish Foreign Minister, Józef Beck.

The Polish Claims

"Chancellor Hitler opened the conversation with me with a statement that events had taken a different turn than he first expected. He then gave a historical outline of the Sudetenland problem, starting from his speech at the Reichstag this February. He laid special emphasis on the events of May 21 which compelled him to take a decision on May 28 to accelerate rearmaments and fortifications in the west. He then remarked that he was taken aback to a certain extent by Chamberlain's proposition to come to Berchtesgaden. It was of course impossible for him not to receive the British Prime Minister. He thought Chamberlain was coming to make a solemn declaration that Great Britain was ready to march. He would, of course, then reply that Germany was aware of such a possibility. The Chancellor declared to Chamberlain that the Sudetenland problem must be settled peacefully *or by war*, resulting in the return of the Sudetenland to Germany. As a result of this conversation Chamberlain, persuaded of the necessity of separating the Sudetenland, returned to London. Up to now the Chancellor has had no further news about London's decisions. Neither has he definite information as yet about the date of the meeting which allegedly is to take place tomorrow. However, incoming news seems to indicate that the Chancellor's claims will be honored. Nevertheless, a version is circulating that the settlement of the Sudetenland problem will be executed not by self-determination but by a new delineation of frontiers. Allegedly where there is an 80 percent German majority, the territory would go to Germany without a plebiscite. The Chancellor declared that he prefers the plebiscite and is standing firm on this. He would of course insist on a plebiscite in order to secure votes for people who left the territory after 1918. The status of 1918 must be restored. Otherwise, it would mean acceptance of Czechization, which has been under way since 1918.

"Occupying the Sudetenland by force would, in the Chancellor's opinion, be a fuller and more definite solution. However, the Chancellor declares that, in case his claims are recognized, then it would not be possible for him not to accept them before his people, even if the rest of the Czechoslovak problem remained unsolved. That is why the Chancellor wonders what could be done with the balance of the problem concerning Hungary and Poland. He therefore invited the Hungarian Prime Minister and me to confer on this problem.

"In reply I declared that I would like to present in detail Poland's point of view....

"With regard to Hungarian demands, I particularly emphasized the question of Carpathian Ruthenia, calling attention to the strategic moment with regard to Russia, the spreading of Communist propaganda over this territory, etc. I had the impression that the Chancellor was particularly interested in this problem. This was even more apparent when I mentioned to him that the Polish-Rumanian frontier is comparatively narrow, and that through a common Polish-Hungarian frontier via Carpathian Ruthenia we would obtain a broader barrier against Russia.

"I wish to add that I pointed out in respect to Carpathian Ruthenia that this territory, not claimed by Slovakia, was entrusted to Czechoslovakia only as a mandate. The very low level of population is strongly mixed; as a matter of fact, Hungary has its greatest interests there.

"Defining our stand with regard to the region of Poland's direct interest (Teschen), I stated:

"a) that we had approached London, Paris, Rome, and Berlin categorically requesting a plebiscite when this idea was brought up for the Sudetenland,

"b) that we had approached the same Powers yesterday with regard to news spread about the alleged plan of territorial delimitations...

"c) that Poland's position is especially strong in view of the assurance received from Prague, which was confirmed at that time by London and Paris, that our minorities in Czechoslovakia would enjoy the same status as the most privileged other minorities.

"I concluded, when questioned by the Chancellor, that we would not retreat at this point from recourse to force if our interests were not recognized.

"Analyzing further tactics to apply in settlement of the Czechoslovak problem as a whole, the Chancellor stated:

"1) If his conditions are not accepted by Chamberlain, the situation is clear, and according to his warning he would use armed force to annex the Sudetenland to the Reich.

"2) In case the Sudetenland condition is accepted and guarantees are claimed from him for the rest of the Czechoslovak territory, he would take the position that he might grant such a guarantee only in case a similar guarantee is given by Poland, Hungary, and Italy. (He considers the introduction of Italy important to counterbalance French and British guarantees.) He understands that neither Poland nor Hungary would issue such guarantees prior to the settlement of the problem of their minorities. Here I gave assurances on behalf of the Polish government.

"3) For my confidential information, remarking that I could use it at my discretion, the Chancellor declared today that, in case a conflict would arise between Poland and Czechoslovakia over our interests in Teschen, Germany would be on our side. (I think that a similar declaration was made by the Chancellor to the Hungarian Prime Minister, though I was not told so.) The Chancellor suggests, in such an eventuality, that we undertake action only after the Germans occupy the Sudeten Mountains, since then the whole operation would be shorter.

"Further in the conversation the Chancellor very strongly stressed that Poland is an outstanding factor safeguarding Europe against Russia.

"From other long deliberations of the Chancellor the following results were clear:

"a) that he does not intend to go beyond the Sudetenland territory; naturally with armed force he would go deeper, especially since, in my opinion, he would then be under pressure from the military elements who for strategic reasons push toward the subjugation of the whole of ethnographic Czechoslovakia to Germany;

"b) that besides a certain line of German interests we have a totally free hand;

"c) that he sees great difficulties in reaching a Rumanian-Hungarian agreement (I think the Chancellor is under Horthy's influence...

"d) that the cost of the Sudetenland operation, including fortifications and armaments, adds up to the sum of 18 billion RM;

"e) that upon settlement of the Sudetenland question he would present the problem of colonies;

"f) that he has in mind an idea for settling the Jewish problem by way of emigration to the colonies in accordance with an understanding with Poland, Hungary, and possibly also Rumania (at which point I told him that if he finds such a solution we will erect him a beautiful monument in Warsaw).

"...I also brought up Polish-German relations in the above conversation. I must mention that the moment was not especially well chosen, since the Chancellor was very much absorbed by his approaching talk with Chamberlain. I referred to the Danzig question, suggesting the possibility of a simple Polish-German agreement to stabilize the situation in the Free City. I cited a series of historical and economic arguments. In reply the Chancellor mentioned that we have the agreement of 1934. He also considers it desirable to take another step forward, instead of simply taking the position that force should be excluded in our relations, and to make a definite recognition of frontiers. He referred here to the concept of the superhighway connected with railways, which you are already familiar with. The width of such a belt would, in his words, reach about thirty meters. This would be a certain *novum*—a time when technical means would serve politics. He said he would not bring this up now, since it could be realized later on. Under these circumstances I did not discuss the matter any further.

"At the close of the conversation I referred to your [Beck's] possible meeting with the Chancellor in the near future in case of necessity. The Chancellor accepted the suggestion with satisfaction, remarking that this might be desirable, especially after his conference with Chamberlain.

"For his part, Ribbentrop asked me to find out if you would be ready to make a declaration regarding Polish demands to Czechoslovakia similar to that made by the Hungarian Prime Minister, in order that it might be used in the conversation with Chamberlain. Besides, Ribbentrop stated that the German press will give wide publicity to our action regarding minorities in Czechoslovakia.

"The above report has been dictated by me before the departure of the courier after my return by plane from Berchtesgaden, so please forgive any possible shortcomings."

Source: Jozef Lipski, *Diplomat in Berlin, 1933-1939*, pp. 408-12.

*　　　　*　　　　*

On 22 September Neville Chamberlain returned to Germany for a second meeting with Hitler, this time at Bad Godesberg. The British Ambassador at Berlin, Sir Nevile Henderson, picks up the story at this point:

Chamberlain and Hitler Meet Again

"In the meantime...the internal situation in Czechoslovakia after Berchtesgaden had gone from bad to worse. Thousands of Sudeten refugees had begun to pour over the frontiers, many undoubtedly at Nazi instigation but some also out of real fear of being caught, in the event of war, between two fires. Ultimately there were about 250,000 of these unfortunate people in Germany. The able-bodied were enrolled as "Free Corps" and started to raid back into Czechoslovakia. The casualty lists began to mount up. The Hodza Government resigned and was succeeded by a Government of National Concentration at Prague led by General Syrovy. A press campaign of unprecedented violence was set loose in Germany, and the Poles and Hungarians joined in the hunt. If Germany was going to get the lion's share of the spoils, Poland and Hungary were not going to leave their own claims unsatisfied. The Hungarian Regent and the Polish Foreign Minister hurried to Berchtesgaden. On the other side of the fence Soviet Russia talked vaguely of supporting the Western Powers; while the Czechs themselves were asking for advice as to what to do in the light of the German military concentrations.

"In view of the agreement between the Prime Minister and Hitler at Berchtesgaden to meet again, the German press campaign was particularly indefensible. But self-determination, now that the principle had been conceded, was no longer enough for Hitler, though Goering at this juncture gave me his word that Germany would take no action before a second meeting had taken place. Nevertheless, as the Field Marshal pointed out, there was no time to waste; and Germany was not bluffing.

"I remember his saying to me on this occasion, 'If England means to make war on Germany, no one knows what the ultimate end will be. But one thing is quite certain. Before the war is over there will be very few Czechs left alive and little of London left standing.' He then proceeded to give me fairly accurate details of the numbers of modern antiaircraft [sic] guns we possessed at the moment as well as of the unpreparedness of England's air defenses generally. He also mentioned, as was doubtless true at the time, that the German Air Force was numerically superior to those of Britain, France, Belgium, and Czechoslovakia combined.

"Such was the position when I was instructed to arrange the second meeting between the Prime Minister and Hitler. It took place this time at Godesberg. The visit to Berchtesgaden had been fixed up literally at a few hours' notice, but the Germans had had a week in which to prepare for Godesberg. Nothing this time was left undone to minister to our comfort and to create the best possible impression. A guard of honour was awaiting Mr. Chamberlain's inspection at the Cologne airdrome, and a band greeted him with 'God Save the King.' He drove from the airdrome to the Petersberg hotel at Godesberg with Ribbentrop. Godesberg itself is one of the beauty spots of the Rhineland, in the country of the Lorelei and the Drachenfels. The Petersberg hotel is famous in Germany. It is situated on a hill, overlooking a wide stretch of country on three sides, with the Rhine on the fourth. The Prime Minister and I were to spend the morning of the morrow pacing the wide balcony, which ran the whole length of the hotel outside the rooms placed at our disposal. It was a lovely autumn morning; and the view was wide and fair to look upon.

" 'Where every prospect pleases, and only man is vile.' It is a hackneyed phrase, but it is astonishing how often in this world it recurs to one. Our accommodation in the hotel was spacious and comfortable, and each room had its own bathroom. The proprietor had filled both bed and bathrooms with the special products of Cologne, scent and soap, bath salts and shaving requisites.

"On the opposite side of the river to us Hitler had taken up his quarters at one of his favourite haunts, a hotel kept by one Dreesen, who had been a companion of his early struggle for power. It was there that he had taken the decision for the 'blood bath' of June, 1934, and it was thence that he flew with Goebbels to Munich for the arrest and execution of Roehm. It was thither that Mr. Chamberlain and his party proceeded for his meeting with Hitler at 5 p.m. on that 22nd of September. To get there it was necessary to cross the river by ferry, which was done under the eyes of thousands of onlookers, who lined the banks in a manner reminiscent of the 'Varsity boat-race day'. Hitler met the Prime Minister at the door of the hotel, and led him without delay to a room upstairs, which was normally used for board meetings. They sat down each at one end of the long baize-covered table, and the proceedings began. The German populace by the river had demonstrated its unconcealed and spontaneous pleasure at seeing the British Prime Minister, whom they recognized as the harbinger of peace; but Hitler himself was in an uncompromising mood.

"Mr. Chamberlain opened the proceedings by recalling that at Berchtesgaden he had agreed in principle to the right of the Sudeten Germans to self-determination; that he had undertaken to endeavour to obtain the assent of his Cabinet and of the French Government; and that it had been agreed that if he were successful he would return in order to consult with Hitler as to the ways and means of putting the agreement into force. Within a very short lapse of time he had, he continued, been able to obtain the assent of the British Cabinet; the French Ministers had visited London and had likewise agreed; and, furthermore, the acquiescence of the Czechoslovak Government had in addition been secured. He accordingly outlined the steps which in his opinion should now be taken to arrange for the peaceful transfer of the Sudeten territory within the shortest possible time.

"When the Prime Minister had finished, Hitler asked whether he was to understand that the British, French, and Czechoslovak Governments had in effect agreed to the transfer of the Sudeten territory from Czechoslovakia to Germany. The Prime Minster replied:

" 'Yes.' There was a slight pause, a silence in which Hitler appeared for a moment to be making up his mind. He then said decisively:

" 'Es tut mir fürchtbar leid, aber das geht nicht mehr.' (I am exceedingly sorry, but that is no longer of any use.) The Prime Minister expressed his surprise and indignation; he could not be expected, he declared, to return to London with fresh proposals and demands only to be faced once more with the rejoinder that they were no longer adequate.

"Hitler thereupon shifted the blame by explaining that it was the Hungarian and Polish claims which had now to be met. His friendship with these two countries demanded, he said, that he should give them full support. To which the Prime Minister retorted that on Hitler's own showing these claims had not the same urgency as the question of the Sudeten Germans and that the Hungarian-Polish claims could only be considered after the Sudeten problem had been solved in an orderly manner. When the discussion thereupon reverted to Mr. Chamberlain's proposals, Hitler declined flatly to consider them on the ground that they involved too much delay. Instead, he demanded that the German-speaking areas should be ceded forthwith and occupied by German troops. This Mr. Chamberlain declined to accept; and after three hours of somewhat exacerbated debate, the meeting adjourned.

"The deadlock that night and most of the next day seemed complete. Hitler, having secured one position, was already advancing on the next. He was no longer prepared to execute his part of the bargain at Berchtesgaden and to discuss quietly the ways and means of a settlement. He was using the claims of the Poles and the Hungarians and the plight of the Sudeten refugees, which his own agents had manipulated, as a pretext, which possibly satisfied his own facile conscience, to break his word to Mr. Chamberlain. Godesberg was the real turning point in Anglo-German relations, and I have always felt that it was there that Hitler made the first of his big political mistakes. He had cheated the British Prime Minister; and, by letting him down, thereby prepared the way for the revulsion of feeling in England against Hitlerism and its methods which was to become complete after the occupation of Prague in March, 1939.

"The first interview at Godesberg thus ended without any reference to a subsequent meeting, and until the late afternoon of the following day it looked as if there might be none. Two written communications were exchanged in the course of the day without producing any modifications of the respective positions. The British press even reported that the negotiations had definitely broken down; and in the interval London informed Prague that it could not advise against a Czech mobilization, while pointing out, nevertheless, that mobilization might precipitate a conflict.

"The Prime Minister's patience was, however, not yet finally exhausted. He was unwilling to refuse discussion of proposals which he had not actually seen in writing; and at 5 p.m. that afternoon he instructed Sir Horace Wilson and myself to see Ribbentrop and to suggest that Hitler should embody the exact nature of his proposals for the occupation of the Sudeten Lands in an official document. It might have been anticipated that Hitler would reject this request on the ground that he had made his proposals sufficiently clear verbally in the course of the conversation on the preceding day. But the war party in Germany was also not yet finally in the ascendant. Mr. Chamberlain's refusal to renew contact had provoked some consternation among the moderates in the German camp; and Hitler, in view of the high hopes placed by the German people in Mr. Chamberlain's intervention, was reluctant to break off the negotiations and anxious for a further meeting. Ribbentrop was accordingly instructed to inform us that a German memorandum would be prepared in the course of the evening and that we should be informed as soon as it was ready. At 10:30 that night the conversations were resumed.

"Although Hitler was in a much less truculent mood and even made an effort to appear conciliatory, his memorandum showed that he had not moderated his demands, which were presented in a most peremptory form and described by Hitler as his last word. In this document he required the Czechs to begin the evacuation of the predominantly Sudeten areas at 8 a.m. on September 28th. Thus, the Czechoslovak Government was to be given a bare forty-eight hours to issue the necessary orders, and only four days in which to evacuate the whole of the Sudeten Lands. It is characteristic of Hitler's methods of argument that, when the Prime Minister pointed out that this was a sheer dictate (the word always applied by Hitler to the Treaty of Versailles) imposed on a country voluntarily surrendering a part of its territory without having been defeated in war, the Chancellor replied: 'It is not a dictate; look, the document is headed by the word 'memorandum.'

"In the course of the long discussion which followed, Hitler agreed to modify his timetable slightly, and he also made in his own handwriting a number of minor alterations designed to attenuate the asperity of the memorandum. 'You are the only man,' he said somewhat bitterly to Mr. Chamberlain, 'to whom I have ever made a concession.' He appeared, however, relieved when the Prime Minister finally said that, while he could not accept or recommend the German proposals, he could nevertheless, as an intermediary, not refuse to submit them to the Czechoslovak Government. Hitler had no desire that the German people should think that the negotiations had broken down as the result of his own intransigency. He was nonetheless bent on the military occupation of Czechoslovakia. He was prepared to risk war with Britain; but, on the other hand, his military advisers were not.

"On the following morning the Prime Minister left by air again for London. Thanks to the energy and drive of Colonel Mason-Macfarlane the German memorandum and the map with the Godesberg line marked on it were in the hands of the Czech Government the same night. It had meant Mason-Macfarlane's flying back to Berlin, motoring to the Czech frontier, and then walking ten kilometers in the dark through Czech barbed wire and other entanglements, at the constant risk of being shot as a raider by either Germans or Czechs."

Source: Nevile Henderson, *Failure of a Mission: Berlin, 1937-1939*,
   pp. 155-62.

*   *   *

Herbert von Dirksen, the German Ambassador to Britain had temporarily returned to Germany on leave in September 1938, where he became caught up in events on the edge of the Czech crisis.

A German View of Godesberg

"When a few days later [after Hitler's speech on Party-Day] I visited the Secretary of State, Weizsäcker, he said that I had come at the right moment, as Chamberlain wished to visit Hitler on the following day at Berchtesgaden and that I was to go to Munich that evening as a member of the delegation. Having arrived there, we drove to the aerodrome to welcome the Prime Minister and Sir Horace Wilson. The German delegates were put up in one of the hotels and remained there until the following morning. Not one of us was consulted...and we also heard little of what was taking place. Then it filtered through: that, contrary to all expectations, the conference had run more smoothly than could have been anticipated. Next morning the German and British delegates started on their return journey to Munich. I travelled with Sir Horace Wilson. He told me that Chamberlain had recognized the self-determination of the Sudeten Germans. A second conference had been fixed. It was to be held within a week at Godesberg. So hope sprang up once more, despite the disloyal action of Hitler and Ribbentrop, who, contrary to what had been agreed upon, issued instructions to withhold the minutes of the conference from the British (the minutes having been drawn up by interpreter Schmidt, the sole witness present).

"A few days later the same Foreign Office officials assembled once more in Berlin for the journey to Godesberg. Whilst the meeting in Berchtesgaden had been small and intimate, the Godesberg Conference resembled Locarno, or similar meetings of world-wide importance. A large German staff filled the modest Hotel Dreesen, which in ordinary times was a meeting-place for tourists who wished to drink Rhine wine on the terrace of the hotel, with a view of the majestic river. Now newspapermen from all parts of the globe congregated, whilst all approaches to the hotel were closely guarded. Party officials turned up to bathe in the sun of highest favors.

"Soon after our arrival we drove to the Cologne aerodrome. Here, too, preparations had been made. A guard of honor—S.S. men, of course—had been marched up. When the Prime Minister with Sir Horace Wilson and Sir William Strang [a Foreign Office official responsible for Central European affairs] descended from the plane he saluted the guard of honor, and then we drove to the beautifully situated Petersberg Hotel, lying on the far bank of the Rhine, opposite to Godesberg. Again I sat in the same car as Sir Horace Wilson. He told me that Chamberlain had done his utmost in London to bring about a compromise. Now he was in a position to make proposals to Hitler which would surely satisfy him. But one should not hurry the Prime Minister, but give him time to bring the entire business to a successful conclusion.

"These favorable reports filled me with joy, and I hastened to pass them on to Ribbentrop, whom I met at the midday meal on the terrace of the Hotel Dreesen. I took it that he, too, would rejoice at the forthcoming satisfactory solution. But when he heard Sir Horace's advice not to press Chamberlain unduly, he put on his iron face, banged the table with his fist, and called out, 'Three days.' These two words left a deep and lasting impression on me and completely changed my ideas about Hitler and Ribbentrop. The hopes which had filled me on taking up my post in London that something useful and lasting might result through an improvement in Anglo-German relations had indeed been shattered during recent weeks. When Hitler declined to receive me and the Minister for Foreign Affairs had expressed the view of not permitting the Ambassadors to return to their posts in times of crisis, it became fairly clear to me what these two men had in mind with regard to responsible officials assigned to responsible posts. They distrusted them, and as the Ambassadors worked in favor of peace, this distrust could only mean that Berlin headquarters was not in favor of peace.

"These vague suspicions were now confirmed by Ribbentrop's words. It was quite obvious to me that he was not at all interested in obtaining autonomy for the Sudeten Germans by peaceful means, or he would have rejoiced at the coming triumph. It surely was immaterial whether this object was attained in two, three, or five weeks. His vexation and the intention of humiliating the Englishmen through a short-timed ultimatum, and so preventing any compromise, clearly proved that for him it was not a matter of achieving a political result, but of humiliating the opponent and possibly of precipitating war. From that time onwards I abandoned any hopes of converting Ribbentrop to a sensible policy, and determined to make myself independent, and to work against him as best I could. My hopes that Hitler desired not war, but perhaps an honorable understanding with Great Britain, had been severely shaken.

"When the conference opened, it was nearly wrecked by Hitler, who declined Chamberlain's offers, although they fulfilled almost all his demands, so the British statesman took refuge in written communications by addressing a letter to the German side. Although Chamberlain adopted this method to determine definitely in writing the responsibility for a rupture, he nevertheless offered Hitler and Ribbentrop the desired opportunity of a tactical delay, which proved itself a dangerous weapon in view of the world's feverish tension.

"In any case the two locked themselves in their rooms for the greater part of the day in order to hatch a reply, without consulting one of their advisers.... The Germans present were Hitler, Ribbentrop, and the interpreter Schmidt; the British were Chamberlain, Sir Horace Wilson, and an interpreter. We were tormented mainly lest an agreement might be prevented by differences of opinion on the delineation of boundaries, in so far as Germany might claim too extensive Czech territories as belonging to the Sudetenland and the British might draw the boundaries too narrow. Thus the conference might have broken up, even though an agreement might have been reached on principle. The hours seemed to drag out endlessly.

"At eleven o'clock came the disastrous news that the Czechs had mobilized. A rupture seemed unavoidable. I was talking with Sir William Strang. At last the doors of the conference room opened. A rupture had been avoided; this, at least, was the confident interpretation ascribed to the result of the conference. Hitler had almost wrecked it with his short-term ultimatum, within which the evacuation was to be carried out. As Hitler had attained his political aims—the freedom of the Sudeten Germans—and as any serious reasons for the short-term ultimatum no longer existed, his further intentions were suspect. A catastrophe had only been avoided because Chamberlain declared himself willing to submit Hitler's demands to the Governments of the Western Powers, but without recommending their acceptance. How irresponsible Hitler's resolve had been to let the conference fail only because of the minor question of a time limit was proved by the fact that complete unity of the Sudeten territory had been agreed upon by both delegations. This problem which might indeed have become a dangerous obstacle, offered no difficulties."

Source: Herbert von Dirksen, *Moscow Tokyo London: Twenty Years of German Foreign Policy*, pp. 208-11.

*   *   *

When Chamberlain returned to London, he had to convince both his own Cabinet and the French that the terms sketched at Godesberg formed a reasonable basis for settlement of the Sudeten question. Sir Alexander Cadogan, the Permanent Under-Secretary of State for Foreign Affairs, recorded the story of those days in his diary.

Three Days in London

Saturday, 24 September

"Hitler's memo. now in. It's awful. A week ago when we moved (or were pushed) from 'autonomy' to cession, many of us found great difficulty in the idea of ceding people to Nazi Germany. We salved our consciences (at least I did) by stipulating it must be an 'orderly' cession—i.e. under international supervision, with safeguards for exchange of populations, compensation, &c. Now Hitler says he must march into the whole area *at once* (to keep order!) and the safeguards— and plebiscites! can be held *after*! This is throwing away every last safeguard that we had. P.M. is transmitting this 'proposal' to Prague. Thank God he hasn't yet recommended it for acceptance. He returned by lunch time. I dropped H[alifax]. at the Palace at 10. He then went to meet P.M. and lunched with him, so I hardly saw H. in the morning....

"Meeting of 'Inner Cabinet' at 3.30 and P.M. made his report to us. I was completely horrified—he was quite calmly for total surrender. More horrified still to find that Hitler has evidently hypnotised him to a point. Still more horrified to find P.M. took nearly an hour to make his report, and there was practically no discussion. J[ohn]. S[imon].—seeing which way the cat was jumping—said that after all it was a question of 'modalities', whether the Germans went in now or later! Ye Gods! And during Thursday and Friday J.S. was as bellicose as the Duke of Plaza Toro. At times he almost went berserk. I gave H. a note of what *I* thought, but it had no effect. P.M. left at 5.10 to rest. I told J.S. and Sam Hoare what I thought: I think the latter shares my view, but he's a puny creature. Cabinet at 5.30 and H. got back at 8 completely and quite happily défaitiste-pacifist. He seemed to think the Cabinet were all right. I *wonder!* They don't yet understand and they haven't seen the map. (They're going round after dinner to have it explained to them by Horace [Wilson]!) Pray God there will be a revolt. Back to F[oreign] .O[ffice]. after dinner. H. got back from No. 10 talk with Labour about 10.30 Drove him home and gave him a bit of my mind, but didn't shake him. I've never before known him to make up his mind so quickly and firmly on anything. I wish he hadn't chosen *this* occasion! I *know* there is a shattering telegram from Phipps about position in France: I *know* we and they are in no condition to fight: but I'd rather be beat than dishonoured. How can we look any foreigner in the face after this? How can we hold Egypt, India and the rest?

"Above all, *if* we have to capitulate, let's be honest. Let's say we're caught napping: that we can't fight now, but that we remain true to all our principles, put ourselves straight into war conditions and *rearm*. Don't—above all—let us pretend we think Hitler's plan is a *good* one! I've never had such a shattering day, or been so depressed and dispirited. I can only hope for a revolt in the Cabinet and Parliament.

"What *will* be written on the remaining pages of this Diary?

Sunday, 25 September
"Cabinet in morning, so I didn't go to F[oreign].O[ffice]. till 11.30. Nothing doing.... Cabinet again at 3.... Monteiro came in to say Franco had offered neutrality in European War. Even crumbs of good news are good! Cabinet up about 6. H. sent for me. He said 'Alec, I'm very angry with you. You gave me a sleepless night. I woke at 1 and never got to sleep again. But I came to the conclusion you were right, and at the Cabinet, when P.M. asked me to lead off, I plumped for refusal of Hitler's terms.' He *is* a frank and brave man. I apologised. He asked me whether I *knew* I was giving him an awful night. I said 'Yes' but had slept very well myself. Seems Cabinet anyhow wouldn't allow P.M. to make any further concessions (and I'm sure country wouldn't). We now have to look forward to frightful ordeal, but we face it with clean hands. I'm *relieved*. French arrived for discussion at 9 p.m. We agreed that we can't accept Hitler's proposals. J.S. was turned on in his best manner, to cross-examine French as to what they would *do*. Awful. But French kept their tempers and they agreed to send for Gamelin. Cabinet about 11.30

Short meeting with French again. Home about 1.30 Record of 3 Cabinets in one day!

Monday, 26 September

"Meeting with French at 10, put off to 10.30. Began with private talk P.M., Daladier, Corbin (then Gamelin). Told French of our new—and further—undertaking to be with them at once if they are 'engaged in active hostilities' as result of German invasion of Cz[echoslovakia]. Full meeting with French about 11. Told them of P.M.'s last message to Hitler being sent by H. Wilson. Told them it hinted at no further concessions but merely appealed for negotiation as against violence. Concocted with French message of warning to Warsaw about Teschen. French left."

Source: Sir Alexander Cadogan, *The Diaries of Sir Alexander Cadogan, 1938-1945*, edited by David Dilks, pp. 103-6.

*   *   *

*A*s Cadogan mentions, it was decided to send Horace Wilson to Berlin to convey the British position directly to Hitler. Ivone Kirkpatrick, at that time serving as First Secretary at the British Embassy in Berlin, recalls those meetings of 26 and 27 September.

Chamberlain's Emissary

"Sir Horace Wilson arrived in Berlin during the afternoon of September 26th bearing a personal letter from the Prime Minister to Hitler. In this letter Mr. Chamberlain said that the Godesberg proposals had been rejected by the Czechoslovak Government. The difference was one of form. He considered accordingly that a further effort should be made to reach agreement and he suggested a meeting with Czechoslovak representatives to consider ways and means of handing over the territory. After a brief consultation Sir Horace Wilson, Henderson and myself set out for the Chancellery where Hitler was to receive us at 5 p.m. Hitler was in one of his worst moods. He was only induced with much difficulty to listen to the

Prime Minister's letter. At intervals he rose from his chair and drifted towards the door as if resolved to leave the room. I gazed at him in fascination. During one of his many tirades I was unable to take my eyes off him and my pencil remained poised above the paper. Sir Horace Wilson noticed this and whispered: 'Are you getting everything down? It's frightfully important.' I whispered back: 'I'm not likely to forget a word.' Nor did I. With only a sketchy note I was able later without the slightest difficulty to reconstruct the whole conversation. At times, particularly when Wilson spoke about the Prime Minister's desire for a peaceful solution, Hitler pushed back his chair and smote his thigh in a gesture of frustrated rage.

"After a long and painful discussion Hitler agreed to the proposed meeting, but only on condition that the Czechoslovak Government accepted the Godesberg memorandum. Moreover, the meeting must terminate satisfactorily in two days. Otherwise the occupation might begin before October 1st. In a word, he agreed to a meeting provided it was understood that the Czechs would give way at every point. Wilson promised to report to the Prime Minister. As we were leaving, Hitler observed that the whole of Germany was behind him. He thought it would be an excellent thing if Wilson could verify this for himself and he accordingly invited him to be present that evening at the meeting in the Sportspalast where he was going to make a speech on the Czech question. Sir Horace Wilson, looking slightly embarrassed, said that he would be able to hear the speech on the radio. 'That is not the same thing,' retorted Hitler. 'You must be present to sense the atmosphere.'

"We returned to the Embassy to dinner. Henderson and Wilson dined in the dining-room, whilst I ate off a tray in front of the radio set to hear as truculent a speech as Hitler ever made. We sat up all that night reporting our conversation with Hitler and his speech. In the early hours of the morning the Prime Minister telegraphed the text of a statement which he was issuing immediately. In it he offered to see that the Czech promises were carried out with reasonable promptitude provided the Germans agreed to a peaceful transfer of the territory. We also received instructions for a second interview with Hitler. By this time it was clear to me that Hitler was bent on having his little war. I felt that the interview could have little result and Hitler's behaviour was so offensive that I wanted never to see him again. He seemed to be enveloped in an aura of such ruthless wickedness that it was oppressive and almost nightmarish to sit in the same room. I therefore asked Wilson if I might be excused from attending. This was very pusillanimous since the interviews were certainly interesting and exciting enough for the most blasé of officials. I can only say that Hitler had inspired me with such a physical repugnance that I could not bring myself to go. Wilson replied that he was very sorry, but that he must ask me to attend. So I put on my hat and we went off once more to the Chancellery. The time for the interview was fixed for 12.15. The ante-room was full of high officials, all manifestly depressed by the turn of events. Bodenschatz, the liaison officer between Goering and Hitler, whispered to Henderson that we must be firm and he wished us well. We went in. Hitler looked as black as thunder. He told us several times, grinding his heel into the carpet, that he had had enough of the Czechs. 'I will smash the Czechs', he shouted. One could sense that he was itching to drop a bomb on Prague, to see Benes in flight. Sir Horace Wilson asked if in the light of the Prime Minister's statement he could take back any message to London. Hitler retorted that there were only two courses open to the Czechs, acceptance or rejection of the German terms. From this attitude he savagely refused to budge.

"Sir Horace Wilson, speaking very slowly and quietly, then said that he had a message to give from the Prime Minster. He would try to give it in the Prime Minister's words and manner. If, he continued, the Germans attacked Czechoslovakia and the French in pursuance of their treaty obligation became engaged in a conflict with Germany, then Britain would feel obliged to support France. Hitler replied angrily that he could only take note of this statement. If France felt obliged to attack Germany, then Britain also felt obliged to commit an act of aggression against Germany. Sir Horace Wilson retorted that Hitler had clearly misunderstood the purport of the message. He must therefore in the interest of history repeat it. Still speaking very slowly, Wilson then repeated the formula to a Hitler who was showing signs of rising exasperation, wriggling in his seat, slapping his knee, drumming on the floor with his heel. But quite unperturbed, Wilson slowly recited his piece to the end. Before the translation was complete Hitler bellowed furiously: 'It's just what I said. If France attacks

Germany, then England must attack Germany too.' He added, 'If France strikes and England strikes, I don't care a bit. I am prepared for every eventuality'; and Ribbentrop sagely nodded his agreement. Sir Horace Wilson, looking very pained, said that it was evident that the Chancellor still misunderstood the message and he must ask leave to repeat it. But this time Hitler was on his feet shouting that he understood the purport of the message only too well. It meant that in six days' time we should all be at war with one another. Thereupon we all coldly shook hands with the infuriated Führer and took our leave. As I grasped his podgy hand I felt an overwhelming sense of relief that war would come and that I should never have to see him again. In the Embassy the feeling was the same. There was general satisfaction that the die had been cast. One member of the staff drove to Wannsee to collect his golf clubs, and I had a long telephone conversation with my wife in England, for which I innocently thought I should never have to pay. After lunch I went to the Tempelhof aerodrome to see Sir Horace Wilson off. We took the opportunity of sending home a member of the staff who had to travel to England on duty. This excited the Gestapo enormously, for they noted that the aircraft was flying away with one more passenger than it had brought. They did not interfere, though they could not refrain from asking who the individual was who had been added to Sir Horace Wilson's suite.

"The same evening the Prime Minister informed Dr. Benes that it seemed likely that German troops would cross the frontier almost at once unless the Czechoslovak Government accepted the German terms forthwith. In this situation the British Government felt unable to tender advice as to what Dr. Benes should do. Later a further effort was made to induce Hitler to come to terms, and at 11 p.m. a note was handed to the German State Secretary embodying a proposed time-table for the evacuation of the Sudeten territory. He replied that the plan was out of date and he did not believe that it could possibly be accepted. While all this was going on our work in the Chancery was disturbed by the rattle of an enormous motorised and armoured column which passed down the Wilhelmstrasse in an easterly direction. The column took over three hours to pass and represented the flower of the German Army. I went out for a moment or two to have a look at it and returned to my desk both impressed and depressed. The people of Berlin who were standing glumly on the pavement stared at the passing troops but showed no emotion whatever. My friends in the Reich Chancellery told me that Hitler, who was watching from a window, was disgusted with the crowd for their apathy."

Source: Ivone J. Kirkpatrick, *The Inner Circle: Memoirs*, pp. 122-27.

*   *   *

Alexander Cadogan describes the discussions of strategy that were being conducted while Horace Wilson was meeting with Hitler, and the events that followed his return.

On the Brink of War

Tuesday, 27 September

"Students of history may be puzzled by recent events.... Gamelin seems to have put heart in to P.M., so we declared 'solidarity with France' in event of her being engaged in 'active hostilities'. Cross-examination of Gamelin showed that 'active hostilities' probably meant a squib offensive (to bring us in) and then retirement on Maginot Line to wait (6 months) for our 'Kitchener armies'! This didn't suit at all, so John S. took up his pen and drafted telegram to Paris emphasising that we must 'fully concert' beforehand any offensive action!

"Frightful afternoon—the worst I have spent. Was sent for to No.10 about 3. Small meeting of Ministers, frightened out of their wits by Gamelin's conversation, by a telegram from Phipps about French feeling, and by Malcolm M[acdonald, Secretary for the Dominions] (and Bruce) on subject of Dominions. P.M. came in and out. Unfortunately Mason Macfarlane (M[ilitary] A[ttaché] in Berlin) also here, and he painted gloomy picture of Czech morale. What does he know about it? Also meeting with Chiefs of Staff who were called in. Not very reassuring. But P.M. authorised Backhouse to mobilise Fleet. But all this produced a glacial period in Ministerial feet. But I got H's authority to send off telegrams proposing my 'timetable'. P.M. due to broadcast at 8. We were turned out of Cabinet room at 7.30 by electricians rigging microphone. P.M., Horace, H. and I adjourned to Horace's room. Horace had drafted telegram of complete capitulation—telling Czechs to accept Hitler memo. H. played up against it, and I spoke my mind. Poor P.M. (quite exhausted) said 'I'm wobbling about all over the place' and went in to broadcast. Back at F.O. after dinner as usual—I never get away before midnight.

Wednesday, 28 September

"4 a.m. this morning Roosevelt and another broadcast proposing Conference. 11.30 P.M. sent telephone messages to Hitler and Musso saying he ready to go to Germany again. About 2.30, while I was listening to T. Inskip [Minister for the Co-ordination of Supply] holding forth to H. on insufficiency of our defences, telegram brought in from Rome saying Musso had got 24 hour postponement of German mobilisation (due 2 p.m. today). H. went off to House to hear P.M. 3.30 N. Henderson rang me to say Hitler invited P.M., Musso (accepted) and Daladier to Munich tomorrow. Dictated message and ran with it to House. Fished H. out of Peers' Gallery and we went along to behind Speaker's Chair and sent it in to P.M., who was still speaking. He used it as peroration—with tremendous effect and House adjourned—Thank God!"

Source: Sir Alexander Cadogan, *The Diaries of Sir Alexander Cadogan, 1938-1945*, edited by David Dilks, pp. 106-9.

*　　　　*　　　　*

*M*ussolini's *Foreign Minister and son-in-law, Count Galeazzo Ciano, tells the story of Mussolini's intervention in the crisis, referred to above by Cadogan, which led to the fateful meeting in Munich on the 29th.*

Mussolini Intervenes

September 28

"10 a.m. Four hours to go before the outbreak of hostilities, when Perth telephones to ask for an interview. I receive him at once. He says, with much emotion, that Chamberlain appeals to the Duce for his friendly intervention in these hours, which he considers the last in which something can be done to save peace and civilization. He repeats the guarantee already offered by England and France for the return of the Sudetenland. I ask Perth whether I am to regard his *démarche* as an official invitation to the Duce to assume the role of mediator. Yes. In that case there is no time to lose—the offer deserves to be given consideration. I tell Perth to wait for me at the Palazzo Chigi. I go to the Duce. He agrees at once on the impossibility of meeting Chamberlain's request with a flat refusal. He telephones Attolico [the Italian Ambassador in Berlin]: 'Go to the Führer and tell him, having first said that in any eventuality I shall be at his side, that I recommend that the commencement of hostilities should be delayed for 24 hours. Meanwhile I undertake to study what can be done to solve the problem.' I go back to the Palazzo Chigi. I inform Perth that hostilities are to begin to-day and confirm that our place is beside Germany. His face quivers and his eyes are red. When I add that nevertheless the Duce has accepted Chamberlain's and has proposed a delay of 24 hours, he bursts into a sobbing laugh and rushes off to his Embassy. A little later he asks for another interview. He brings with him a message from Chamberlain to the Duce and a copy of another sent to Hitler: a concrete proposal for a Conference of Four with the task of reaching a radical solution of the Sudeten problem within seven days. It cannot be rejected—by rejecting it Hitler would draw the hatred of the world upon himself and have the sole responsibility for the conflict. Palazzo Venezia—the Duce decides to support the English request, particularly as the Führer has now, at Mussolini's desire, had a phonogram of instructions made. I telephone to Perth, to inform him, and to Attolico, to give him directions. Naturally I cancel the meeting with Ribbentrop and Keitel [chief of the supreme command of the German armed forces] arranged yesterday.

"Blondel [the French Ambassador in Rome] too, it transpires from a telephone call, is preparing to make a '*démarche*'. Not a hope—it is not our intention that France shall interfere. The whole face of the question would be changed and the Germans would, rightly, smell a rat. I telephone to Perth [the British Ambassador in Rome]: 'It transpires that France is preparing to put her oar in. I advise you that any *démarche* by Blondel would simply defeat its own ends. Find a way of preventing it. Our work would be imperilled.' He agrees and undertakes to comply with my request.

"3 p.m. Attolico telephones that Hitler agrees in principle, making certain reservations of secondary importance. He lays down one condition, however: the presence of Mussolini, which he regards as the sole guarantee. The Duce accepts. We leave at 6 to-night, in order to be in Munich, where the Conference is to take place, at 10.30 in the morning.

"I return to the Duce with the American Ambassador, bearing a very tardy message from Roosevelt. I remain alone with the Duce. 'As you see,' he says, 'I am only moderately happy, because, though perhaps at a heavy price, we could have liquidated France and Great Britain for ever. We now have overwhelming proof of this.'

"We leave at 6. The unanimous prayers of Italy are with us.

September 29-30

"In the train the Duce is in a very good humor. We dine together and he speaks with great vivacity on every subject. He criticizes Britain and British policy severely. 'In a country where animals are adored to the point of making cemeteries and hospitals and houses for them, and legacies are bequeathed to parrots, you can be sure that decadence has set in. Besides, other reasons apart, it is also a consequence of the composition of the English people. Four million surplus women. Four million sexually unsatisfied women, artificially creating a host of problems in order to excite or appease their senses. Not being able to embrace one man, they embrace humanity.'

"At Kufstein we meet the Führer. We get into his carriage, where spread out on a table are all the maps of the Sudetenland and the western fortifications. He explains the situation: he intends to liquidate Czechoslovakia as she now is, because she immobilizes forty of his divisions and ties his hands *vis-à-vis* France. When Czechoslovakia has been, as she must be, deflated, ten divisions will be enough to immobilize her. The Duce listens with concentration. The programme is now fixed: either the Conference is successful in a short time or the solution will take place by force of arms. 'Besides,' adds the Führer, 'the time will come when we shall to fight side by side against France and England. All the better that it should happen while the Duce and I are at the head of our countries, and still young and full of vigor.'

"But all that seems superseded by the atmosphere which in fact has been created—an atmosphere of agreement. Even the people waving as the train passes make one realize their joy at the event which is in the air.

"After a brief stop at the palace where the Duce and I are staying, we go to the Führerhaus, where the conference is to take place. The others have already arrived and are gathered round a table on which snacks and drinks are set out. The Führer comes half-way down the stairs to meet us and, with the rest of his suite, singles out us, the Italians, by a marked distinction of treatment. Brief, cold handshakes with Daladier and Chamberlain—then the Duce, alone, goes over to a corner of the room where the Nazi leaders surround him. There is a vague sense of embarrassment, particularly on the part of the French. I talk to Daladier, and then to François-Poncet, about trivial things. Then to Chamberlain, who says he wants to talk to the Duce. He thanks him for all that he has already done. But the Duce, coldly, does not take advantage of the opening, and the conversation peters out.

"We enter the conference room. The four chiefs; Ribbentrop, Leger, Wilson, and I; and Schmidt, the interpreter. The Führer speaks—a few words of thanks and an exposition of the situation. He speaks calmly, but from time to time he gets excited and then he raises his voice and beats his fist against the palm of his other hand. Then Chamberlain. Then Daladier. Lastly the Duce, who affirms the necessity for a rapid and concrete decision, and with this end in view proposes to use as a basis for discussion a document which has in fact been telephoned to us by our Embassy the previous evening, as expressing the desires of the German Government.

"The discussion develops formally and without very much animation. Chamberlain is inclined to linger over legal points; Daladier defends the cause of the Czechs without much conviction; the Duce prefers to remain silent and sum up and draw conclusions when the others have finished their dissertations.

"We adjourn for lunch, which takes place in the Führer's private house—a modest apartment in a large building full of other residents. It has, however, many very valuable pictures.

"The conference is continued in the afternoon and virtually breaks up into little groups which try to work out the various formulas. This permits us to talk with greater confidence, and the ice is broken.

"Daladier, particularly, is loquacious in personal conversation. He says that what is happening to-day is due solely to the pig-headedness of Benes. In the last few months he has repeatedly suggested to Benes that the Sudetens should be given autonomy. That would at least have deferred the present crisis. He grumbles about the French warmongers, who would have liked to push the country into an absurd and indeed impossible war—for France and England would never have been able to do anything really useful for Czechoslovakia, once she was attacked by the forces of the Reich.

"The Duce, slightly annoyed by the vaguely parliamentary atmosphere which conferences always produce, moves round the room with his hands in his pockets and a rather distracted air. Every now and then he joins in the search for a formula. His great spirit, always ahead of events and men, has already absorbed the idea of agreement and, while the others are still wasting their breath over more or less formal problems, he has almost ceased to take any interest. He has already passed on and is meditating other things.

"However, he joins in the discussion again, when it turns to the question of including in the agenda the problem of the Polish and Hungarian minorities. The others, without exception, would gladly have said nothing about it. In fact they try to evade its discussion. But when there is a strong will, the strong will always predominates and others coalesce around it. The problem is discussed and solved by means of a formula which I do not hesitate to describe as very brilliant.

"Meanwhile conversations à deux are taking place. There is a hint at the possibility of the Duce delaying his departure in order to permit a meeting between him and Chamberlain. But the idea is ruled out by the Duce, as he thinks that this might offend German susceptibilities. First I and then the Duce talk to Chamberlain. We tell him more or less the same things: we disinterest ourselves in Spain; withdrawal of 10,000 volunteers in the near future; goodwill for a speedy implementation of our Pact of April 16. Chamberlain hints at the possibility of a Conference of Four to solve the Spanish problem.

"At last, at one in the morning, the document is completed. Everybody is satisfied, even the French—even the Czechs, according to what Daladier tells me. François-Poncet has a moment of shame while he is collating the document. 'Voilà comme la France traite les seuls alliés qui lui étaient restés fidèles,' he exclaims.

"We sign, shake hands, and depart.

"In Italy, from the Brenner to Rome, from the King down to the peasants, the Duce receives welcomes such as I have never seen. He says himself that this enthusiasm was only equalled on the evening when the Empire was proclaimed.

"Ribbentrop has handed me a project for a tripartite alliance between Italy, Germany, and Japan. He says it is 'the biggest thing in the world'. He always exaggerates, Ribbentrop. No doubt we will study it quite calmly and, perhaps, put it aside for some time."

Source: Count Galeazzo Ciano, *Ciano's Hidden Diary, 1937-1938*, translated by Andreas Mayor, pp. 165-68.

*   *   *

The French Ambassador to Germany, André François-Poncet, has provided us with another impression of the meeting.

A French Perspective

"The meeting began at 12.45 in an adjoining room. The ambassadors were not admitted. Two hours later, as the meeting adjourned, I was informed that the four participants exposed their points of view in turn in general terms. Hitler delivered a diatribe of extreme violence against Czechoslovakia. Thereupon Daladier clearly and vigorously posed the crucial question. Did the Conference wish Czechoslovakia to exist or not? Was the amputation intended to make her healthier and to give her better chances for life in the future? Or was it but a means to weaken her, a mutilation bound to bring about her death? If the point was to prepare the dismemberment and disappearance of Czechoslovakia, then he, Daladier, had no business in this place. He refused to be associated with such a crime and would take his leave. If, on the contrary, the point was to assure Czechoslovakia's future, then he was prepared to concur with the others in a spirit of reciprocal concession and collaboration. The French Premier spoke in accents of a determination and nobility that moved his hearers.

"Mussolini declared that Hitler's idea had been misunderstood, and, like the Duce, all protested that they wished to consolidate and to respect the existence of the Czechoslovakian State.

"At three o'clock luncheon was served.

"There was a second session at the close of the afternoon. This time I entered by permission and sat behind Daladier. The delegates were grouped in a semi-circle around a vast fireplace, the British on the left, the Italians and the Germans in the center, the French on the right. Within the British group there was scant conversation; within the German and Italian groups there was much. Mussolini was deeply ensconced in his armchair. His extraordinarily mobile features were never at rest for a moment; his mouth would part for a wide smile or contract in a pout; his eyes, generally curious and amused in expression, would suddenly dart lightning.

"Standing at his side, Hitler gazed intently upon him, subject to his charm and as though fascinated and hypnotized. Did the Duce laugh, the Führer laughed too; did Mussolini scowl, so scowled Hitler. Here was a study in mimicry. It was to leave me with the lasting and erroneous impression that Mussolini exercised a firmly established ascendancy over the Führer. At any rate that day he did.

"No one presided at this session and there was no methodical agenda. For want of directive, the discussion proved difficult, confused, and interminably long. Hampered by the necessity of a double translation, it kept constantly changing its topic and ceased whenever a contradiction arose. The atmosphere grew thicker and heavier. At last toward evening the British produced a type-written memorandum from their files. It had been drawn up by Horace Wilson with Strang's assistance. The debate, which had wavered, now concentrated upon this proposal for an agreement.... At 1:30 a.m. the agreement was signed.

"It provided for the evacuation, in four stages, of districts 'preponderantly' German; this was to begin on October 1 and be completed by October 10. Conditions were to be determined and supervised by an international commission composed of representatives of Britain, Italy, Germany, and Czechoslovakia. The commission was also to rule upon what districts were to hold plebiscites and, until these had been completed, international contingents were to occupy the territory. Previous plebiscites in the Saar were to serve for models and the operation was to be concluded by the end of November at latest. Inhabitants of these transferred districts were to enjoy an interval of six months before opting between inclusion and exclusion. A German-Czechoslovak commission would assure the details governing the right of option and would arrange the exchange of populations.

"Compared to the Godesberg ultimatum the Munich agreement marked a considerable withdrawal of German claims. But that fact did not lessen the painful character of the Munich decisions. The French felt it fully. A land which had always been their loyal ally was suffering a large-scale material reduction and horrible moral humiliation. It was being deprived of cities and regions which formed a valuable part of its riches. It had perforce to yield to the threats of might. It had been sacrificed to the cause of peace.

"We were bitterly aware of the cruelty of the event. Daladier shook his head, muttered, and cursed circumstances. He refused to take part in the congratulations exchanged by the other delegates. Worst, the most painful step had not yet been taken; we had now to break the news to the Czechoslovaks who were awaiting the outcome of the Conference at their hotel. Mastny, their minister in Berlin, broke into tears. I consoled him as best I could. 'Believe me', I said, 'all this is not final. It is but one moment in a story which has just begun and which will soon bring up the issue again.'

"Returning to our hotel at 2.30 a.m. I called Bonnet by telephone to inform him of what had happened, while Daladier, still cursing and lost in gloomy thought, weighed the difficulties he was likely to meet on his return to Paris. Bonnet swept aside my detailed explanations. 'Peace is assured,' he said. 'That is the main thing. Everybody will be happy.'

"Whatever may be the truth about the meeting, Daladier was resigned to giving way. But in doing so he was the prey of extreme distress. Sadness showed on his face, but he was well aware of the price of this surrender!"

Source: André François-Poncet, *The Fateful Years: Memoirs of a French Ambassador in Berlin, 1931-1938*, translated by Jacques LeClercq, pp. 270-73.

*   *   *

*E*ugen Dollman, *a translator working in the German Embassy at Rome, accompanied the Italian delegation to Munich.*

Pray for Peace

"It saddens me that my pen does not have the mordant power of a Saint Simon or Cardinal de Retz. How much material Munich would have given both men for what, as Ranke says, 'in the normal way passes only fleetingly from mouth to mouth'! Never have 'world figures' seemed more puny to me, and never have I cherished less respect for them than I did during those hours in the Prinz-Karl-Palais, the Führerbau and Hitler's private flat in Munich's Prinzregentplatz.

"Daladier alternated between apathy and tearful agitation. Not the least of his worries was that there should be an adequate supply of Pernod in the conference hall, and Herr Walterspiel delivered it with the same nonchalant efficiency he had shown when supplying Himmler's Tegernsee kitchen. Ciano felt sorry for his colleague from Paris and devised 'frivolous trifles' to amuse him and François-Poncet, the smooth, subtle schemer who was then French Ambassador to Berlin. Chamberlain, whose umbrella bearing arrival had evoked delighted grins from the élite troops who ringed the airport, certainly seemed to be in close communion with some invisible Anglican or Puritan deity, but he had none of the imperial aura of Benjamin Disraeli, who had so greatly impressed Bismarck at the Congress of Berlin. He played the martyr, and one can only speculate sadly as to what might have happened if the dictators had been confronted by a man like Churchill.

"The dictators, too, were in very different moods. Adolf Hitler obviously lamented the frustration of his war aims from the outset, and his disappointment was shared by all the other Nazi leaders with the single exception of Hermann Göring, whose delight at the success of the conference struck me as genuine and sincere. Mussolini, who had engineered the conference almost single-handed, obviously felt that he was at the zenith of his fame and glory

"Years later, when his fame and glory had evaporated, he talked to me about Munich. It was my last private audience with him, only a few days before he was lynched at Dongo in April 1945. A miracle had happened, he told me, and the miracle's name was Munich. The still impressive eyes glowed with their old fire and the weary, shrunken figure with the balding head of a Roman emperor drew itself erect in memory of the day. I remembered it too. Mussolini had, in effect, been chief interpreter at the Conference. His laborious English, Italianate French and questionable German were the linguistic highlights of a gathering at which none of the other three participants spoke a language other than his own. The Duce was, of course, able to enlist the services of the indefatigable Dr. Schmidt of the Foreign Office, but this did not prevent him from scintillating, from mediating, from holding Europe's trembling scales in balance....

"I took advantage of the lunch at Hitler's rather grisly private apartment in the Prinzregentenplatz to savor the bad taste of the devoted Party members, male and female, who had paid homage to their idol by presenting him with frightful specimens of home-handiwork and countless other souvenirs and tributes of every description.

"Mussolini, who was not overburdened with an aesthetic sense, found the sight quite undaunting, and his wife Donna Rachele would doubtless have revelled in it....

"After lunch, world history resumed its course. Thanks to the fact that Benito Mussolini was acting as interpreter-general, I did not find myself overworked. I spent most of the time standing around in corners with the Prince of Hessen or other members of the Italian party, watching with amusement as the Duce, striking a faintly bored dictatorial pose, paced up and down the room with his hands in his pockets. He was so carried away by his role that one would not have been surprised to see him don the imperial purple and plant a laurel-wreath on his bald pate. Daladier, fortified with Pernod, vented all his annoyance at the Munich fiasco on Benès and the Czechs. The people of Munich having given him a wild ovation outside the Vier Jahreszeiten, where he was staying, he had now donned the pose of a Parisian barrister whose case is lost but whose rhetorical brilliance is bound to win the court's acclaim. The British premier still awaited divine intervention and took comfort in his sense of personal decency, little realising that in this company such a quality spelt mortal danger.

"Just when things were getting interesting I was summoned from the room. A security guard outside the door told me excitedly that a veiled woman had appeared in the guard-room and demanded to speak to me on a matter of the utmost urgency. There was something intriguing and romantic about this feminine intrusion into the rude masculine world. Since my presence at the conference had not so far averted war or saved the peace, and since I knew nothing about the demands of the Sudeten Germans or Czechs, justified or unjustified, I hurried to the guard-room.

"There, surrounded by a group of young men of heroic stature and Nordic appearance, stood an extremely elegant lady of unmistakably Latin appearance. A dense black veil obscured most of her face. The uniformed youngsters continued to ogle her until she greeted me with a *'Carlo Dollmann—finalmente!'* I knew at once who it was. Only Donna Eleonora Attolico would have ventured so far along the corridors of power. A respectful circle formed round us. Then I had to laugh. She insisted that I ask Herr Hitler 'immediately and without delay' how the conference was going. Although I was much further from events than her husband, the Italian Ambassador, she seemed to find it entirely natural that I should step into the breach. The guards trembled with awe. I sent for a chair and asked her respectfully why the matter was so urgent. The mystery was soon solved: she had promised her favourite Madonna, the Madonna in the Pilgrims'

Church at Loreto, that she would bring her a fat golden candle in person if the conference went well and the peace of the world were assured. Her train left in half an hour, hence the urgency of her request. I told her that it would be out of the question for me to accost Hitler, but that I would gladly ask Benito Mussolini or Galeazzo Ciano. This did not suit her at all. With a meaningful glance, she instructed me to ask Heinrich Himmler, who knew everything.

"I went in search of Himmler and found him standing around looking important. Like his lord and master, he was not in a rosy mood—a nice gory war would have suited him better—but Donna Eleonora's name, coupled with an allusion of her proposed pilgrimage and the candle, put him in a more indulgent frame of mind. His initial surprise gave way to amusement. He authorised me to announce that peace was assured and further instructed me to take one of the guards on duty—one who was equipped with all the necessary permits—and convey the Lady Attolico to her sleeping-car with his compliments.

"I transmitted the joyful tidings. To the renewed astonishment of the guards, who may have been Christians but may equally have been devotees of Wotan, Donna Eleonora crossed herself. There was a brief argument as to who should drive us—an argument won, needless to say, by the man with the largest number of official passes. We climbed into a beflagged Maybach and raced through the crowded streets to Munich's main railway station. My companion had relapsed into silence and was probably praying. I do not know who the crowds thought we were, but they cheered us enthusiastically. The sleeping-car for Italy and Loreto was on the point of leaving when we arrived. The ecstatic driver received a handshake and I, to the amazement of the bystanders, a light kiss, Roman-style, on both cheeks.

"That was my chief contribution to the world-famous Munich Conference of 1938. I found on my return that the Western Powers had retired, worn out and dispirited, to their hotels to eat, while the representatives of the Axis-to-be settled down to an excessively long and substantial dinner. Mussolini cheerfully ignored the chilly mood of his confederates. He ate and drank with relish, his only kindred spirit at the table being Hermann Göring. Ciano, who had taken me aside at the beginning of the conference and begged me, as a native of Munich, to show him the city's night-life, became increasingly taciturn as the meal dragged on. I never managed to take him on a conducted tour, as it happened, nor did he get a chance to satisfy his curiosity.

"It was approaching 1 a.m. by the time everything was signed. The crowds cheered again, far more loudly than they had done during my ride with Donna Eleonora Attolico—in fact I had never heard the inhabitants of Munich cheer louder, even during the Oktoberfest or at carnival time. Benito Mussolini, who relished his triumph, bore the peace of the world home with him like a trophy."

Source: Eugen Dollman, *The Interpreter*, pp. 126-33.

* * *

Was Hitler happy with the agreement? Ribbentrop afterwards insisted that he was, that he had no desire to press his demands to the point of warfare.

A Happy Hitler?

"The solution made the Führer and me exceedingly happy, for the Munich solution was indeed an extraordinary political event. Dr. Hjalmar Schacht, my co-defendant at Nuremberg, a strong opponent of National Socialism, said repeatedly during the trial that Britain 'made Germany a present' of Czechoslovakia at Munich.

"During an interrogation after my arrest Mr. Kirkpatrick asked me whether 'the Führer had been very sorry' that Munich had led to a settlement because he had 'not got his war'; for Hitler had said in Munich that the next time, he wanted to 'throw Mr. Chamberlain and his umbrella down the stairs'. It can only be said that this is completely untrue. The Führer was very satisfied with Munich; I never heard as much as a hint to the contrary. He telephoned me immediately after the Prime Minister's departure, to tell me with joy of Mr. Chamberlain's call and the signing of the supplementary protocol. I congratulated Hitler because this had clarified relations with England.

On the same afternoon at the station Hitler again expressed his pleasure and satisfaction with the Munich Agreement.

"Any other version of the opinions held by Hitler or myself at the time is complete fiction."

Source: Joachim von Ribbentrop, *The Ribbentrop Memoirs*.

*   *   *

*H*ubert Ripka, the diplomatic correspondent of the Prague news-paper, Lidove Noviny, has recorded the public reaction of the Czechoslovak government and people to the agreement signed at Munich.

The Czech Reaction

"Meanwhile Prague was trembling in suspense, full of indescribable anxiety. Political conferences of the Government and representatives of the various parties were being held incessantly with the President of the Republic. The people of the whole country waited breathlessly. There were not many people who slept in the night from September 29th to 30th. In the morning of September 30th our diplomats brought the text of the Munich Agreement together with the relevant maps. It was a fearful blow—worse than the Anglo-French Ultimatum of September 21st.... The leading political administrators and the Government were in conference with the President of the Republic the whole morning. At 12 a.m. the Government, under the lead of the President, decided the following:

'After deep deliberation and examination of all important recom-mendations which were conveyed by the French and British Governments, and in full knowledge of its responsibility to poster-ity, the Czechoslovakian Government decided, in agreement with the responsible executives of the political parties, to accept the resolutions of the Four Great Powers. This was done with the conviction that it was indispensable to the preservation of the nation, and that there was no other alternative. Having decided to adopt this resolution, the Government of the Czechoslovak Republic were determined at the same time to register to the world a protest against these recommendations, which are one-sided, and were made without the nation's participation.'

"This resolution was communicated to the Czechoslovak nation on the wireless at 5 p.m. by their Prime Minister, General Syrovy. His declaration read as follows:—

'I have experienced the most tragic moment of my life. I am fulfilling the most painful duty which has ever fallen to my lot, a duty which is worse than death.... We have had to choose between useless fighting, and sacrifice. We have had to choose between the annihilation of all our citizens—men, women and children alike, and the acceptance of terms which were imposed on us by exterior pressure, and without defeat by war, and which, in their total lack of all consideration, have no parallel in history. We wanted to make our contribution towards Peace. Gladly would we have done so, but never in such a form as was forced upon us. We were forsaken, we remained alone. All European States, also our neighbours in the North and South, are mobilised. We are in the real sense of the word surrounded by forces far more powerful than our own. With the deepest concern, all your leaders, and the Army, and the President of the Republic were weighing up the possibilities which remained open to us.

'We have recognised that in the choice between the contraction of the frontiers and the death of our nation, our sacred duty was to preserve the life of our people, that they might emerge un-weakened from this terrible period, and that we might not abandon hope that our nation might rise again, as it has so often done in past history....'

"Nobody can realise the poignant grief and desolation which overwhelmed the Czechoslovak people. The streets of Prague were filled with endless crying and sobbing groups, and of course many outcries of desperate anger and defiance. Despite this, these assemblies were disciplined, feeling instinctively that in these tragic hours dissension and anarchy must not enter the ranks of the Czechoslovak people. Not Prague only, but also the smallest Czechoslovak hamlet where the shattering news was received, shook with despairing groans and fruitless defiance. Many hardened men and soldiers collapsed and fainted, unable to bear the news of the terrible wrong which was perpetrated on their nation...."

Source: *Four Days*, edited by Lord Killanin, pp. 120-24.

*   *   *

As the Poles had made clear beforehand, there was more to the Czechoslovakian situation than the issue of the Sudetenland. Juliusz Lukasiewicz, the Polish Ambassador to France, recorded the Polish reaction to the Munich agreement.

The Polish Ultimatum

"The decisions of the four-power conference in Munich...contained no definite resolutions concerning adjustments in Czechoslovak territories inhabited by minorities other than the Germans. Moreover, they stated in an additional declaration that, if within three months the problems of the Polish and Hungarian minorities were not settled by agreement with the governments in question, they would become the subject of further conferences of the prime ministers of the four powers. In this way, despite Czechoslovak commitments and French assurances that the problem of the Polish minority in Czechoslovakia would be settled simultaneously with that of the German minority, the matter was left open. At the same time the four powers whose representatives met in Munich reserved the right to return to these problems, not even asking for the agreement of the governments concerned.

"An especially disturbing element, from this point of view, was the declaration signed in Munich on September 30 by Chamberlain and Hitler. It stated that both sides considered 'the agreement signed last night and the Anglo-German Naval Agreement as symbolic of the desire of our two peoples never to go to war with one another again,' that they 'are resolved that the method of consultation shall be the method adopted to deal with any other questions that may concern our two countries,' and that they 'are determined to continue...efforts to remove possible sources of difference, and thus to contribute to assure the peace of Europe.'

"Since in this solemn declaration the problem of the Sudeten Germans was recognized as one which could concern the two countries, i.e., England and Germany, there were, of course, no formal reasons why in other circumstances Danzig or even Silesia could not become problems concerning the two countries.

"Another circumstance weighing on the Munich conference, from the Polish point of view, was the absence of Czechoslovakia. In all efforts designed to defend the rights of the Polish minority, we scrupulously followed the principle of not bypassing Prague. We sought French and British assurances only when it became clear that the Czechoslovak government had decided to surrender the problem of the German minority to Paris and London. But we always considered Czechoslovakia's own commitments, made to Poland directly, as most important.

"Thus appraising the situation we found ourselves in immediately after the announcement of the Munich agreements, I spent September 30 awaiting further news and instructions from Warsaw. Before I received them, about 8 p.m., M. Bonnet telephoned me. In an excited and irritated voice he told me that he had received news from Warsaw that the Polish government had supposedly demanded from Czechoslovakia in the form of an ultimatum the immediate cession of lands inhabited by a Polish majority, and that the deadline for this ultimatum was to run out on the following day, i.e., at noon on October 1. He finally asked whether I knew anything about this. I answered truthfully that I had no information on the subject but that I believed the news which had reached M. Bonnet was likely correct. I asked whether M. Bonnet remembered the declarations I had presented to him repeatedly over the past few months and the assurances he had given me. Clearly startled by my reply, Bonnet admitted that he remembered my declarations, as well as his own assurances, but he had not supposed that our reaction to Munich would be so grave and peremptory. I could do nothing but suggest to M. Bonnet as politely as possible that in the future he should not make light of the declarations of our government or of his own assurances.

"Later during this conversation Bonnet tried to induce me to intervene in Warsaw against employing too harsh methods toward Czechoslovakia. He stressed that he considered it intolerable that Poland should create new tensions in the international situation precisely at the moment that France and England were rejoicing that peace had been saved. I answered that there was nothing unexpected in our behavior, and that there would have been no question of new tensions in relations between Warsaw and Prague had the Czechoslovak government fulfilled its commitments and the French government kept the assurances made to me. This ended our talk.

"We resumed it two hours later when Bonnet telephoned me again; this time, without indignation or any attempt to put pressure on me, he asked about news from Warsaw. On the basis of cables I had received in the meantime, I was able to inform Bonnet that as a result of the unsatisfactory response to our note of September 27, and the resolutions of the Munich conference, the Polish government had demanded that Czechoslovakia fulfill its commitments toward us not later than noon of the next day, i.e., October 1. I added that I hoped the French government, for its part, would honor the assurances made to us and would advise the Czechoslovak government as emphatically as possible that it should not delay with an affirmative answer. Bonnet said that he would be very happy to contribute to a rapid and peaceful settlement of the problem, but he doubted whether in the mood prevailing in Prague following the decisions of the Munich conference the intervention of the French envoy could be effective.... In a further exchange of ideas we agreed, on my initiative, that Bonnet would try to reach President Benes by telephone directly and advise him to accept the Polish demands as consistent with commitments contracted by the Czechoslovak government in June.

"M. Bonnet's remark that he did not have much faith in the effectiveness of the intervention of his envoy in Prague was especially valuable to me. It fully confirmed what I had told M. Bonnet many times—that at the moment the tension caused by the problem of the Sudeten Germans passed, France's influence on Prague would prove insufficient to ensure the fulfillment of obligations toward Poland, and that for this reason our demand that the problem of the Polish minority be settled not only parallel, but simultaneously, with that of the Sudeten Germans was fully justified.

"It must be noted here that although the answer of the Czechoslovak government to our note of September 27, not given until September 30, did contain acceptance of the principle of a rectification of frontiers, at the same time it prolonged the procedure of taking care of this matter to two months, and offered no other guarantees of its final loyal settlement outside of declarative assurances and pledges. A condition of the effectiveness of the procedure proposed by the Czechoslovak government was, of course, agreement of the interested parties on the frontier changes. Prague did not take into consideration what would happen if such agreement was not reached. Prague's position was automatically supplemented by the Munich resolutions on this point; they provided that, if the interested governments did not reach agreement within three months on the problems of the Polish and Hungarian minorities, a new conference of the four powers would take care of them. So, then, besides the bad experiences in the period before Munich, and the prospect of a considerable weakening of French influence in Prague, there were also pressing substantial reasons which did not allow the Polish government to place its confidence in Czechoslovakia's proposals or to consider them adequate.

"When I finished my telephone conversations with M. Bonnet and our Foreign Ministry in Warsaw late on the evening of September 30, I was fully convinced that Prague would accept the demands we presented, and that a conflict would not erupt. On the morning of October 1, Bonnet informed me by telephone that he had been in touch with President Benes during the night. Although he had not achieved any decisions, he told me that he was less pessimistic about the whole situation. A moment later I received news from Warsaw that the Czechoslovak government had proposed that the deadline for our ultimatum be postponed for one hour, and that we had agreed. At the same time I received the text of a press interview of Minister Beck, who said that he expected that, after the long-standing dispute over Teschen Silesia was settled, Polish-Czechoslovak relations could develop in a friendly and positive fashion. I immediately passed both pieces of information on to M. Bonnet, who received them with apparent satisfaction. Finally, at 1 p.m. news came from Warsaw that the Czechoslovak government had accepted our terms and that on this basis our troops and civil authorities were preparing to take over the Polish part of Teschen Silesia from the Czech administration. It turned out then that our apprehensions about German territorial claims were justified. When we were taking over Bohumin, it was only with great effort that incidents were avoided with German forces, who had planned to occupy it. Our suppositions also proved correct concerning the fact that if we had not gotten Czechoslovakia to carry out its obligations toward Poland immediately after the Munich conference we would have run the risk of having the whole matter turned over to decisions dependent on Berlin. This was the fate which befell the problem of territories inhabited by the Hungarian minority. It was settled by German-Italian arbitration, which enhanced the tremendous growth of Hitler's influence in Central Europe and paralyzed the possibility of any effective British or French intervention.

"Naturally, it was impossible for Poland to accept such a procedure. It would not only mean acceptance of the Munich decision on the problem of the Polish population of Czechoslovakia, taken without our participation or agreement, but it would also create a precedent on the basis of which the Munich Four would undoubtedly try to apply similar methods to Danzig, Pomerania, and Silesia...the Polish government had two choices: either to defend the rights of the Polish minority in Czechoslovakia by our own efforts, and the rights of the Polish Republic to Teschen Silesia, or by acting passively, to forget the objections made by Paderewski and Witos in 1920 to the resolutions of the Paris Ambassadors' Conference that gave the Polish part of Silesia to Czechoslovakia.

"The wishes of the Polish minority in Czechoslovakia, who since 1920 had felt themselves to be grievously wronged and were fighting for their rights, also played a large role in our decision. From the time that Premier Hodza confirmed the need for reforms in the minority setup in Czechoslovakia during a debate in the Prague parliament at the end of March, 1938, the Polish minority had demanded the same rights which were to be granted to others. Of course, this was completely natural and understandable.

"By means of diplomatic action undertaken in May, 1938, the Polish government received a formal commitment from the Czechoslovak government in the middle of June, as well as French guarantees, that the Polish population in Czechoslovakia would enjoy the so-called most-favored-nation clause with regard to national rights and the time they were to be granted. Formally, then, there was every reason to hope that the problem of Teschen Silesia would be settled peacefully, without undue tension. Unfortunately, neither the commitments of the Czechoslovak government nor the French assurances were fulfilled. This brought on the independent action of the Polish government in the form of an ultimatum presented to Prague on September 30. It was only this note that induced the Czechoslovak government to carry out its long-promised commitments with regard to Teschen Silesia."

Source: Juliusz Lukasiewicz, *Diplomat in Paris, 1936-1939*, pp. 141-46.

List of Sources

Abrikossow, Dmitrii I. *Revelations of a Russian Diplomat: The Memoirs of Dmitrii I. Abrikossow*. Ed. George Alexander Lensen. Seattle, Wash.: University of Washington Press, 1964.

Acheson, Dean. *Present at the Creation: My Years in the State Department*. New York: Norton, 1969.

Alfieri, Dino. *Dictators Face to Face*. New York: New York University Press, 1955.

Andrassy, Gyula. *Diplomacy and the War*. Trans. J. Holroyd Reece. London: Bale, 1921.

Apponyi, Albert. *The Memoirs of Count Apponyi*. New York: Macmillan, 1935.

Armstrong, Hamilton Fish. *Peace and Counterpeace: From Wilson to Hitler*. New York: Harper, 1971.

Badoglio, Pietro. *Italy in the Second World War: Memories and Documents*. London: Oxford, 1948.

Balabanoff, Angelica. *My Life as a Rebel*. New York: Greenwood, 1968.

Ball, George W. *The Past Has Another Pattern: Memoirs*. New York: Norton, 1982.

Bandholtz, Harry H. *An Undiplomatic Diary*. New York: Columbia University Press, 1933.

Barmine, Alexandre. *Memoirs of a Soviet Diplomat: Twenty Years in the Service of the U.S.S.R.* Trans. Gerard Hopkins. Westport, Conn.: Hyperion, [1938] 1973.

Baruch, Bernard M. *The Making of the Reparation and Economic Sections of the Treaty*. New York: Harper, 1920.

————. *The Public Years*. London: Odhams, 1960.

Baudouin, Paul. *The Private Diaries*. London: Eyre and Spottiswoode, 1948.

Beaufré, André. *1940: The Fall of France.* New York: Knopf, 1968.

Beaulac, Willard L. *Career Ambassador.* New York: Macmillan, 1951.

Beck, Jozef. *Final Report.* New York: Speller, 1957.

Benes, Eduard. *Memoirs: From Munich to New War and New Victory.* Boston: Houghton Mifflin, 1954.

Berle, Adolf A. *Navigating the Rapids, 1918-1971.* New York: Harcourt, 1973.

Bernadotte, Folke. *The Curtain Falls: The Last Days of the Third Reich.* New York: Knopf, 1945.

Bernstorff, Johan. *Memoirs of Count Bernstorff.* New York: Random House, 1936.

Bernstorff, Count. *My Three Years in America.* New York: Scribner's, 1920.

Bessedovsky, Grigory Z. *Revelations of a Soviet Diplomat.* Westport, Conn.: Hyperion, [1931] 1977.

Bethmann-Hollweg, Theobald von. *Reflections on the World War.* London: Butterworth, 1920.

Beyens, Napoleon. *Germany before the War.* London: Nelson, 1916.

Biddle, Anthony Joseph Drexel. *Poland and the Coming of the Second World War.* Columbus: Ohio State University Press, 1976.

Birse, Arthur Hubert. *Memoirs of an Interpreter.* London: Joseph, 1967.

Blondel, Jules-François. *Entente Cordiale: Fifty True Stories, Mostly from Diplomatic Experience.* Trans. Eugen Millington-Drake. London: Caduceus Press, 1971.

Bogicevic, Milos. *Causes of the War.* London: Allen and Unwin, 1920.

Bohlen, Charles E. *Witness to History, 1929-1969.* New York: W.W. Norton, 1973.

Bolín, Luis. *Spain: The Vital Years.* Philadelphia: Lippincott, 1967.

Bonsal, Stephen. *Suitors and Supplicants.* New York: Prentice-Hall, 1946.

————. *Unfinished Business.* Garden City, N.Y.: Doubleday, 1944.

Bowles, Chester. *Promises to Keep: My Years in Public Life.* New York: Harper & Row, 1971.

Bowers, Claude G. *Chile through Embassy Windows, 1939-53.* New York: Simon and Schuster, 1958.

Braunthal, Julius. *The Tragedy of Austria.* London: Gollancz, 1948.

Bridges, George Tom. *Alarms and Excursions.* London: Longmans, Green & Co.

Bruce, Henry James. *Thirty Dozen Moons*. London: Constable, 1949.

Brzezinski, Zbigniew. *Power and Principle: Memoirs of the National Security Adviser, 1977-1981*. New York: Farrar-Straus-Giroux, 1983.

Buchanan, George. *My Mission to Russia*. Vols I & II. New York: Arno Press, [1923] 1970.

Buchanan, Meriel. *Ambassador's Daughter*. London: Cassell, 1958.

Bullitt, William C. *The Bullitt Mission to Russia*. New York: Huebsch, 1919.

————. *The Great Globe Itself*. New York: Scribner's, 1946.

Bülow, Bernhard von. *The Memoirs of Prince von Bülow*. Boston: Little, Brown, 1932.

Burian, Stephan. *Austria in Dissolution*. London: Benn, 1925.

Child, Richard Washburn. *A Diplomat Looks at Europe*. New York: Duffield, 1925.

Butler, Lord. *The Art of the Possible*. Boston: Gambit, 1972.

Byrnes, James F. *Speaking Frankly*. New York: Harper & Brothers, 1947.

Campbell, Gerald. *Of True Experience*. New York: Dodd, Mead, 1947.

Carton de Wiart, Sir Adrian. *Happy Odyssey: The Memoirs of Lieutenant-General Sir Adrian Carton de Wiart*. London: Jonathan Cape, 1950.

Casey, Lord. *Personal Experience, 1939-46*. London: Constable, 1962.

Chamberlain, Austen. *Down the Years*. London: Cassell, 1935.

Childs, James Rives. *Foreign Service Farewell: My Years in the Near East*. Charlottesville: University Press of Virginia, 1969.

Ciano, Count Galeazzo. *Ciano's Hidden Diary, 1937-1938*. Trans. Andreas Mayor. New York: E.P. Dutton, 1953.

Ciechanowski, Jan. *Defeat in Victory*. New York: Doubleday, 1947.

Clark, Mark. *Calculated Risk*. New York: Harper & Bros., 1950.

Cleugh, Eric. *Without Let or Hindrance*. London: Cassell, 1960.

Clemenceau, Georges. *Grandeur and Misery of Victory*. London: Harrap, 1930.

Colville, John R. *Footprints in Time*. London: Collins, 1976.

Cretzianu, Alexandre. *The Lost Opportunity*. London: Cape, 1957.

Crocker, W.R. *Australian Ambassador: International Relations at First Hand*. Melbourne: Melbourne University Press, 1971.

Cudahy, John. *The Armies March: A Personal Report*. New York: Scribner's, 1941.

Czernin, Ottokar. *In the World War*. New York: Harper, 1920.

Dahlerus, Birger. *The Last Attempt*. London: Hutchinson, 1948.

Daniels, Josephus. *The Wilson Era*. Chapel Hill, N.C.: University of North Carolina Press, 1944-46.

Davies, Joseph E. *Mission to Moscow*. Garden City, N.Y.: Garden City Publishing, 1943.

Deane, John R. *The Strange Alliance: The Story of Our Efforts at Wartime Co-operation with Russia*. New York: Viking, 1947.

Dirksen, Herbert von. *Moscow Tokyo London: Twenty Years of German Foreign Policy*. Norman, Oklahoma: University of Oklahoma Press, 1952.

Dixon, Pierson John. *Double Diploma*. London: Hutchinson, 1968.

Dodd, Martha. *Through Embassy Windows*. New York: Harcourt, 1939.

Dollmann, Eugen. *Call Me Coward*. London: Kimber, 1956.

————. *The Interpreter*. London: Hutchinson, 1967.

Dumba, Constantin. *Memoirs of a Diplomat*. Boston: Little, Brown, 1932.

Dunham, Donald. *Envoy Unextraordinary*. New York: John Day, 1944.

Eeman, Harold. *Clouds Over the Sun: Memories of a Diplomat, 1942-1958*. London: Hale, 1981.

————. *Inside Stalin's Russia: Memories of a Diplomat, 1936-1941*. London: Triton, 1977.

Egan, Maurice F. *Recollections of a Happy Life*. New York: Doran, 1924.

————. *Ten Years Near the German Frontier*. New York: Doran, 1919.

Einstein, Lewis D. *A Diplomat Looks Back*. Ed. Lawrence Gelfand. New Haven: Yale University Press, 1968.

Elibank, Arthur Cecil Murray. *At Close Quarters: A Sidelight on Anglo-American Relations*. London: John Murray, 1946.

Ford, Gerald R. *A Time to Heal*. New York: Harper & Row, 1979.

Fotitch, Constantin. *The War We Lost: Yugoslavia's Tragedy and the Failure of the West*. New York: Viking, 1948.

Franckenstein, George. *Diplomat of Destiny (or Facts and Features of My Life)*. New York: Alliance, 1940.

François-Poncet, André. *The Fateful Years: Memoirs of a French Ambassador in Berlin, 1931-1938*. New York: Harcourt, 1949.

Francis, David R. *Russia from the American Embassy*. New York: Scribner's, 1921.

Gafencu, Grigore. *The Last Days of Europe: A Diplomatic Journey in 1939*. New Haven: Yale University Press, 1948.

————. *Prelude to the Russian Campaign, from the Moscow Pact to the Opening of Hostilities in Russia*. Westport, Conn: Hyperion, 1981.

Galbraith, John Kenneth. *Ambassador's Journal: A Personal Account of the Kennedy Years*. Boston: Houghton Mifflin, 1969.

Gerard, James W. *Face to Face with Kaiserism*. New York: Doran, 1918.

————. *My Four Years in Germany*. New York: Doran, 1917.

Gibson, Hugh S. *A Journal from Our Legation in Belgium*. Garden City, N.Y.: Doubleday, 1917.

————. *The Education of a Diplomat*. London: Longmans, Green and Co., 1938.

Giolitti, Giovani. *Memoirs of My Life*. London: Chapman, 1923.

Gladwyn, Hubert M.G.B. *The Memoirs of Lord Gladwyn*. New York: Weybright, 1971.

Gore-Booth, Paul. *With Great Truth and Respect*. London: Constable, 1974.

Granatstein, J.L. *The Ottawa Men: The Civil Service Mandarins, 1935-57*. Toronto: Oxford University Press, 1982.

Gregory, John. *On the Edge of Diplomacy: Rambles and Reflections, 1902-1928*. London: Hutchinson, 1929.

Grew, Joseph C. *Ten Years in Japan*. New York: Simon & Schuster, 1944.

Gripenberg, Georg A. *Finland and the Great Powers: Memoirs of a Diplomat*. Lincoln: University of Nebraska Press, 1965.

Hägglöf, Gunnar. *Diplomat: Memoirs of a Swedish Envoy*. London: Bodley Head, 1972.

Haig, Alexander M. Jr. *Caveat: Realism, Reagan and Foreign Policy*. New York: Macmillan, 1984.

Hambro, Carl Joachim. *I Saw It Happen in Norway*. New York: Appleton-Century, 1940.

Halifax, The Earl of. *Fulness of Days*. London: Collins, 1957.

Hardinge, Arthur. *A Diplomatist in Europe*. London: Cape, 1927.

Hardinge of Penshurst, Charles. *The Old Diplomacy*. London: Murray, 1947.

Harriman, Florence J. *Mission to the North*. Philadelphia: Lippincott, 1941.

Harriman, W. Averell and Elie Abel. *Special Envoy to Churchill and Stalin, 1941-46*. New York: Random House, 1975.

Hayes, Carlton J.H. *Wartime Mission in Spain, 1942-1945*. New York: Macmillan, 1945.

Hayter, William G. *The Diplomacy of the Great Powers*. New York: Macmillan, 1961.

————. *A Double Life*. London: Hamish Hamilton, 1974.

Hedin, Sven. *German Diary, 1935-1942*. Dublin: Euphorian Books, 1951.

Herwarth, Hans von. *Against two Evils*. New York: Rawson, Wade, 1981.

Hilger, Gustav. *The Incompatible Allies: A Memoir History of German-Soviet Relations, 1918-1941*. New York: Macmillan, 1953.

Hodgson, Robert M. *Spain Resurgent*. London: Hutchinson, 1953.

Hoettl, Wilhelm. *The Secret Front: The Story of Nazi Political Espionage*. New York: Praeger, 1954.

Hoffmann, Heinrich. *Hitler Was My Friend*. Trans. R.H. Stevens. London: Burke, 1955.

Hoover, Herbert. *The Memoirs of Herbert Hoover: The Cabinet and the Presidency, 1920-1933*. New York: Macmillan, 1952.

Horthy, Nicholas. *Memoirs*. New York: Speller, 1957.

Horton, George. *Recollections Grave and Gay: The Story of a Mediterranean Consul*. Indianapolis: Bobbs, 1927.

House, Edward M. *What Really Happened at Paris. The Story of the Peace Conference, 1918-1919*. New York: Scribner's, 1921.

Howard, Esme. *Theatre of Life*. Vols I & II. Boston: Little, Brown, 1935-36.

Hugessen, Hughe Montgomery Knatchbull. *Diplomat in Peace and War*. London: Murray, 1946.

Ishii, Kikujiro. *Diplomatic Commentaries*. Baltimore: Johns Hopkins, 1936.

Ismay, Hastings L. *The Memoirs of General Lord Ismay*. New York: Viking, 1960.

Iswolsky, Alexander. *The Memoirs of Alexander Iswolsky*. Ed. and trans. Charles Louis Seeger. Gulf Breeze, Florida: Academic International Press, 1974.

Johnson, Hallett. *Diplomatic Memoirs, Serious and Frivolous*. New York: Vantage, 1963.

Johnson, Lyndon B. *The Vantage Point: Perspectives of the Presidency, 1963-1969*. New York: Holt, Rinehart & Winston, 1971.

Jonescu, Tuke. *The Origins of the War: The Testimony of a Witness*. London: Council for the Study of International Relations, 1917.

————. *Some Personal Impressions*. New York: Stokes, 1920.

Kallay, Nicholas. *Hungarian Premier: A Personal Account of a Nation's Struggle in the Second World War*. New York: Columbia University Press, 1954.

Kalmykow, Andrew D. *Memoirs of a Russian Diplomat: Outposts of the Empire, 1893-1917*. Ed. Alexandra Kalmykow. New Haven: Yale University Press, 1971.

Károlyi, Michael. *Fighting the World: The Struggle for Peace*. New York: Boni, 1925.

————. *Memoirs of Michael Károlyi: Faith without Illusion*. New York: Dutton, 1957.

Karski, Jan. *Story of a Secret State*. Boston: Houghton Mifflin, 1944.

Kelly, David Victor. *The Ruling Few*. London: Hollis and Carter, 1952.

Kennan, George F. *Memoirs, 1925-1950*. Boston: Little, Brown & Co., 1967.

Kennedy, John Noble. *The Business of War*. New York: Morrow, 1958.

Kennedy, Robert F. *Thirteen Days: A Memoir of the Cuban Missile Crisis*. New York: W.W. Norton, 1968.

Kessler, Harry von. *In the Twenties: The Diaries of Harry Kessler*. New York: Holt, 1971.

Keynes, John Maynard. *Two Memoirs: Dr. Melchior: A Defeated Enemy, and My Early Beliefs*. New York: Kelley, 1949.

King, Ernest J. *Fleet Admiral King*. New York: Norton, 1952.

Kirkpatrick, Ivone J. *The Inner Circle: Memoirs*. London: Macmillan, 1959.

Kissinger, Henry. *White House Years*. Boston: Little, Brown & Co., 1979.

Kleffens, Eelco N. van. *The Rape of the Netherlands*. London: Hodder and Stoughton, 1940.

Kleist, Peter. *The European Tragedy*. Isle of Man: Times Press, 1965.

Konoye, Fumimaro. *Memoirs of Prince Fumimaro Konoye*. Tokyo: Okuyama Service, 1946.

Kot, Stanislaw. *Conversations with the Kremlin and Dispatches from Russia*. Trans. H.C. Stevens. London: Oxford, 1963.

Kuter, Laurence S. *Airman at Yalta*. New York: Duell, Sloan and Pearce, 1955.

Kybal, Vlastimil, "Czechoslovakia and Italy: My Negotiations with Mussolini, 1922-1924." *Journal of Central European Affairs*, 13 & 14. 1954; pp. 352-68, 65-76.

Lane, Arthur Bliss. *I Saw Poland Betrayed*. Indianapolis: Bobbs-Merrill, 1948.

Lansing, Robert. *The Big Four and Others of the Peace Conference*. Boston: Houghton Mifflin, 1921.

––––––. *The Peace Negotiations: A Personal Narrative*. Boston: Houghton Mifflin, 1921.

––––––. *War Memoirs of Robert Lansing*. Indianapolis: Bobbs-Merrill, 1935.

Laval, Pierre. *The Unpublished Diary of Pierre Laval*. London: Falcon, 1948.

Lawford, Valentine. *Bound for Diplomacy*. Boston: Little, Brown, 1963.

Leahy, Fleet Admiral William D. *I Was There*. New York: Whittlesley House, 1950.

Lee, Raymond E. *The London Journal of General Raymond E. Lee, 1940-1941*. Boston: Little, Brown, 1971.

Leeper, Reginald. *When Greek Meets Greek*. London: Chatto and Windus, 1950.

LePan, Douglas. *Bright Glass of Memory*. Toronto: McClelland and Stewart, 1979.

Lichnowsky, Karl Max von. *Heading for the Abyss: Reminiscences*. New York: Payson and Clarke, 1928.

Lipski, Jozef. *Diplomat in Berlin, 1933-1939*. New York: Columbia University Press, 1968.

Lloyd George, David. *Memoirs of the Peace Conference*. 2 vols. New Haven: Yale University Press, 1939.

Lomax, John G. *The Diplomatic Smuggler*. London: Barker, 1965.

Lukasiewicz, Juliusz. *Diplomat in Paris, 1936-1939*. New York: Columbia University Press, 1970.

Lyttelton, Oliver. *The Memoirs of Lord Chandos: An Unexpected View from the Summit*. New York: New American Library, 1963.

MacVeagh, Lincoln. *Ambassador MacVeagh Reports: Greece, 1933-1947*. Princeton: Princeton University Press, 1980.

Madariaga, Salvador de. *Morning without Noon: Memoirs*. Farnborough: Saxon House, 1974.

Maisky, Ivan. *Memoirs of a Soviet Ambassador: The War, 1939-1943*. New York: Scribner's, 1968.

Macmillan, Harold. *Pointing the Way, 1959-1961*. New York: Harper & Row, 1959.

Marchal, Léon. *Vichy: Two Years of Deception*. New York: Macmillan, 1943.

Martel, Giffard. *An Outspoken Soldier: His Views and Memoirs*. London: Sifton Praed, 1949.

Marye, George Thomas. *Nearing the End in Imperial Russia*. Philadelphia: Dorrance, 1929.

Masaryk, Tomas Garrigue. *The Making of a State: Memories and Observations, 1914-1918*. New York: Stokes, 1927.

Massey, Vincent. *What's Past is Prologue*. New York: St. Martin's, 1964.

Meriweather, Lee. *The War Diary of a Diplomat*. New York: Dodd, Mead, 1919.

Miliukov, Pavel. *Political Memoirs, 1905-1917*. Ann Arbor: University of Michigan Press, 1967.

Miller, David Hunter. *The Drafting of the Covenant*. Vols I & II. New York: Putnam's, 1928.

Moffat, Jay Pierrepoint. *The Moffat Papers*. Cambridge, Mass.: Harvard University Press, 1956.

Monnet, Jean. *Memoirs*. Garden City, N.Y.: Doubleday, 1978.

Montgomery, John F. *Hungary: The Unwilling Satellite*. New York: Devin Adair, 1947.

Morgan, John Hartman. *Assize of Arms*. Vol. 1. London: Methuen, 1945.

Morgenthau, Henry. *All in a Lifetime*. Garden City, N.Y.: Doubleday, 1922.

Morris, Ira N. *From an American Legation*. New York: Knopf, 1923.

Munemitsu, Mutsu. *Kenkenroku: A Diplomatic Record of the Sino-Japanese War, 1894-95*. Ed. and trans. Gordon Mark Berger. Princeton: Princeton University Press/University of Tokyo Press, 1982.

Murphy, Robert D. *Diplomat Among Warriors*. Garden City, N.Y.: Doubleday, 1964.

Nabokoff, Constantin. *The Ordeal of a Diplomat*. London: Duckworth, 1921.

Nekludoff, Anatoly V. *Diplomatic Reminiscences Before and During the War, 1911-17*. London: Murray, 1920.

Newman, Peter C. *The Distemper of Our Times*. Toronto: McClelland and Stewart, 1968.

Nicholas, Prince of Greece. *Political Memoirs, 1914-1917*. London: Hutchinson, 1927.

Nixon, Richard M. *RN: The Memoirs of Richard Nixon*. New York: Grosset & Dunlap, 1978.

Noel-Baker, Philip John. *The First World Disarmament Conference, 1932-33, and Why It Failed*. Oxford: Pergamon, 1979.

Nowak, Jan. *Courier from Warsaw*. Detroit: Wayne State University Press, 1982.

Oliphant, Lancelot. *An Ambassador in Bonds*. London: Putnam, 1947.

O'Malley, Owen. *The Phantom Caravan*. London: Murray, 1954.

Oudendyk, William J. *Ways and By-Ways of Diplomacy*. London: Peter Davies, 1939.

Paléologue, Maurice. *An Ambassador's Memoirs*. Vol. I. London: Hutchinson, 1923.

Papen, Franz von. *Memoirs*. New York: Dutton, 1953.

Parrott, Cecil C. *The Tightrope*. London: Faber & Faber, 1975.

————. *The Serpent and the Nightingale.* London: Faber & Faber, 1977.

Pearson, Lester B. *Mike: The Memoirs of the Rt. Honourable Lester B. Pearson*. Toronto: University of Toronto Press, 1972.

Peterson, Maurice. *Both Sides of the Curtain: An Autobiography*. London: Constable, 1950.

Phillips, William. *Ventures in Diplomacy*. London: Murray, 1955.

Poincaré, Raymond. *Memoirs of Raymond Poincaré*. London: Heinemann, 1926-30.

Ponsonby, Charles E. *Ponsonby Remembers*. Oxford: Alden, 1965.

Quaroni, Pietro. *Diplomatic Bags: An Ambassador's Memoirs*. New York: Davies White, 1966.

Raczynski, Edward. *In Allied London*. London: Weidenfeld, 1962.

Randall, Alec. *Vatican Assignment*. London: Heinemann, 1956.

Reid, Escott. *On Duty: A Canadian at the Making of the United Nations, 1945-1946*. Kent, Ohio: Kent State University Press, 1983.

Reid, P.R. *Winged Diplomat: The Life Story of Air Commodore "Freddie" West*. London: Chatto & Windus, 1962.

Rendel, George. *The Sword and the Olive*. London: Murray, 1957.

Reynaud, Paul. *In the Thick of the Fight, 1930-1945*. New York: Simon and Schuster, 1955.

Reynoso, Francisco de. *Reminiscences of a Spanish Diplomat*. London: Hutchinson, 1933.

Ribbentrop, Joachim von. *The Ribbentrop Memoirs*. London: Weidenfeld and Nicolson, 1954.

Ribot, Alexandre. *Letters to a Friend: Recollections of My Political Life*. London: Hutchinson, 1925.

Riddell, George Allardice. *Lord Riddell's Intimate Diary of the Peace Conference and After*. London: Gollancz, 1933.

————. *Lord Riddell's War Diary, 1914-1918*. London: Ivor Nicholson and Watson, 1933.

Ritchie, Charles. *Diplomatic Passport: More Undiplomatic Diaries, 1946-62*. Toronto: Macmillan, 1981.

Ritchie, Charles. *Storm Signals: More Undiplomatic Diaries, 1962-71*. Toronto: Macmillan, 1981.

Robien, Louis Comte de. *Diary of a Diplomat in Russia, 1917-1918*. New York: Praeger, 1970.

Ryan, Andrew. *The Last of the Dragomans*. London: Bles, 1951.

Salandra, Antonio. *Italy and the Great War: From Neutrality to Intervention*. London: Arnold, 1932.

Salter, Arthur. *Memoirs of a Public Servant*. London: Faber, 1961.

Satow, Ernest. *A Diplomat in Japan*. Philadelphia: Lippincott, 1921.

Savinsky, Alexander. *Recollections of a Russian Diplomat*. London: Hutchinson, 1927.

Sawyer, Charles. *Concerns of a Conservative Democrat*. Carbondale: Southern Illinois University Press, 1968.

Sazonov, Serge. *The Fateful Years, 1909-1916*. London: Cape, 1928.

Schelking, Eugene de. *Recollections of a Russian Diplomat: The Suicide of Monarchies*. New York: Macmillan, 1918.

Schmidt, Paul. *Hitler's Interpreter*. New York: Macmillan, 1951.

Schoen, Wilhelm von. *Memoirs of an Ambassador*. London: Allen and Unwin, 1922.

Sforza, Carlo. *Diplomatic Europe since the Treaty of Versailles*. New Haven: Yale University Press, 1928.

————. *Makers of Modern Europe: Portraits and Personal Impressions*. Indianapolis: Bobbs-Merrill, 1930.

Sharp, William Graves. *The War Memoirs of William Graves Sharp*. London: Constable, 1931.

Shigemitsu, Mamory. *Japan and Her Destiny: My Struggle for Peace.* New York: Dutton, 1958.

Shotwell, James T. *The Autobiography of James T. Shotwell.* Indianapolis: Bobbs-Merrill, 1961.

—————. *At the Paris Peace Conference.* New York: Macmillan, 1937.

Spaak, Paul-Henri. *The Continuing Battle: Memoirs of a European, 1936-1966.* Boston: Little, Brown, 1971.

Spears, Edward Louis. *Assignment to Catastrophe.* 2 vols. New York: A.A. Wyn, 1954-55.

—————. *Fulfillment of a Mission.* London: Cooper, 1977.

Standley, William H. *Admiral Ambassador to Russia.* Chicago: Regnery, 1955.

Stetinnius, Edward R., Jr. *Roosevelt and the Russians: The Yalta Conference.* Garden City, N.Y.: Doubleday, 1949.

Stimson, Henry L. *On Active Service in Peace and War.* New York: Harper, 1948.

Stovall, Pleasant Alexander. *Switzerland and the World War.* Savannah, Ga.: Mason, 1939.

Strang, William. *Home and Abroad.* London: Andre Deutsch, 1956.

—————. *The Moscow Negotiations, 1939.* Leeds: Leeds University Press, 1968.

Strong, Kenneth. *Intelligence at the Top.* Garden City, N.Y.: Doubleday, 1969.

Swinton, Ernest. *Over My Shoulder.* Oxford: George Ronald, 1951.

Swinton, Philip Cunliffe-Lister. *I Remember.* London: Hutchinson, 1948.

—————. *Sixty Years of Power: Some Memories of the Men Who Wielded It.* New York: Heinemann, 1966.

Tanner, Väinö. *The Winter War: Finland against Russia, 1939-1940.* Stanford, Calif.: Stanford University Press, 1957.

Tardieu, André. *The Truth about the Treaty.* Indianapolis: Bobbs, 1921.

Temperley, Arthur C. *The Whispering Gallery of Europe.* London: Collins, 1938.

Thayer, Charles W. *Bears in the Caviar.* Philadelphia: Lippincott, 1951.

—————. *Hands across the Caviar.* Philadelphia: Lippincott, 1952.

Thompson, Geoffrey. *Front Line Diplomat.* London: Hutchinson, 1959.

Togo, Shigenori. *The Cause of Japan*. New York: Simon and Schuster, 1956.

Tolley, Kemp. *Caviar and Commissars: The Experiences of a U.S. Naval Officer in Stalin's Russia*. Annapolis: Naval Institute Press, 1983.

Trudeau, Margaret. *Beyond Reason*. Toronto: General Publishing, 1979.

Truman, Harry S. *Memoirs: Year of Decisions*. Garden City, N.Y.: Doubleday, 1955.

Vansittart, Robert G. *Bones of Contention*. London: Hutchinson, 1945.

————. *Even Now*. London: Hutchinson, 1949.

————. *Events and Shadows*. London: Hutchinson, 1947.

————. *Lessons of My Life*. London: Hutchinson, 1943.

Varè, Daniele. *Laughing Diplomat*. London: Murray, 1938.

————. *The Two Imposters*. London: Murray, 1949.

Villard, Henry Serrano. *Affairs at State*. New York: Crowell, 1965.

Viviani, René. *As We See It*. New York: Harper, 1923.

Vopica, Charles J. *Secrets of the Balkans*. Chicago: Rand McNally, 1921.

Webster, Charles Kingsley. *The Historian as Diplomat: Charles Kingsley Webster and the United Nations, 1939-1946*. London: Martin Robertson, 1976.

Wheeler-Bennett, John. *Action this Day: Working with Churchill*. New York: St. Martin's, 1969.

————. *Knaves, Fools and Heroes: In Europe between the Wars*. New York: St. Martin's, 1974.

————. *Special Relationships: America in Peace and War*. London: Macmillan, 1975.

Whitlock, Brand. *Belgium: A Personal Narrative*. 2 vols. New York: Appleton, 1919.

Wilhelm II, Emperor of Germany. *The Kaiser's Memoirs*. New York: Harper, 1922.

Willert, Arthur. *Washington and Other Memories*. Boston: Houghton Mifflin, 1972.

Wilson, Hugh R. *The Education of a Diplomat*. New York: Longmans, 1938.

————. *Diplomat between Wars*. New York: Longmans, 1941.

————. *A Career Diplomat. The Third Chapter: The Third Reich*. New York: Vantage, 1961.

Winant, John Gilbert. *Letter from Grosvenor Square*. Boston: Houghton Mifflin, 1947.

Windischgraetz, Lajos. *My Adventures and Misadventures*. London: Barrie and Rockliff, 1966.

————. *My Memoirs*. London: Allen and Unwin, 1921.

Winterbotham, Frederick W. *The Nazi Connection*. New York: Harper, 1978.

Wood, Eric Fisher. *The Note-Book of an Attaché*. New York: Century, 1915.

Woodhouse, Christopher Montague. *The Struggle for Greece, 1941-1949*. London: Hart-Davis, 1976.

Yost, Charles W. *History and Memory*. New York: Norton, 1980.

Extracts

Eugen Dollmann, *The Interpreter*, © 1967 Hutchinson. Reprinted by permission of Random Century Group.

Sir Neville Henderson, *Failure of a Mission: Berlin 1937-1939*. Reprinted by permission of Hodder & Stoughton Limited.

Michael Killanin (ed.), *Four Days*. Reprinted by permission of William Heinemann Limited.

Viscount Templewood, *Nine Troubled Years*. Reprinted by permission of Harper Collins Publishers.

Index